Women and ETA

Women and ETA
The gender politics of radical Basque nationalism

Carrie Hamilton

Manchester University Press
Manchester and New York

distributed exclusively in the USA by Palgrave

Copyright © Carrie Hamilton 2007

The right of Carrie Hamilton to be identified as the author of this work has been asserted by her in accordance with the Copyright, Designs and Patents Act 1988.

Published by Manchester University Press
Oxford Road, Manchester M13 9NR, UK
and Room 400, 175 Fifth Avenue, New York, NY 10010, USA
www.manchesteruniversitypress.co.uk

Distributed in the United States exclusively by
Palgrave Macmillan, 175 Fifth Avenue,
New York, NY 10010, USA

Distributed in Canada exclusively by
UBC Press, University of British Columbia, 2029 West Mall,
Vancouver, BC, Canada V6T 1Z2

British Library Cataloguing-in-Publication Data is available

Library of Congress Cataloging-in-Publication Data is available

ISBN 978 0 7190 8906 0 paperback

First published by Manchester University Press in hardback 2007

This paperback edition first published 2013

The publisher has no responsibility for the persistence or accuracy of URLs for any external or third-party internet websites referred to in this book, and does not guarantee that any content on such websites is, or will remain, accurate or appropriate.

Printed by Lightning Source

Contents

Acknowledgements	*page* vi
Introduction: gender, nationalism and memory	1
1 Growing up nationalist	19
2 Gendering the roots of radical nationalism	39
3 Nationalism goes public	62
4 Constructing the male warrior and the homefront heroine	84
5 From the domestic front to armed struggle	105
6 The final front: arrest and prison	125
7 Nationalism and feminism	148
8 Women and the Basque conflict in the new millennium	165
Conclusion	176
Glossary	184
Appendix 1: interviews	187
Appendix 2: women in ETA	188
Notes	194
Select bibliography	234
Index	246

Acknowledgements

During the course of researching and writing this book I have been privileged to receive support from numerous individuals and institutions in Canada, the UK, Spain and the Basque Country.

I am grateful to the Commonwealth Scholarship Commission, the Social Sciences and Humanities Research Council of Canada and the British Academy for funding different stages of the research on which the book is based. I also want to thank Helen Graham of the History Department at Royal Holloway, University of London, for her academic guidance during the first few years of this project, and especially for sharing with me her vast knowledge of Spanish history.

During my two years in the Basque country I benefited from the generosity and ideas of many people. I am particularly indebted to Father Juan José Agirre of the library and archive at the Benedictine monastery in Lazkao, Guipúzcoa, where I accessed most of the printed primary sources. Several colleagues and friends at the Universities of the Basque Country and Deusto provided support and inspiration. Gracias a Arantxa Elizondo, Patxi Juaristi, Eva Martínez, Garbiñe Mendizabal and María Silvestre. I am also grateful to Regina Tolosa and her family in Bilbao for their help and hospitality. Many other friends in the Basque country gave me a place to stay and showed endless patience in helping me learn the Basque language, *euskera*. To Izaskun, Idoia, Ane, Arantza and Cristina – *mila esker*.

In the UK I have been privileged to work with outstanding colleagues at the University of Southampton and Roehampton University, London. For their ongoing intellectual inspiration and friendship, thanks to Carole Sweeney, Nicky Marsh, Florence Myles, Liz Dore, and especially Jackie Clarke. I have also enjoyed the support of friends in Hispanic studies, among them Nuria Triana-Toribio, Isabel Santaolalla and David Vilaseca. I owe special thanks to Anny Brooksbank Jones and Jo Labanyi for their advice and support on the book and other aspects of my work and career over the years.

Several people read and made recommendations on earlier versions of the book, including Clare Mar-Molinero, Anna Davin, Kate Hodgkin and Susannah Radstone. The anonymous readers at MUP made excellent suggestions. I am especially indebted to and Caitlin Adams, Jesus Casquete and Annabelle Mooney for proofreading the final draft, and for their encouraging words.

On a personal level, I want to thank my mother, Mimi, for her ongoing emotional support and sharp mind, and to remember my father, Carl, my first intellectual and political mentor.

Finally, I owe my greatest thanks to the women I interviewed for this book. Their participation is what has made this project most meaningful for me as a feminist oral historian. As this book was in its final stages, ETA announced a permanent cease fire(March 2006). I share with most Basques and Spaniards the hope that this announcement will open the way for a peace process in the Basque country. In the meantime, I respect the anonymity of my interview narrators. But, although their names are absent, their stories remain with me and I try to remain faithful to their memories in the pages that follow.

Introduction: gender, nationalism and memory

In 1959 a small group of young men in the Basque city of Bilbao founded the organisation Euskadi ta Askatasuna (ETA – Basque Homeland and Freedom), which was to have an enormous impact on Basque and Spanish politics and society from the late 1960s to the present day. A fascination with ETA's commitment to armed struggle as the principal strategy for attaining independence for the Basque country,[1] as well as the organisation's seemingly endless ability to regenerate itself in the face of ongoing police repression and diminishing popular support, have made ETA the focus of ongoing popular and academic interest. The growing bewilderment of outsiders (and indeed of many Basques) over ETA's continued existence thirty years after the death of General Franco in 1975 and Spain's subsequent transition to liberal democracy, has increased rather than diminished this interest.

Publications on ETA and radical nationalism[2] (so called not only for its revolutionary claims, but also to distinguish it from the majority mainstream nationalism represented by the Basque Nationalist Party or PNV) cover broad ground, from scholarly research to populist accounts of the lives of ETA 'terrorists'.[3] But to date one area has been largely ignored: the role of women in ETA and the gender politics of radical nationalism. To the extent that women have been considered at all in the academic literature, it has been primarily as mothers.[4] But no study has looked in detail at the other roles of women in the radical nationalist movement, including female members of ETA.[5]

This book restores gender to a central position in the history of radical nationalism through a study of women's participation as members and supporters of ETA during the organisation's first two decades (1959 to 1982), and an analysis of the wider gender politics of radical nationalism. Women were active in all areas of ETA – including the military front – from the mid-1960s onwards; throughout the 1970s they participated in the growing number of radical nationalist organisations that developed around ETA, including trades unions, political parties, neighbourhood collectives (and, later, feminist organizations). As ETA stepped up its military campaign during that decade, and greater numbers of its members (mostly men) were arrested and imprisoned, or killed 'in action', mothers of ETA activists became increasingly visible as part of the growing prisoners' rights movement. These women were continuing a long tradition of women's intervention in the political sphere 'as mothers', but this was only one example of women's radical nationalist activism.

Women and the history of radical Basque nationalism

Women's participation in Basque nationalism dates to the early twentieth century, when women from urban, Catholic, middle-class nationalist families associated with the PNV participated in public political activities that were considered a natural extension of their duties as wives and mothers at home: charitable works, teaching Basque language and promoting Basque culture. Following the Spanish Civil War (1936–39) and the repression meted out against Basque nationalists by the Franco dictatorship (1939-75), these cultural and linguistic activities became more explicitly political. Historians of Basque nationalism have noted that during the first twenty years of the dictatorship Basque traditions – and a memory of Basque nationalist resistance – were preserved largely in those spaces that had a degree of autonomy from the State, namely the family and the Church.[6] Such analysis places women in the private sphere, but a gender analysis of the origins of ETA shows that the reproduction of nationalism was carried out through the interaction of families with other social, political and economic institutions (including the Church, educational institutions, workplaces and social groups) and that women as well as men were active in this process. Moreover, if women had some limited access to the public domain, men could also play important political roles in the private sphere. Such observations indicate a need to reconsider the conclusions of some comparative studies of nationalism, which attribute to women a privileged role in the reproduction of national communities through their status as mothers.[7]

The gender politics of early ETA were inextricably linked to the historical context of Franco Spain. The substantial structural changes of Spain's 'economic miracle' during the 1960s, including the partial reversal of restrictions on women's paid labour, provided unprecedented opportunities for women to enter into historically male domains. During this decade, which coincided with ETA's first ten years, increasing numbers of young Basque women left their family homes on a daily basis to work, and consequently were more likely than women of the previous generation to come into contact with emergent social organisations and political movements, including nascent radical nationalist groups. At the same time, the continuing emphasis on culture and language as the defining elements of the Basque nation meant that women were given a privileged place in nationalist rhetoric as the guardians of Basque tradition. Although radical nationalism remained a male-dominated movement, the convergence of traditionalist nationalist gender discourse with economic and social change meant that small numbers of radical nationalist women could, unlike their predecessors in previous generations, become involved in areas of activism conventionally reserved for men, including ETA's political and military fronts.

The history of women's entry into ETA in the 1960s also cautions us against making generalisations about the impact of nationalist movements on women's lives. The proliferation of studies of gender and nationalism in the 1990s was spurred in part by the high-profile war in the former Yugoslavia, with reports of systematic sexual abuse and torture of women by soldiers fighting in the name of the fatherland.[8] In the light of the reactionary and often violent nature of European ethnic nationalisms, as well as the rise of fundamentalist movements and regimes in some Islamic countries, many feminist scholars understandably emphasised the dangers of nationalism for women. As Valentine Moghadam stressed in 1994, the politics of nationalist movements in the late twentieth century, which typically defined the nation as a large extended family, had 'distinct implications for definitions of gender, for the position of women, and for feminism as an emancipatory project'.[9]

But, notwithstanding its conservative gender rhetoric, the new radical Basque nationalism of the 1960s (which emerged in the midst of a military dictatorship that defined gender in binary and hierarchical terms and associated women primarily with the home) actually provided new spaces for women's social, cultural and political activity. Although a division of roles was clearly evident during ETA's first decade, the push towards more restricted and hierarchical gender relations in the radical nationalist community intensified during the 1970s with the increased militarisation of the movement. It was during this period that mothers came to occupy a privileged place in the public image of radical nationalism. Although early ETA rhetoric paid homage to a universal Basque Mother, in practice the majority of women who became nationalist activists in the 1960s were young, single and childless. Mothers became more active in the radical nationalist movement as increasing numbers of young male activists were imprisoned or killed following ETA's first fatality in 1968.

Like all forms of maternity, therefore, radical nationalist motherhood was ideological. It was a role constructed first and foremost in relation to ETA's central protagonist: the armed activist son.[10] The idealisation of a particular form of nationalist motherhood not only heightened the visibility of male militants; it also had the effect of making less visible other forms of women's nationalist activism, including their roles in ETA. If women were associated above all with the home, ETA itself was constructed as a place of male domination separate from the domestic sphere. Paradoxically, however, it was precisely inside ETA that a small number of female activists had the opportunity to gain access, even if under very restricted conditions, to one of the historically privileged sites of male power: the sanctioned violence of military activity.

Gender, nationalism and oral history

One of the challenges of writing a history of women in radical Basque nationalism is the location of adequate and accurate sources. This study draws on a variety of written sources, including press reports and radical nationalist documents. Evidence of women's membership in ETA has been established primarily through lists of arrests and prison statistics.[11] But, in the absence of significant written records of women's participation in radical Basque nationalism, this study also depends on oral history interviews with former activists for evidence of the changing patterns of women's activism in ETA. Equally importantly, the interviews are a valuable qualitative source. They provide the opportunity for the study of changes and continuities in women's consciousness, and the ways in which memory has shaped the history of ETA, including its gender politics.

Oral history has occupied a privileged place in the development of contemporary women's history. Both fields arose out of a political and intellectual commitment to the recuperation of the voices of social groups silenced by traditional documentary history.[12] Since the 1980s, moreover, both areas have been shaped by the turn to theory in history, characterised by increased attention to language and subjectivity, and the relationship between discourse and the lived experiences of people in the past.[13] These insights have had a particularly strong impact on oral history, whose unique feature is the creation of a historical document through the interaction of interviewer and narrator(s). This inter-subjective process provides opportunities for the analysis of memory and language in representations of the past, as well as the relationship between the personal memories of the narrators and the wider historical context in which such memories are formed. As a document looking backwards from the perspective of the present, the oral history interview also offers the chance to assess how current conditions shape understandings of the past. In other words, oral history is about the relationship between history and memory.

Memory, like history, is shaped by gender relations. This is not to say that women and men always remember differently, or that there are universal features that distinguish women's narratives of the past from those of men. Differences among women – including diverse gender identities – are as likely to condition their memories as the similarity of being female. But because in most societies, past and present, gender has been a central organising principle and power relation, it is bound to condition memory. Oral history can help trace the contradictions and shifts in the development of social relations, underlining how they inflect with class, race, nationality, age, and other factors. Memories can highlight moments in the past when gender relations were particularly rigid and hierarchical, but equally they can reveal how historically contingent and even fragile and malleable gender roles can be.

Debates about memory have also come to the fore in studies of nationalism. In recent years it has become common to speak of 'collective' or 'social memory'[14] to designate those representations of the past shared by members of a particular social group, including national communities.[15] But although I have used the term 'collective memory' in previous publications I have become increasingly wary of this and related concepts.[16] Significant conceptual and methodological problems arise when one attempts to trace the construction of collective memories, and to measure the extent to which these are actually shared by members of a specific social group.[17] The study of memory in national and other collectives often seems to refer to public *narratives* or *representations* of the past – monuments, films, architecture, museums, and so on. There has been less critical attention to how these narratives and representations are negotiated, accepted, rejected or contested by individuals and groups.[18]

Part of the problem here is a lack of definition of key terms in much work on memory.[19] Another dilemma raised by the idea of collective memory is the relationship between the memories of different groups. Whereas in earlier work I talked about a 'collective' (and, by implication, 'male') nationalist memory that could be 'contested' by women's memories, I now see this relationship between different forms of memory – individual and collective, 'national' and 'women's' – as much more dynamic.[20] It is too simplistic to conceive a women's private memory in direct conflict with a public male national memory. Oral narratives suggest instead a complex process of negotiation and reworking whereby women's memories are formed both in identification with, and in response to, dominant representations of nationality and of gender.

Nor should it be assumed that women's oral narratives are only instructive about constructions of femininity, for gender, like national identity, is always constructed in relation to a perceived 'other'. In her oral history of British women in the Second World War, Penny Summerfield uses women's memories of male work colleagues to analyse women's constructions of wartime masculinities.[21] She then places these memories in the context of wider social discourses of work and masculinity during and after the war. By showing the extent to which women's memories of men drew on these wider discourses, Summerfield highlights the often precarious nature of male power, as well as the challenges many men faced in trying to live up to strict standards of militarised masculinity. At the same time, she demonstrates that women's self-representations, and their evaluations of gender equality and difference in the workplace, depend upon their perceptions and representations of the men around them. This example is particularly suggestive for the history of ETA, an area in which the overwhelming academic emphasis has been on men as the protagonists of the radical nationalist movement, but where there has been no comprehensive analysis of masculinity.[22] Although its emphasis is on women, this book contributes to the development of a history of radical nationalist masculinity, in particular with reference to the importance of fatherhood to the reproduction of radical nationalism (see especially chapters 1 and 4).[23] I attempt to avoid the trap of creating a generic and undifferentiated image of the male activist while showing the historical richness of women's roles. As Wendy Bracewell has argued in relation to Serbian nationalism, even if nationalism is premised on male bonding and privilege, nationalisms do not privilege all men in the same way.[24]

Moreover, to position women as the victims of an all-powerful male nationalist discourse would be to ignore the ways in which women themselves, through their actions and narratives, have helped to construct the myth of male nationalist heroism and martyrdom. This does not imply that women and men are represented equally in nationalist rhetoric, or that they are equal participants in memory's 'struggle over meaning'.[25] One group of oral historians argues, for example, that a central question for oral historians is 'why and how power relations between men and women have caused some memories to prevail over others. What makes some memories more significant, and how is this dominance related to other types of subjugation?'[26] As Katharine Hodgkin and Susannah Radstone remind us, memory is intimately tied to questions of power, questions that are always related in turn to the historical contexts in which memories are formed.[27] Against this background, an ongoing challenge for feminist oral history is to incorporate the theoretical insights about memory, subjectivity and language within a historical analysis that is grounded in social and economic relations. As Joan Sangster insists, these two aims cannot ultimately be separated: 'While it is important to analyse *how* someone constructs an explanation for their life, ultimately there are patterns, structures, systemic reasons for those constructions which must be identified to understand historical causality.'[28]

Interviewing Basque nationalist women

In 1996–97 I conducted a series of interviews with women who had been active in ETA and radical Basque nationalism from the mid-1960s to the early 1980s. In identifying the narrator group, I aimed to choose a sample that represented a range of backgrounds (age, region, class and ethnic group) and experiences of activism, while maintaining a particular focus on women who had participated directly in ETA and/or the radical nationalist feminist movement. With these criteria in mind I made contact with potential narrators through references from four sources: Basque women's organisations; radical nationalist organisations; academics, activists and other acquaintances in the Basque country; and narrators themselves.[29]

Following the methodology preferred by many oral historians, I conducted the interviews in the life story format.[30] Each narrator was encouraged to narrate her personal history in her own manner, prompted at points by my guidance or questions, a process that allowed the interviews to be shaped as much as possible by the narrators' memories. Each interview lasted between one hour and two and a half hours, and in all but one case (#22, b. 1943) – in which the interview was held in a location with excessive background noise – was taped with prior agreement of the narrator.

I subsequently transcribed the tapes and analysed them in detail. In order to preserve as much as possible the 'orality' of the original interviews,[31] I transcribed all the interviews literally, indicating pauses, gaps, repetitions, part words, and filler words. The spoken nature of the original texts (including laughter, pauses, repeated words, slips of the tongue, and so on) formed an important part of my analysis. However, quotations have been slightly edited for readability in this text because several readers of earlier versions found the direct transcriptions difficult to follow.[32] I then translated into English all the excerpts used in the text.[33] Finally, I cross-checked the information in the interviews as much as possible with written documents. The small sample size means that in places I have stressed the tentative nature of the conclusions, in hopes that others may continue the project of establishing an empirical base of evidence for the history of women in ETA.

The interviews are used primarily in the book as qualitative sources. The main themes which appear throughout the book, such as identification with motherhood, religion, the importance of the media in shaping radical nationalist identities, were chosen precisely because they were prominent in many or all of the interviews. Unlike most formal histories, the interviews are rarely chronological, and the weaving of themes through the chapters reflects this tension between the historical narrative and the more free-flowing memories as expressed in the interviews. In order to give the reader an impression of this interplay, and ways in which the interaction between the narrators and me as interviewer has shaped the book, each chapter explores one or two interviews in some detail.

The oral history project began in the mid-1990s at a time when women and nationalism was becoming a popular academic topic. Having grown up in English-speaking Canada during the premiership of Pierre Trudeau, when René Levesque led the Parti Québecois government in Quebec, I was familiar from childhood with debates about federalism, nationalism and 'separatism'. I spent my first few months in the Basque country in the autumn of 1995 researching in the archive of the Benedictine monastery in the small, largely Basque-speaking town of Lazkao in the heart of the Goierri region of Guipúzcoa, which is a traditional area of support for radical nationalism. During this period Basque nationalists were following closely the Quebec referendum on sovereignty association. The referendum (which was lost by less than one percentage point) provided a useful opening with many of the people I spoke to over the following year, for whom the fact that I had recently lived in Montreal seemed enough to suggest I might be sympathetic to Basque nationalism. Several comments also led me to understand that, had I been either American or Spanish – or indeed Basque – people's reception of me would not have been so warm. Thus my particular outsider status opened doors and provided some perceived common ground.

In addition, the fact that I was a woman allowed some narrators to appeal to an assumed common gender position, or at least perception, when sharing stories about personal relations, sexuality and experiences of sexism. This shared ground did not override substantial differences of age, ethnicity, life experience and, in several cases, class and level of education, but it did help to structure the interviews around what could broadly be called 'women's issues'. Some narrators took up my interest in their experiences 'as women' enthusiastically and in explicitly political terms, as in the case of the first woman I interviewed:

Well, hell, I wish all our feelings were reflected. I'd like that. I think it'd be better for all of us . . . Because I have the impression that the feelings that are reflected are men's. And I'd like it if society were seen through women's eyes. (#1, 1947)[34]

Others, however, cautioned that I should not listen to women's stories at the expense of men's, an attitude particularly common among women whose partners or male relatives had been killed, imprisoned or exiled.

Yet, whether the narrators embraced feminism as a political project or not, their interpretations of their life histories and their roles in the radical nationalist movement were fundamentally shaped by an awareness of the changes in gender roles and relations from their youth during the Franco regime to the time of the interviews thirty or forty years later. They made frequent references to the lack of feminist consciousness in the 1960s and 1970s as compared to the 1990s. Moreover, even among those narrators who criticised the lack of progress in the nationalist movement with regard to women's roles, the changing social position of women was a yardstick with which the distance from the past could be measured, and prospects for the future gauged.

This discourse of progress and optimism stands in marked contrast to the language used to describe the Basque conflict, which in the interviews seems to be caught in a time warp: a never-ending cycle of violence and repression.[35] Images in the interviews of an epic struggle between 'Basques' and 'Spain', stretching backwards in time to collective pre-memory, and threatening to extend endlessly into the future, echo radical nationalist rhetoric about the conflict. But they also reflect the political climate of the mid-1990s when the interviews were conducted. As Ronald Grele has noted, '[t]he documents we produce are artefacts of the time of their creation, not the period under discussion.'[36] The summer of 1995 saw what would prove to be a landmark in the aftermath of the dirty war against ETA.[37] In Valencia, on Spain's eastern coast, police discovered the remains of two young men, presumed to be ETA members, who had been tortured and killed over a decade earlier by the anti-terrorist organisation GAL and the Spanish Civil Guard, with the complicity of members the Socialist government in Madrid. The cases against those accused of the murders of Joxean Lasa, Joxe Zabala and two dozen others in the mid-1980s dominated the news much of the time I was in the Basque country. Several of my narrators knew people, including partners, who had been killed by the GAL. In March 1996, after I had done only a few interviews, the Socialists were defeated by the conservative Popular Party. Although the Socialists were universally reviled by radical nationalists, and indeed many Basques who did not support ETA but were nevertheless appalled by the GAL affair, the prospect of a government led by a party with direct links to the Franco regime was hardly met with enthusiasm.

Luisa Passerini has written that '(p)eople's memories of their own past lives, what they remember and what they forget, are shaped by their own expectations for the future, and also by whether they have children or young people for whom they care and who may outlive them.' [38] The general mood of pessimism about a resolution to the Basque conflict, as well as narrators' personal circumstances, informed the interviews as much as their experience of the history they were recounting. In contrast to Passerini's studies of fascist Italy and the Italian underground of the 1970s[39] – work that has been particularly inspirational for my own – neither my Basque narrators nor I had historical distance from ETA and the Basque conflict. This was a history project, but it was about a history that was 'still happening'.[40]

Throughout the period of the interviews – February 1996 to April 1997 – ETA pursued its campaign of violence, carrying out sporadic bombings and murders of politicians, police and other Basque and Spanish citizens. None of these killings inspired the level of public loathing that would be seen just a few months after my departure, with the murder of the young town councillor Miguel Angel Blanco in the Basque town of Ermua in July 1997. But reaction to ETA attacks, both in Spain and the Basque country, indicated that support for ETA was dwindling. This period also coincided with the years of the *kale borroka* or street struggle, involving organised acts of violence against public property and police officers by gangs of hooded radical nationalist youths in towns and cities throughout the Basque country.[41] Non-nationalist reporting of these actions seemed to intensify the already widespread view that all radical nationalists, and not just ETA members, were inherently and incurably violent. While in public the radical nationalist community retained a united front in the face of what ETA supporters perceived as a conspiracy against them, there were indications that years of conflict were taking their toll on radical nationalist supporters.

This impression, which I gained through observation, conversation with people of many political persuasions, and media-watching, was generally confirmed by the interviews. The narrators represented a wide spectrum of opinion about the conflict. A minority remained staunch supporters of mainstream radical nationalism and gave no hint of criticising ETA or its actions. These narrators were most likely to tell their stories in epic tones of 'us' and 'them', and focused more on collective history than personal experience and emotions. Another minority continued to support nationalist aims, but had abandoned radical nationalism because of ETA's actions. These narrators were most likely to look to the past for clues to what had caused the current crisis. Whereas for the first group ETA was a constant, an organisation unchanged in thirty-five years, for the second, history could be divided into a good period and a bad period: a time, broadly corresponding with the narrator's own activism, when ETA represented hope and the collective dream of a better future, followed by a fall, when dreams turned to nightmares, heroes became villains, and the narrator could no longer 'support the unsupportable' (#7, b. 1943). The timing of the fall sometimes coincided with a landmark in the history of ETA (for example, the Hipercor bombing in Barcelona in 1987, which killed over twenty people), but the break with radical nationalism reflected equally events in the narrator's personal life.[42] The majority of the narrators occupied positions between these two groups. They continued to support nationalism in some form, more or less critical of ETA, but typically were more willing openly to condemn the Spanish and Basque governments for what they considered repeated failures to end the conflict – and in particular to solve the problem of more than 400 ETA prisoners spread throughout Spain and France.

But if the current situation of the conflict provided a solid and sinister backdrop, casting a shadow over the interviews, and making narrators stress what had not changed, in reality much had changed since ETA's founding in 1959. The organisation's development was spurred by the confluence of Francoist repression and unprecedented industrial renewal and economic growth. During the1960s the province of Vizcaya, whose capital is the urban centre Bilbao, enjoyed the highest standard of living in Spain.[43] By the following decade, however, in the wake of global downturn, the Basque economy had set into a long decline. The region, one of the most highly industrialised in Spain during the late Franco period, and particularly dependent on heavy industry, was badly affected by the economic restructuring introduced by the Socialists during the 1980s. By the 1990s the Basque country had one of the highest youth unemployment rates in the country.[44]

Like the GAL, the recession acted more as a sustaining mechanism than a cause of the ongoing political violence. Nonetheless, it may have helped some of my interview narrators, and radical nationalists generally, to continue to justify a strategy that had taken an enormous personal toll and proven utterly ineffective in political terms. Although the young people (mostly teenage boys) who participated in the street violence during the 1990s did not necessarily come from the most deprived areas of the Basque country, their future employment prospects were certainly limited. This probably served, in the eyes of their supporters, to excuse their violence as a righteous expression of personal, political and social injustice. For narrators with adolescent and young adult children, unemployment was exacerbated by the perception that young radical nationalists had, in the words of one narrator, 'certain doors closed' to them because of their politics (#11c, b. 1945).

This view corresponds with the generally moralistic tone of radical nationalist language, in which activism is posited as a sacrifice that only the strongest can sustain. But the economic crisis also facilitated the construction of a history in which radical nationalists were the only ones who did not 'sell out' during the transition to democracy. One narrator pointed to the 'betrayals' of the Socialist and Communist parties, arguing that the recession meant that history had 'proved us right' (#8a, b. 1948). The economic crisis may have enabled narrators to map on to their personal memories the 'official' radical nationalist history of ETA as a movement rooted in class, as much as nationalist, struggle. Although the majority were of middle- or lower-middle-class social status as adults, many of the narrators alluded to the economic and employment crisis during their interviews. In other words, the economic crisis may have provided an excuse for a retrospective construction of a radical nationalist movement grounded in class conflict, a version of history that contradicted evidence of the material prosperity of the 1960s, but resonated with the economic reality and the subjective situation of the narrators in the 1990s.

Finally, international events also informed interpretations of the past and hopes for the future. One narrator, explaining at the end of the interview why she continued to support radical nationalism, drew a contrast between what she remembered of the project she had supported in the 1970s and 1980s and what she saw around her in the mid-1990s:

> What I do think has been lost is that other component of creating another society . . . [our project] yes it was about getting independence and everything but always thinking about how we would create another world, live in a different way, we're going to build something different. I don't see that so much any more. People don't dream so much about that. It was my dream and the dream of the people around me. Maybe it has to do with the fact that the socialist block has fallen. I think that has a lot to do with it . . . I mean ideologically to think you can live in a different way, the situation in Cuba . . . Maybe the fact that all that has been erased a bit. I do notice that. (#17, b. 1958)

In a 1973 radio interview with a group of oral historians in Chicago, Saul Benison raised the question of how to deal with the 'hopes and aspirations' of people in the past, and the inadequacy of conventional historical evidence in capturing such information:

You know what makes life bearable for everybody? The fact that they can have a secret life that they don't reveal to anyone. That secret life can really inform history. This is what I mean. You could get data on the rise of income in Great Britain from 1800 to 1830 and you could say in statistical terms 'things got better'. The one thing that's missing is the hopes and aspirations of these people that make those figures viable. Should you go after the dreams? Should you go after the hopes and aspirations? Should you go after the secret life? I'm not sure.[45]

In response to Benison's question, I would say that we should go after the hopes and aspirations, even if, as I discuss below, there are some secrets we must respect as outsiders. In the case of the narrator quoted above, memories of shared dreams of a better future help explain the disappointments expressed in some interviews, as well as the pessimism about the future. Such memories also help to account for the nostalgia notable in many of the interviews about what I call the 'golden years' of radical nationalist activism, when radical change seemed possible, even imminent.

Benison's question – what information the interviewer should 'go after' – is part of the wider issue of the ethics of oral history. The power dynamic between interviewer and narrator has been much debated by oral historians, sociologists and ethnographers. Notwithstanding attempts to 'level the field' by adopting as balanced a relationship as possible between narrator and interviewer, most scholars agree that the relationship can never be an equal one; after all, even with the best training and intentions, the final decision about how to use narrators' stories rests with the researcher.[46] But debates about the interviewer – narrator relationship have been valuable in raising awareness about the ethical dimension of interviewing, and in particular the responsibility of the interviewer to her subjects and their stories.

As my example of nationality indicates, the interaction between interviewer and narrator is informed as much by assumed identities as actual social positions. Moreover, one cannot assume that the interviewer is in an unambiguously privileged position vis-à-vis the narrator. A narrator's attitude towards an interviewer's professional status, like any other aspect of her social position (class, ethnicity, age, sexuality, gender – to name only the obvious ones) will be conditioned by the narrator's own position and experience of these factors outside the interview context. Thus one should be wary of assuming that academic qualifications afford automatic esteem from narrators. I was reminded of this in the course of one interview with a narrator who had spent many years in exile as the partner of a high-profile male ETA member, returning home to the Spanish Basque country after his death. A kind and reserved woman, and somewhat nervous interviewee, she claimed at the outset that she had nothing of value to tell me (a common refrain in interviews with people who have rarely been asked to tell their life story to a stranger). But in response to a question about whether she had been involved in politics since her return to Bilbao, she answered:

> No, no . . . I've dedicated myself to the house, to financial concerns. And culture. Look, when you get here you realise you've got a terrible cultural void. I'd been over there for years . . . On a human level I'd had some amazing experiences. If you like, I'd done a PhD. (#6, b. 1946)

The narrator may not have consciously or deliberately asserted her credentials in the face of my own, but in the context of the specific story she was telling she was highlighting the value of her hard-earned knowledge. The mythologising of ETA's early years, and the kudos accorded to those who had lived through that period, is well established in the radical nationalist community. Despite her modesty, the narrator's direct experience of the GAL and her personal relationship with many of ETA's legendary activists, gave her credibility and esteem in her own community, and in my eyes as a researcher, a fact of which she was no doubt aware.

Daniel James encountered a similar scenario in his analysis of the life story of María Roldán, a working-class Argentine woman and Peronist activist whom he interviewed in the 1980s. Contemplating Doña María's assertion that she had not learned from the university, but rather from 'the book of life', James argues that this claim is a warning against the idea – found in some postmodernist ethnographic work – 'of the interviewee/narrator as victim whose memory and identity are appropriated and exploited',[47] a view that 'seriously underestimates the power of the interviewee to negotiate the conditions under which communication takes place in the interview situation.'[48] James grants that the reference to the 'the book of life' 'is certainly a claim to establish footing, to equalise the gap in cultural status between a university professor and a meatpacking worker',[49] but argues that it also serves as a reminder that there are certain parts of the narrator's past that the interviewer cannot know and understand.[50] In answer to his own question about how the oral historian should respond to such a claim, James suggests we follow the advice of Doris Sommer in an essay on Latin American *testimonio*, 'in which she enjoined the reader/critic to respect the secret, to treat the claim as an ethically unpassable border that no form of interpretative representation should seek to cross'.[51]

All the chapters of this book contain examples of moments when narrators have clearly chosen not to reveal all. This is especially true of stories involving controversial or painful events, including the use of violence or death of a family member or friend. At times I attempted to push the narrator a little farther, asking her how she had felt about these experiences. At other moments, sensing that further questioning would constitute an invasion of the narrator's privacy, I allowed that 'unpassable border' to stand as its own kind of evidence, as an example of the importance of silence.

Memory, silence and violence

A great deal of the recent literature on memory is preoccupied with memories of violence. Indeed, the study of memory in the late twentieth century developed in close connection with Holocaust studies, and more broadly with personal or political memories of violence often characterised as trauma. The voices typically represented in this literature are those of victims. Much has been written, particularly in the scholarship on Holocaust survivors, about the difficulties encountered by victims in recounting their tales in a cultural context in which there is no public language into which to fit these tales and no wider public willing to listen to the survivors' stories. Yet, from the 1980s onwards, there has been growing interest in such stories, both in the academy and in the wider public sphere, with testimonies of the survivors of war, genocide and state terror, and with the question of witnessing.[52] But the current attention afforded tales of survival is not without its problems and paradoxes. Some scholars have expressed concern with what they see as a tendency to encourage identification of readers and listeners, in the words of Susannah Radstone, with 'pure victimhood'.[53]

The study of the Basque conflict presents particular difficulties in relation to the categories of victim and perpetrator. Unlike in the case of the Holocaust or other genocides, the distinction between victims and perpetrators is not always easy to ascertain and maintain. Former members of ETA who have committed or supported acts of violence against others have almost invariably been victims – direct or indirect – of state violence, including police repression, torture (in some cases sexual torture), right-wing paramilitary attacks and killing. To draw attention to different forms of violence is not to suggest a direct parallel between the violence suffered by ETA members and supporters and their victims.[54] It is, rather, to try to understand ETA violence in its wider historical and cultural context, and to be aware of the risks involved for narrators in remembering violence. In her interviews with women imprisoned for their participation in underground organisations in Italy in the 1970s, Passerini describes the absence from the interviews of the very facts of terrorism, the repression of violence, which she eloquently calls 'lacerations in the memory'.⁵⁵ There may be a number of explanations for these silences, but she insists on the necessity of reading them in their 'global context':

> In a society in which violent death is so frequent, is this repression part and parcel of every kind of murder? Hasn't all previous violence, whether committed by fascism or by antifascism, been pushed aside, in a sort of collective repression mechanism?⁵⁶

I have argued elsewhere for the need to read memories of violence in interviews with Basque nationalist women within the wider context of the silences around other forms of violence in Spain's past, including acts committed by the Franco regime.⁵⁷ As Passerini insists, the responsibility for acts of violence lies with those who commit them; only by accepting that responsibility can the actor be considered a subject in the full sense of the term.⁵⁸ The responsibility of the interviewer, on the other hand, lies in a willingness to listen to and record accounts of political violence from the perspective of those who have participated in or supported it, without either justifying or sensationalising that violence. The interviewer must be especially aware that the interview might, in Passerini's words, 'constitute a trap in the sense that it is an inducement to indulge in the old identities, to think of oneself only as a character in illegal stories'.⁵⁹ I have therefore avoided using the label 'terrorist', in order not to equate narrators with their histories of violence or to freeze them in the past. I agree with Ronaldo Munck that '[p]ractitioners of political violence need constantly to (re)interpret the sense of their actions. Yet we should also be aware that violence is usually only a part, often a small one, of the broader construction of political identity.'⁶⁰

While violence is at the centre of most studies of ETA, this book offers a new perspective by analysing political violence from the perspective of gender. Moreover, I have been careful throughout the book not to emphasise violence at the expense of other elements of radical nationalist history, or other memories. If the book departs from many feminist approaches to women and conflict by placing equal emphasis on women as victims *and* agents of violence, it also calls for a reconsideration of the place of violence in much recent memory work. In her study of the 'afterlives' of May 1968, Kristin Ross argues that the study of memory has been constrained by the very terms with which it has come to be identified. Locating the rise of the 'memory industry' in studies of the Second World War – in particular, of the Holocaust and the 'Gulag' – Ross contends that the widespread application of the psychoanalytic concepts of trauma and repression to the study of collective memory has 'defamiliarised' us with mass events not associated with catastrophe: ' "Masses" . . . have come to mean masses of dead bodies, not masses of people working together to take charge of their collective lives.'[61]

In contrast to the proliferation of studies of memory as trauma, Ross stresses that participants' memories of 1968 often emphasise the pleasures of partaking in collective action and forming new solidarities.[62] My interviews with radical Basque nationalist women similarly underscore the limitations of the trauma paradigm for understanding the history of political movements. Although memories of violence figure prominently in most of the interviews, they sit alongside memories of the pleasures of activism. This phenomenon is related to something else Ross notes: the feeling of intensity associated with living through a period when time seems to be accelerated, and the distinction between everyday life and politics collapses.[63] The following example of what I call 'activist time and space' comes from a narrator who lived in hiding through most of the 1980s before being arrested and imprisoned for four years:

> You live in a reduced space, because you're not in the street, you don't have any social life. So you don't know what's going to happen the next minute. So there are intense relationships, every minute is like a whole lifetime. So you create really deep friendship ties. You experience all your feelings a hundred per cent. Because you're always in the pendulum of time. Another time exists, which is our time, inside real space. (#18, b. 1961)

In searching for explanations for ongoing ETA violence, some scholars have emphasised the hatred that motivates ETA members, in particular a hatred of all things associated with Spain.[64] There is no doubt that radical nationalist rhetoric constructs an overwhelmingly negative image of the Spanish state, helping to sustain support for radical nationalist violence. But the maintenance and reproduction of a radical nationalist community over several generations cannot be explained primarily in terms of hatred. One study has suggested, for instance, that the rituals of radical nationalism are best understood not as demonstrating defiance towards the enemy, but as creating and consolidating ties within the community.[65] In his classic study of nationalism Benedict Anderson stresses that the language of nationalist movements is more often characterised by images of love of nation than of fear and loathing.[66] Likewise, the interviews explored in this book highlight the importance of feelings of love and happiness, often above anger and hatred, in memories of radical nationalist activists.

The book's layout combines a more traditional narrative history with the themes as they appear through memories in the interviews. Chapters 1 to 4 are loosely chronological, focusing on the prehistory and history of

ETA's first two decades (1959–82). Chapter 1 covers the postwar period, looking at the reproduction of Basque nationalism in the 1940s and 1950s, the years of most intense Francoist repression, through the childhood and adolescent memories of narrators. Chapter 2 moves ahead to the 1960s, when the older group of narrators became politically active. This chapter looks at the roots of radical nationalism through the lens of gender, exploring some of the key institutions from which the movement emerged, including the Church. Chapters 3 and 4 focus more directly on the development of ETA through the 1960s and 1970s, and in particular the relationship between the militarisation of radical nationalism and the movement's gender politics.

Chapters 5, 6 and 7 focus on three areas of women's experience in radical nationalism from the mid-1960s to early 1980s: ETA activism, prison and feminism. Chapter 5 analyses the gender roles, relationships and politics inside ETA, as well as evidence of women's changing activities and media representations of female 'terrorists' in this period. Chapter 6 looks at women's memories of arrest and prison. Here, forms of state violence, including torture, which is typically portrayed as neutral in terms of gender, are analysed within the context of a gendered discourse of conflict. In addition, prison is examined as a space that simultaneously isolated women from the wider nationalist community and brought them into contact with new communities and political ideas, including feminism. Chapter 7 extends the examination of feminism through an exploration of radical nationalist feminist organisations in the 1970s and 1980s, and their often frustrated attempts to introduce a feminist agenda into radical nationalism. Chapter 8 examines the changes and continuities in women's roles in ETA and radical nationalism over the past twenty-five years, as well as contemporary representations of female 'terrorists'. Finally, the Conclusion suggests some areas for future research on gender and ETA, and includes a brief discussion of the gender politics of postnationalism. It closes with some suggestions about how the history of women in ETA can contribute to understandings of Spain's 'memory wars' at the turn of the millennium.

1

Growing up nationalist

> We were born Basque. Our work, our whole lives, take place in this territory, seat of our ethnicity, which we call Euskadi. (ETA, 'Carta a los intelectuales', *Zutik*, June 1965)

> I've been a nationalist by calling since I was tiny. (#2, b. 1959)

The history of Basque nationalism over the past hundred years, as recorded in nationalist literature and recounted in personal narratives and historical texts, is heavily infused with the notions of family and generation. 'Family' and 'nation' are often portrayed as overlapping or even interchangeable, making it appear that nationalist sentiment and ideology are natural or innate, as suggested by the quotes above. Yet this narrative of tradition and continuity tends to obscure a history shaped equally by transformation and even rupture. With its roots in the social upheavals generated by rapid industrialisation in the late nineteenth century, Basque nationalism developed in the twentieth century against a background of uneven development in Spain and Europe, through civil and international wars, economic boom and bust. Within the ranks of nationalism itself divisions have given rise to new movements, new communities and even new nationalisms.

This book is concerned with the most decisive of these breaks, that which occurred in 1959 when a group of young men disillusioned with the politics of the Basque Nationalist Party (PNV) founded ETA. Like other landmarks in the history of Basque nationalism, this split took place at a juncture of broader social, economic and political change. The new radical nationalist movement that developed in the 1960s represented itself simultaneously as a revolutionary break with a more conservative nationalist past, and a movement that continued to defend a timeless Basque tradition, associated above all with a dwindling rural community centred on the family farmstead. Thus, in common with other European nationalist discourses, in radical nationalist rhetoric the family operated as a trope, a symbol of stability and tradition in an era of upheaval. Yet family structures in the Basque country, as elsewhere, differed between rural and urban contexts and across ethnic communities and socioeconomic classes. Nor were families in any of their forms free from internal flux and conflict.

This chapter will look at the role of the family in the history of the Basque nationalist movement in the post-Civil War period. It looks at the family both as a symbol in the language of nationalism, and as an institution that shaped the movement's development. In particular, it focuses on the different and changing places of women in relation to family life. It argues that the family should not be considered a separate, private sphere, but must be understood in the context of the complex and changing relationship between private and public realms during the Franco dictatorship. Moreover, while mothers played an important role in the history of Basque nationalism under Franco, the privilege accorded motherhood in many histories of the movements has tended to obscure the roles of both fathers and unmarried and/or childless women. This means that the process of the development of Basque nationalism under Franco must be reconsidered.

The gender politics of early Basque nationalism

The language of gender in Basque nationalism during the first third of the twentieth century, with its emphasis on women's maternal position as caregivers and preservers of national tradition, was typical of late nineteenth-century middle-class European nationalisms. For instance, the writings of Sabino Arana, who founded the PNV in 1895, constructed an idealised image of Basque community in contrast to everything he designated 'Spanish'. Yet in the area of gender Arana's nationalist rhetoric did not so much challenge hegemonic Spanish ideas as mimic them, incorporating the dominant middle-class Catholic vision of women as mothers and guardians of the home. If nationalist womanhood was presented as an idealisation of motherhood, it was nonetheless based upon a Western dualist model of femininity as simultaneously sacred and profane. Thus, in a familiar nationalist trope, for Arana 'Woman' represented the land and the *patria*, revered but also feared as vulnerable to seduction, attack or penetration by the foreign enemy.[1]

The patrolling of women's sexuality was central to the early nationalist project of protecting what Arana claimed was a separate Basque 'race'. While nationalist men were sometimes permitted to marry outside the national collective, a woman's marriage to a Spaniard was considered a threat to the purity of the Basque nation.[2] Paradoxically, the corrupt 'Spanish' phenomena from which the Basque country was to be protected (socialism, secularism, and so on) were decried as 'feminine', while Basque patriotism was hailed as a 'virile' virtue.[3] This underscored the extent to which gender functioned as a discourse, intersecting with those of race and class, to construct a nationalist world view based on the opposition Basque and Spanish.[4] Far from operating merely on a symbolic plane, these discursive relations constructed and reinforced power relations based on gender within the nationalist community.

If the family represented the symbolic centre of Basque tradition, in practice the middle-class nationalist family was the basic unit of the early nationalist community. In their political rhetoric, early Basque nationalists frequently represented the nation as 'one big family'.[5] Yet the nascent nationalist community comprised a network of Catholic, middle-class Bilbao families, which blurred the distinction between personal and political alliances.[6] In her landmark history of women in the early Basque nationalist movement, Mercedes Ugalde analyses the history and membership of the Basque nationalist women's organisation Emakume Abertzale Batza (EAB) from the beginning of the twentieth century to the outbreak of the Spanish Civil War (1936). Like the roles of middle-class Christian women in much of the industrialised world at the turn of the last century, the activities of the EAB (predominantly in the areas of Basque culture and language, education and charity) were conceived by nationalists as an extension of women's duties in the home. In this way, women's nationalist activism fit within collective values of urban, middle-class Basque families. It also resonated with the daily realities of most EAB members, for whom motherhood and other forms of family and community care were a central experience.[7]

EAB members also, however, made use of the association between womanhood, motherhood, family and nation in order to leave their homes and enter new spaces of social, cultural and political activity. The creation of women's groups affiliated to the early Basque nationalist movement allowed a limited number of middle-class women from ethnic Basque nationalist families to extend their activities into the public political sphere, without threatening the gender hierarchy within the nationalist movement, or within Basque society more generally.[8] At the same time – and this would constitute one of the enduring paradoxes of nationalist gender politics, in the Basque country as elsewhere – the move of women into limited spheres of public activity opened the way to some renegotiation of gender roles, and even, in a few isolated cases, to the possibility of criticising women's subordinate social and political position.[9]

Ugalde's study therefore highlights the abiding tensions between traditionalist nationalism, with its conservative gender politics, and the ways in which nationalist women took advantage of the central place of the family in nationalist ideology to create new spaces of women's activity. The majority of early Basque nationalist women never directly challenged the gender hierarchy in their movement and in society. Indeed, during the Spanish Second Republic and Civil War (1931–39) the Catholicism and social conservatism of the EAB created a distance from other Republican women's organisations,[10] which supported basic reforms in the area of family and gender relations (such as the legalisation of divorce).[11] This was a fundamental ideological difference that mirrored the wider divide between Basque nationalists and other Republican groups.[12] Nevertheless, the liberal reforms of the Second Republic, including women's suffrage in 1931, provided an environment favourable to women's political activism, benefiting even conservative, Catholic organisations such as the EAB.[13] The emergency brought on by the outbreak of the Civil War in July 1936 opened opportunities for such activity, although unlike many socialist, communist and anarchist women's groups, the EAB never expanded women's activism beyond the 'home front'.[14] But even women's traditional forms of activism were crushed by the reactionary rebel forces under Francisco Franco. In the summer of 1937, the fall of the Basque provinces of Vizcaya and Guipúzcoa signalled the end of the EAB, and of Basque nationalist aspirations for autonomy.[15] By the time of the final Republican surrender in April 1939, the Basque nationalist 'family' had been forcefully incorporated into Franco's 'great household' of united Spaniards.[16]

Nationalist families and the post-war crisis

The first fifteen years following the victory of the Franco forces saw a Spain devastated by economic destruction and widespread political and social repression. Although these were felt to varying degrees in all regions of the country, the relatively higher standard of living in the Basque country helped to ameliorate – if by no means to eliminate – some of the worst effects of disease and devastation in these notorious 'years of hunger'. Moreover, while for many communities that had supported the Republic – most notably the urban proletariat – punishment was characterised by mass arrests, imprisonment and executions, in the Basque country (where support of the conservative, Catholic PNV for the Spanish Republic had been ambivalent at best),[17] repression manifested itself above all in the realm of culture and language. In an endeavour to impose General Franco's imagined unified Spanish nation, the new regime banned the open expression of any national identity other than that which it identified as 'Spanish'. In Catalonia and the Basque country the use of Catalan and the Basque language *euskera* was forbidden, the flying of national flags prohibited, and the symbols of a victorious Spanish National Catholicism imposed.

While anti-Basque measures were aimed particularly at supporters of the PNV, the direct effects of linguistic and cultural repression were felt most profoundly in those areas where the Basque language had been best preserved, namely in the rural and coastal zones of the provinces of Guipúzcoa and Vizcaya and the Basque-speaking areas of Navarre. Like early Basque nationalists before them, postwar nationalists idealised these zones as the repositories of a true, timeless Basque culture. From the 1920s the PNV had broadened its base of support, winning followers beyond Bilbao in smaller Basque-speaking fishing and farming communities.[18] By the postwar period the new nationalist supporters in these areas, many of whom had participated directly in the war, faced what some believed was the demise of their rural way of life – not only economically, but culturally and linguistically too. The threat to *euskera*, which was already in declining use, and the social insecurity stemming from the decreased viability of traditional rural and fishing communities, was heightened from the 1950s by a new wave of industrialisation that attracted large numbers of Spanish-speaking workers to Basque-speaking areas.[19]

In the nationalist symbolic order, these changes to rural traditions – and the decreasing use of *euskera* in particular – represented a danger to the nation itself. For Sabino Arana's generation, the rural family farm (*baserri*) had represented the antithesis to industrialisation.[20] This myth of ancient rural harmony was common to nineteenth-century lower-middle-class European nationalisms,[21] but in the Basque case the myth of the countryside was enhanced by its association with medieval foral laws (*fueros*) allowing for primogeniture and 'universal nobility'.[22] These were reworked in the late nineteenth-century nationalist imagination into a kind of primitive democracy granting nobility and equality to all Basque citizens.[23] By celebrating medieval and early modern Basque society as egalitarian and free of class conflict, therefore, early nationalists (who were mainly middle-class men from Bilbao) had essentially 'invented' an idyllic Basque rural haven: the opposite of the perceived corruption of the rapidly modernising world around them.[24]

Historically, the *baserri* had been a unit of economic and familial production and reproduction. The all-encompassing nature of the *baserri*, and its relationship to the people (*herri*), the land (*lur*) and the family, are encompassed within the basic unit *etxe* (house). The land is commonly referred to in *euskera* in the feminine as *amalur* (motherland), and the *etxe* is associated in traditional *baserri* culture with women, and above all mothers.[25] This association helps explain the popular stereotype of the strong Basque mother who ran the traditional family farm and controlled its economy. This image was underpinned by the nationalist interpretation of the foral laws, which stressed that the same traditions that granted Basques of all classes universal equality also extended to relations between men and women.[26] The notion of an age-old Basque gender equality goes far beyond the nationalist writings of the early PNV, to popular images of the strong Basque mother in contemporary Basque society. The stereotype of the strong mother and the belief in historical gender equality associated with traditional rural culture have given rise to frequent claims that a long tradition of matriarchy is one of the unique features of the Basque country.[27]

The matriarchy theory has been a source of significant debate among academics and the wider Basque public.[28] Likewise, there are disagreements regarding the nature of women's power in the rural household. Teresa del Valle and the other authors of an early feminist contribution to the study of women in contemporary Basque society stress that the popular image of women running the *baserri* did not reflect the actual division of labour in many rural households in the twentieth century.[29] Although women did take part in decision-making and were instrumental in the daily running of the family farm, much of the most prestigious economic work – notably that related to the outside world – was done by men.[30] The gap between women's and men's experience of life outside the farm was reflected as well in leisure time: while men regularly went to bars and Sunday-afternoon games and sports, women tended to live and work almost exclusively on the *baserri*, with little free time to themselves, and few regular outings beyond weekly trips to mass and market.[31]

When explaining its resilience in the decades following the Civil War, scholars of Basque nationalism have tended to portray the family as a kind of haven from Francoist repression and social and economic upheaval.[32] In other words, it is portrayed as an institution relatively protected from wider social and political conflict, with the home as a privileged space for the protection of national identity and the reproduction of nationalism itself. Implicit in this is the assumption that women were instrumental as mothers and housekeepers in preserving and transmitting Basque culture and language inside the home. Yet the academic literature on nationalism has relatively little to say about the actual structure of Basque families in the postwar period, their variance across class and region, or the gender and generational relations inside different families. Nor do studies of the origins of ETA and radical nationalism provide details of the interaction between the family and other social, economic and political institutions under Franco.

In contrast, other scholars have turned their attention to gender relations and discourse under Francoism, and in particular to the ideological construction of motherhood under the regime. As one has noted:

> In Francoist Spain, as in other authoritarian or totalitarian regimes (such as Nazi Germany, Fascist Italy, or Stalin's Soviet Union), the drive to nationalize the female populations implied the politicization of the private sphere . . . Women were the 'heart' of the family in National-Catholic Spain . . . The glorification of the maternal role of women under totalitarianism is essential for understanding how gender was and is central to authoritarian politics. Motherhood represented the essences of national strength and orchestrated an orderly relation between the sexes.[33]

The parallels with Basque nationalist gender ideology are striking. The similarity between these two forms of Catholic and nationalist motherhood, and of gender relations generally, undermines any simplistic view of Basque families as spaces that were 'protected' from the Franco state, or that represented unequivocal resistance to Francoism. In the area of gender relations in particular, middle-class Basque nationalist families to a large extent followed, rather than challenged, dominant ideology. This is not to say that Basque women from nationalist families supported the Franco regime any more than men did, or that they did not feel the repressive effects of the regime in their day-to-day lives. But a perspective on the reproduction of Basque nationalism under Franco that takes gender into account raises new questions about the relationship between families and the State. Rather than defining the family as a site of resistance against Francoism, an alternative model for understanding the relationship between the family and the State considers the movements of individuals and groups between the family and other institutions.

Mothers between private and public

In contrast to a popular image of a matriarchy in which women ran the rural home and family economy, in some interview narrators' childhood memories, Basque family farms under Franco had what would more appropriately be called patriarchal power structures. Some narrators implicitly call into question the idea that men and women had equal inheritance rights by stressing the need for women as well as men to look for paid work outside the farm during difficult financial times. This corroborates the thesis of del Valle and her colleagues that women and men had uneven access to leisure time and places.[34] In other interviews the division of roles is represented through a series of vivid contrasts between women's and men's activities, and in particular their different levels of access to the public sphere. Such interviews also stress men's authority and economic privilege within the family.

The following two interview excerpts come from narrators who grew up in rural areas in different parts of the Basque country (the first in Guipúzcoa, the second in Vizcaya) during the 1950s and 1960s:

> My father, apart from all that stuff he loved his time off. He loved going out. He loved a party . . . More than anything what my mother did was work. And the one in charge was my father. She worked loads . . . She's been a burden, a beast of burden. But that's the way the majority of women were. (#20, b. 1945)

> I'm from a farm family, from a farm in one of the poorest areas of Euskadi, Encartaciones. There's a point at which young people think 'We're big families, and the whole family can't live on the farm.' Since there was a big [industrial] expansion in greater Bilbao, and everyone has relatives around Bilbao, you think about starting your life over in industry. In our case, since we're women, it's not considered proper for women to go into the factories with men. But at that point women also saw that they couldn't go on living on the farm because that wasn't a life for a woman. First of all because the older brothers always kept the farm. So in one way or another the daughters had to sort out their own lives. (#8a, b. 1948)

There is no suggestion in these or other interviews that women's work was looked down upon; on the contrary, the narrators emphasise the physical labour performed by women, whether on the farm or in the factory. Such examples reflect a wider tension in the interviews as a whole, between the value placed on women's traditional roles and a recognition of gender hierarchies and divisions of labour. Thus the narrators express a dilemma similar to that in much contemporary feminist commentary on the family, between the ideal of gender equality and a celebration of values and roles associated with traditional femininity, in particular motherhood.[35]

Memories of mothers' activity in public are most frequent in stories of women's work with political prisoners. Alongside activities associated with Basque culture and language, prison support was one of women's traditional political activities, and was likewise often perceived as a natural extension of their family duties.[36] During the 1940s and 1950s, in Republican communities all over Spain, women with family members in prison formed informal support groups, whose aims were to raise funds for the prisoners, initiate liberation campaigns and denounce the maltreatment of prisoners.[37] The following excerpts, each taken from the opening of the oral history interview, highlight the importance of prison in the memories of postwar Basque nationalist families. Both narrators were raised in Basque nationalist families in the postwar period and were later active in ETA circles during the 1960s. The first speaker was born near the largely Basque-speaking town of Guernica, the historical centre of Basque claims to independence and site of the notorious bombardment by German war planes in April 1937, which was immortalised in Picasso's painting of the same name. The second narrator was born to a Basque-speaking mother who had migrated to Bilbao to work as a young woman.

> Well, I was born into an *euskaldun* [Basque-speaking] family, that I think had participated quite a bit in the war, even though nothing was ever said clearly, because people were afraid of talking, but they did talk. My father, was a *gudari* [Basque soldier] and my mother, I don't know, but I think she went around to the prisons a lot and organised help, that kind of thing . . . My grandmother lived with us, and my grandmother, of course, didn't shut up. Because a son of hers had died in the bombing of Guernica . . . my grandmother didn't forget; and, she constantly told us things about the war. (#1, b. 1947)

> I was born in Bilbao, in an *euskaldun* family . . . I was raised only by my mother. [My father] was in prison because he was a *gudari*, *ertzaina* [Basque soldier], in the war, and he came home very sick, in the year 1940 . . . My parents were married in '43. They met in prison. My father was a prisoner, and my mother was a PNV *emakume* [member of the EAB], and she went to wash his clothes, to look after the prisoners . . . And she met my father there. They fell in love and waited for him to get out of prison, and they got married in '43. And in '46 – he came home really sick from the front – and in '46 he died. So we were left alone in '46. I was 2 and my mother was 30. (#3, b. 1944)

These excerpts can be understood on one level as an attempt to establish, from the outset of the interview, an individual ethnic, cultural or nationalist identity. They can equally be taken together as testimony to the particular social and political alienation experienced by Basque-speaking communities during the harshest years of Francoist repression. Although not necessarily representative of the experience of women who became radical nationalist activists in the 1960s, these excerpts describe a set of social relations that collectively helped to define a postwar Basque nationalist and anti-Francoist consciousness. This would later give rise to a new nationalist movement. Moreover, these narrators recall not only the heavy physical and psychological toll of the Civil War, but also the division of women's and men's roles in managing this toll. Stories of nationalist men killed or imprisoned by Franco forces form part of a public nationalist narrative in which the Basque soldier or *gudari* is the protagonist. These two narrators acknowledge and validate this tradition. But in their stories it is older female family figures who are left to cope with the effects of the death and destruction wrought by war.

Stories about mothers can also serve as the basis for political identity. This is the case particularly among narrators whose fathers were entirely or largely absent from their childhood homes. In some cases the father had died, while in others he was often away at sea. The latter was the case with this woman from a Vizcayan fishing village:

Where was your mother from?

My mother was *abertzale*. My mother in that period was a socialist. Yes. She was a socialist. I don't know if she was –

Socialist and abertzale.

Yes. Yes, the two things. That's a bit what I carry as well. They have always told me that that isn't possible. It can be, because I'm it, I say . . . My mother has never directed me at all. No way. But of course, I absorbed her experiences. A lot of feeling of justice, above all. But with a feeling for the national, for your own, for your culture, on top of everything else . . . 'I feel socialist, and I feel *abertzale*. And the rest of you can say what you want, but what goes is what I feel.' [*laughter*] . . . 'You want to give me better parents?' I always said to them, 'Better than my parents? I have parents who for me are the best in the world'. (#4, b. 1936)

This narrator's sense of political parentage is underlined by the use of phrase 'the best [parents] in the world' to explain her dual commitment to nationalism and socialism. The comparison gains currency with the allusion to the wider debate about the compatibility of socialism and nationalism, a debate which raged in ETA circles (in which the narrator was active) during the 1960s. Rejecting an ideological or theoretical defence of her identification as socialist *and* nationalist, the narrator instead claims the logic of her political choice through the commitment inherited from her mother. On one level this story corresponds with a broader nationalist narrative in which, as Jeremy MacClancy has written, '(r)adical ideologues speak of *la gran familia abertzale*, a social unit where political attitudes are often inherited and one broad enough to accommodate both militant nationalism and revolutionary socialism'.[38] But on another level it offers an alternative to this narrative by providing an example of the transmission of political identity from mother to daughter.

Memories of fathers

Following the end of the Second World War, and the subsequent onset of the Cold War, the staunchly anti-communist Franco regime was gradually recognised by Western liberal democracies as the legitimate government of Spain. This international acceptance prompted disillusionment and further division among Spanish Republican forces in exile, including Basque nationalists. By the 1950s, moreover, inside the Basque country nationalism was entering a period of crisis. Following more than a decade of repression and economic austerity, the Basque middle class – the traditional stronghold of the PNV – had begun to benefit financially from the new economic developments in Spain, and thus from the political status quo under Franco.[39]

It was in these circumstances that, in 1952, a group of male students formed a secret association at Deusto, the Jesuit university in Bilbao. These young Basque men came from urban, middle-class, professional, nationalist families. Most had studied previously in seminaries, and many later graduated with degrees in the liberal professions.[40] In other words, their socioeconomic profile was in important ways parallel to that of the generation of students from middle-class Francoist families who had begun to rally against the regime (and, by extension, the politics of their parents) in other Spanish cities in these same years.[41] But in spite of their class status, the young Basque men with anti-Francoist backgrounds faced an uncertain future in an authoritarian state where career advancement depended largely upon connections with Madrid.[42] The Deusto group eventually took on the name Ekin, meaning 'to persist'. The Ekin members were concerned with the repression of Basque culture and language, and the national problem in general. In particular, they were convinced that the failure of the PNV – the official voice of Basque nationalism – to challenge Franco was a direct result of its enduring aim of establishing Basque autonomy within a revived Spanish Republic. Ekin, in contrast, promoted the creation of a separate Basque state, and therefore shunned cooperation with Spanish opposition forces. In 1959 this position led the younger set to break with the older party to found ETA.[43]

Some commentators have detected in the schism between Ekin and the PNV a story of generational conflict.[44] Moreover, some individual ETA members have considered their participation in ETA in terms the need of young nationalists to avenge the loss of their fathers' generation in the Civil War.[45] The image of the weak father who lost the war and subsequently failed to stand up to the Franco regime stands in contrast to the common image of the strong mother who plays a generally positive role in her son's political formation.[46] But the generational conflict model is problematic in a number of ways. Kristin Ross, for example, argues that the generational model, especially as formulated by Karl Mannheim in his classic sociological study, offers a biologist interpretation of history. This interpretation reduces social movements to a 'family drama' instead of locating them in their wider historical contexts. According to Ross, in this generational model '[c]hildren, by means of "acting out", end up confirming all the more strongly their parents' endowment; thus, contestation is useful, functional, a rite of passage to the status of adulthood.'[47] Ross hints at another fundamental problem in the generational interpretation of history: the 'family drama' it typically represents takes place between fathers and sons. Thus, if the idea of generational conflict provides a way of containing and depoliticising history by converting it into a kind of 'sociobiological destiny', it also assumes men to be the natural actors of that history.

The generational narrative does not, of course, represent the truth of men's historical experience of nationalist activism. But what interests me here is the role women are assigned in this story: the supportive mother. Without proposing a universal model of women's political formation, interviews with female narrators offer alternatives to this story. The model of male generational conflict is undermined by tales, such as that quoted above, of daughters who 'inherited' their political commitment from their mothers. It is also called into question through childhood stories of narrators who remember fathers who encouraged them to become politically conscious and active, first at home and later outside. Memories of supportive fathers may be shaped in reaction to a wider representation of the 'weak' father, or may occur as resistance to other cultural models that privilege the mother–daughter relationship, including some forms of feminism. A narrator who grew up in the French Basque country and later had contacts with the French psychoanalytical feminist group Psych et Po (Psychoanalyse et Politique) recalls that she resisted what she saw as the group's idealisation of the mother–daughter relationship:

> In my life the important person was my father . . . But they were all good friends with their mothers, and the fathers were bad . . . Their fathers were wild, brutal and all that. And the mothers were darlings. And by chance I hadn't experienced that kind of parental relationship. I experienced the reverse. (#13, b. 1941)

In the following quotations we see more detailed memories of the positive father–daughter relationship. The first narrator is from Pamplona and came to radical nationalist politics through trade union activism in the 1970s. The second is from a rural Basque-speaking family in rural Guipúzcoa and became active in ETA in the 1960s. In each narrator's childhood a landmark memory is of accompanying her father to an illegal public political event.

> I was born in Iruña [Pamplona], in Nafarroa [Navarre], which is one of the *herrialdes* [provinces] of Euskal Herria . . . In Nafarroa . . . they're very

Catholic. My family is basically Catholic, and traditionalist. My father had fought as a volunteer with Franco. He had been a *requeté*[48] ... So even though my father fought with Franco ... he had been a Carlist ... So I start my initiation into politics at Montejurra. Montejurra is ... the mountain where all the Carlists went to proclaim God, foral rights. ... That's where I start to become politicised. I remember the first time I went, it's the first time I see the Civil Guard disrupt a demonstration. Because a picture of Franco had been burned. Because the Carlists felt betrayed by Franco. (#5, b. 1949)

I would've been around 14, 15. My father wasn't a supporter of the PNV but he admired José Antonio Agirre.[49] So when he died, I remember we were listening to the BBC from London, because when my father finished his work, the livestock and everything, at night he always stayed and listened to Radio Paris and the BBC from London. And I always stayed with him. I was the oldest, and I stayed and listened. I didn't understand Spanish, but he explained to me in *euskera*. Since I was really little. And I remember ... the news arrived that José Antonio Agirre had died, and my father was really moved. So the funeral was going to be held in the Basilica at Loyola. And my father said, 'The whole family is going to go to the funeral.' And I got a bit scared and said, 'Are we going to go just us? And what about the police?' ... And my father says to me, 'You'll see. The Basilica is going to fill up and the people won't fit in.' 'Really?' I said to him, since there was so much repression ... The whole family, the children and our mother, we all went to the funeral. And I was shocked because the Loyola Basilica looked small during the funeral. Those are my first memories of the whole thing. (#19, b. 1944)

In this last excerpt the common association of women with the household, and with the transition of language and culture to their children, is undermined by the memory of a father who very much occupied the family home, both as the head of household and as a role model for his daughter's social, cultural and political formation. In this interview the father occupies a very specific place in the domestic sphere: the realm of leisure, of intellectual and political information and exchange, the place at home where the global intersects with the local through the foreign radio and press (and, later, television). By inviting the daughter to share this privileged space at home the father enabled her to envision herself as an active political subject in the public sphere beyond it. By providing a crucial link between the world of family, and the potentially dangerous outside world – personified by the security forces – such a father fulfilled the role not only of mentor, but also to some extent of hero: he who faced the enemy on their own territory.

The interview from which the second story above is taken is a particularly rich source because the narrator manages to combine an impression of the emotional intensity of decades of activism with a wealth of factual information about debates, events and other activists. She was one of the first generation of women to join ETA in the late 1960s and early 1970s. She spent some time in prison under Franco before joining a far-left party in the late 1970s. Hers was an atypical political trajectory in that she became critical of, and distanced herself from, nationalism for many years before returning to radical nationalist activism in the years prior to the interview. The narrator consequently had both a cogent critique *and* committed defence of radical nationalist strategy, including ETA violence, which comes through in another memory. Here she is listening to the radio with her father, three years after the incident recounted above:

Do you remember the first time you heard about ETA?

The first time, I think was in '61 or '62. With one of ETA's first actions. Old members of the *requete* army were going to a *fiesta* . . . they put a bomb and a little girl got hurt[50] . . . I heard it on the radio. I was listening with my father. And my father explained to me, 'Look, it's not good to injure people, that a little girl got hurt, but if I was 20 years old, I'd be in ETA,' he said to me, 'because those people in the PNV said they were going to do this, that and the other thing. And they've done absolutely *nothing*' . . . And later he always said if he'd been 20 he would've joined ETA. (#19, b. 1944)

It is interesting to compare this excerpt with that of another narrator born in the same period and also raised in a Basque-speaking family. The two women had spent time in prison together in the early 1970s, and had later remained in contact (in fact, I got the contact for narrator #19 from #15, quoted below). Given their shared experience as early female ETA activists, their memories of their fathers are compelling in their similarity. In the story of the second narrator, the television replaces the radio as the source of political commentary in the home, as her father becomes a kind of armchair activist:

They [my family] were very nationalist. My father said the people in the PNV were bloody bourgeois. The leaders. And he wasn't wrong. And later my father became *etarra* [pro-ETA] . . . In his place. In front of the TV. He made us die laughing. He called them Carlists, fundamentalists. And if ETA killed a policeman, he used to say to me, 'Hey! That way we'll get nowhere. One by one?' And he was a good conversationalist, peaceful. My father was wonderful. He had spent many years in Argentina before the war. He was educated, and in my house my father did everything except iron. Because he'd lived alone in Argentina, and he cooked, he washed, everything except ironing. He did everything. And he became totally *etarra*. (#15, b. 1946)

In the memories of these two women fathers figure prominently as political examples to be followed, not only in the public arena but also at home. By performing some domestic chores, the father helped to break down gender dichotomies in the home. Yet these interviews also express the narrators' ambivalence about their parents' roles. A nervous laugh or a verbal stumbling can suggest discomfort, an awareness that the breaking down of gender divisions was perhaps more fantasy than reality. The following excerpt, like that above, came in the context of a series of memories about childhood and family with which the narrator opened the interview:

> [My father] was open. He taught us to respect other people's ideas . . . I still admire my father a lot because he instilled this in us. My mother as well, but my mother was more rural, shyer, because she never went out, she didn't see things. Although my mother always obeyed what my father said. That was, was sacred [*laughter*] . . . My father, of course, was macho like the whole society. But in that regard too I remember when I was little he helped my mother cook, clean . . . from that point of view he was a little special. (#19, b. 1944)

The importance of these memories lies not in their factual accuracy but rather in their representation of a father perceived as exceptional because he performed household chores associated with women's work and shared his political views with his daughter, an image preserved in the daughter's memory as a model to be followed. In these stories the father provides political guidance and emotional support to a daughter at a time when politics were still almost exclusively the domain of men, thereby suggesting alternative futures in a largely gender-segregated world. It was the father's age, and not his weakness, that marked his fundamental difference from his daughter, preventing him from carrying on the war against Francoism. Having been born after the Civil War, the daughters had the option of taking the route they imagine their fathers would have chosen had the fathers been younger. In contrast to those histories of the founding of ETA that stress the break between generations of men, these women's stories show that continuity across generations was an important factor in the political formation of some future activists.

These passages have implications beyond the case of Basque nationalism. They indicate further areas for work with regard to intergenerational relationships and women's personal and political identities. In her essay 'Memory, generation and history', Sally Alexander, drawing on both the psychoanalytic and feminist movements of the twentieth century, takes inspiration from the following words of Virginia Woolf: 'we think back through our mothers if we are women'. Alexander's interest is in writing a history that 'retrieves the maternal dimension', and considers the ways in which such a project may go 'beyond the history of femininity to remap the history of twentieth-century structures of feelings'.[51] The writing of Alexander and others on feminist history and psychoanalysis has provided an important counterpoint both to the masculine bias of mainstream history and to an Oedipal model that privileges the father, and an inspiration for my own work. However, I caution against a model of history or memory that starts from the assumption that women 'think back' through their mothers. The diversity of women's childhood memories presented in this book indicates the need for a broader understanding of what Alexander calls 'intergenerational lineages' passed through oral and other traditions.[52]

The example of 'independent women'

If these examples help to expand our knowledge of the roles of families and generations in the reproduction of postwar Basque nationalism, one final element is worth considering: the roles of single and childless women. In the memories of female narrators born in the postwar period, such women figure frequently as participants in nationalist politics – through direct activism and as an inspiration to younger activists. One narrator, who was among the first women to be arrested, tried and imprisoned for ETA membership in the late 1960s, recalls her earliest encounter with Basque identity:

> All that came to me through some single aunts of mine. My aunt was also a teacher . . . I don't think generally political topics were discussed in families. Of course the war was taboo. But these aunts of mine broke with that, but with me. I was the only girl in the house, there were three boys and me . . . but I was the one who broke the blockade, I went to the aunts' house, the one who listened to all that, the one who had access to all that. (#21, b. 1945)

In this narrator's memory the aunts chose to speak to her alone about the 'taboo' topic of national identity precisely because she was the only daughter in the family. Like her own mother, who had died when the narrator was 15, the aunts worked as schoolteachers. Teaching was one of the few professions available to middle-class women in the early Franco period and the opportunity of paid labour was important in shaping women's social and political awareness. In this sense, in the narrator's memory the aunts were carrying on a role already initiated by the mother, who before her death had instilled in her daughter the idea 'that we women had the same rights and the same obligations as men' (#21, b. 1945).

The role of single women was not necessarily restricted to the example they set for younger women within their own families. Other narrators remember single women known for their political activism. One recalls a wave of arrests of accused supporters of ETA in her Basque-speaking hometown in the late 1960s:

> I think the people who were committed, that woman I told you about who had seven children and I don't know why they put her in prison, I think the rest were single.
>
> *Single?*
>
> You have to keep that in mind. Single –
>
> *Even at your age? At your age or older?*
>
> Older. I think the older people that in some way were in solidarity, or collected money for the prisoners, or did things like that . . . I have the impression they were reli,[53] that is, single. At least in my hometown. In the rest I don't know . . . Why? Well from the moment you take on other commitments, a husband and some children or whatever, you can't take on anything else any more. (#1, b. 1947)

These stories indicate that single and childless women made important contributions to the development of the new radical nationalist movement in the 1960s. Moreover, there is strong evidence that a significant proportion of women directly involved in ETA in the 1960s and 1970s were not mothers. Several of the women interviewed for this project were childless, tending to confirm the observation of the last narrator that women had to choose between political and familial commitments, or at least that certain types of activism – in particular, the illegal, clandestine activity associated with ETA – were incompatible with the day-to-day responsibilities of motherhood.

The editors of the volume *Nationalisms and Sexualities* draw an important connection between the idealisation of mothers in nationalist discourse and 'the distinctly homosocial form of male bonding' favoured by nationalism':[54]

> The idealization of motherhood by the virile fraternity would seem to entail the exclusion of all nonreproductively-oriented sexualities from the discourse of the nation. Indeed, certain sexual identities and practices are less represented and representable in nationalism.[55]

This link is particularly suggestive for the case of ETA, an organisation whose early structure was based, as described in the next chapter, on close interpersonal relations, secrecy and separation from the outside world. This recalled the all-male institutions, including the seminary, in which its founding members had been socialised. The emphasis on nationalist motherhood had the effect of rendering 'unrepresentable' single and childless women, but one way of representing such women has been through their relationships to the younger generation, in a form of surrogate motherhood. Thus PNV founder Sabino Arana believed that even women who had not physically given birth could be mothers of 'second rank', expected to perform maternal duties for the next generation.[56] However the 'surrogate mother' scenario ignores evidence that the example set by single and childless women offered some younger women an alternative way of envisioning family life, as well as a model of personal and political independence.

In considering the relationship between 'homosocial' male bonding, the idealisation of motherhood and 'compulsory heterosexuality' in nationalism, the editors of *Nationalisms and Sexualities* are concerned to address the under-representation of queer, and especially lesbian, sexualities in nationalist rhetoric. But in so doing they miss an important point: that not all forms of 'reproductively-oriented sexuality' are validated in nationalist discourses, and not all forms of maternity are idealised. An analysis of the language of early radical Basque nationalism shows that its central preoccupation was not with biological or even cultural reproduction per se, but rather with the ideological reproduction of male nationalist activists. Not all mothers were therefore visible or idealised in radical nationalist representations; special privilege was preserved for mothers of sons and, more specifically, mothers who shared their sons' ideological commitment to nationalism, including (at least from the 1970s onwards) a commitment to nationalist violence. This fact explains the vilification of mothers who questioned or rejected their sons' political choices, as well as the omission of the mother–daughter relationship from most nationalist imagery. This was in spite of the fact that since the late 1960s there has been a slow but steady rise in the number of women active in ETA – including, increasingly, in armed actions.

In an earlier article on gender and generation in ETA I argued that both women's memories of fathers, and the presence of single and/or childless women acting as political mentors, called into question the Oedipal model of the father–son–mother at the heart of nationalist narratives and much academic analysis of the origins of ETA.[57] Today I would alter this argument, taking into account Gilles Deleuze's and Félix Guattari's critique of Freud's formulation of the Oedipus complex.[58] Deleuze and Guattari stress that families and parental figures are never isolated, but are always part of wider social, political and economic power relations, including historical figures such as 'the soldier, the cop, the occupier, the collaborator, the radical, the resister, the boss, the boss's wife'.[59]

Furthermore, every family has its outsiders: 'an uncle from America; a brother who went bad; an aunt who took off with a military man; a cousin out of work, bankrupt, or a victim of the Crash; an anarchist grandfather; a grandmother in the hospital, crazy, or senile.'[60] These observations serve as a warning against any temptation to interpret as literal references to 'the Basque nationalist family' or to see nationalist archetypes (for example, 'the soldier, the cop, the occupier') as actual family members. Most important of all, the work of Deleuze and Guattari serves as a reminder that those figures who fall outside the Oedipal triangle, and whose stories may fall outside convention, are not exceptions, but are as much a part of family history as parents and children.

My earlier interpretation that narrators' stories of fathers and 'independent women' offered alternatives to a more conventional family model was therefore too literal a reading of the interviews. This points to a methodological problem in oral history itself. By focusing on the role of the individual protagonist in history, the oral history interview may encourage a heroic narrative that emphasises the idea of the 'exceptional' life. Ronald Grele cautions that:

> Because we usually interview one person at a time and ask people about what they themselves did, there is a tendency to move our narrators to stage center, seeing the world through their eyes and attributing to them or allowing them to attribute to themselves a choice, prescience, or motive which may not be historically valid. Oral history, like all biography or autobiography, encourages the view that individuals shape their own destinies.[61]

Equally, narrators may feel encouraged to construct their own histories as special, outside the norm, in particular if they have subsequently played a prominent public role in their movement. Indeed, as seen in the examples already explored, some narrators insist on the exceptional nature of their own childhoods: a father who shared in housework, a mother who believed in equality between women and men. In subsequent chapters, several narrators who later became involved directly in ETA present themselves as 'rebels', distancing themselves from a norm of female behaviour. As Grele rightly notes, '[c]oncepts of the role of individuals is class based both at a deep structure level and at the level of social relations.'[62] Tales of exceptional childhoods and female rebellion may reflect in part the middle-class backgrounds of some narrators. But they should equally be understood as memories shaped by gender. As such, they are attempts to make sense of a past that led to a life of political activism at a time when such activism was still considered largely the domain of men. In the light of Deleuze and Guattari's critique, I would argue that childhood memories of exceptionality should not be read literally, and much less as a straightforward explanation for later political activism. Instead, narratives of exceptional childhoods can be understood as strategies for understanding individual political trajectories in the face of dominant models (both inside the nationalist community and more generally) that ignore the reality of the fragmented family and the complexity of female activists' experiences.

2

Gendering the roots of radical nationalism

> The Resistance is many-sided: peaceful women dedicated to cultural and humanitarian work; violent men who await only a little more strength and an order; honest priests, who fearlessly raise the voice of the Truth.
> (ETA, *Zutik*, 10, 1961)

In the scholarly literature on radical nationalism three institutions are habitually cited as central to the preservation of Basque nationalist culture under Franco and as major political influences on early ETA: the family, the Church and the *cuadrilla* or friendship group.[1] The previous chapter looked at some of the roles of nationalist families in the reproduction of Basque nationalism in the post-war period. This chapter will analyse the place of the Church and *cuadrilla* in the development of ETA in the 1950s and 1960s. It will also examine patterns of paid labour in the 1960s, and how differences between women and men influenced access to politics. While women were largely excluded from those institutions in which men came into contact with nationalism, they were more likely to become active through cultural organisations. ETA's early association of culture with the feminine thus opened the way for small numbers of women to participate in the new radical nationalism, while keeping largely intact gender divisions within the radical nationalist movement.

The Church

A major defining feature of Basque nationalism historically has been its close relationship to the Catholic Church. The middle-class and confessional character of Basque nationalism helps to explain its paradoxical position in the Spanish political landscape throughout the twentieth century. During 1930s the PNV supported the Second Republic against the Spanish nationalists forces of the Right. But the party's conservatism and Catholicism brought it into frequent conflict with the largely secular,

Republican forces on the Left. Under Franco the regime's extreme centralism caused a rift between the Church hierarchy and local Basque priests. Consequently, the resurgent Basque nationalism of the 1950s and 1960s was to find some of its strongest supporters among a new generation of lower clergy.

By the late 1950s nationalist Basque priests, like their Catalan counterparts, increasingly spoke out in support of regional rights. In 1960 a group of over 300 Basque priests sent a letter to their bishops protesting political and cultural repression. This step towards open resistance was facilitated by a shift in Church–regime relations. By the early 1960s, encouraged in part by the reforms of Vatican II, the Spanish Catholic hierarchy began to adopt more liberal policies on social justice. Equally important was the radicalisation of the Church's most dedicated lay disciples. During the 1950s and 1960s, working-class Catholic organisations came to the forefront of the growing popular resistance to Francoism. The most prominent of these were Juventud Obrera Católica (JOC – Catholic Workers Youth) and Hermandad Obrera de Acción Católica (HOAC – Catholic Action Workers' Brotherhood), which, had their roots in the Catholic Action groups of the 1940s.[2] While not officially engaged in political activity, JOC and HOAC activists, with their commitment to Christian service among workers, inevitably came face to face with the stark injustices of Francoism. Given official status under the Church, the lay Catholic movement became a prime location for the clandestine political activity of a new generation of anti-Francoist youth.

The grassroots Christian movement in the Basque country was parallel to that in the rest of Spain, with the added factors of cultural/linguistic difference, a tradition of nationalism, and a particularly intense history of devotion. A sociological study carried out by the state Institute for Youth in the early 1960s concluded that Basque youth were the most dedicated young churchgoers in Spain.[3] Especially in Basque rural areas, religious belief and practice played a central role in the everyday life of all generations. In small towns most members of the community were active in one of several sodalities (religious fellowships) established by the categories of gender, age and marital status.[4] In addition, for young men the Church offered one of the few routes out of the local community through secondary education in seminaries.[5] Both JOC and HOAC were firmly established in the Basque country, particularly in the industrial belt around Bilbao, one of the primary sites of worker unrest and illegal strike action during the 1960s. In the rural and coastal areas of Vizcaya and Guipúzcoa, the organisation Herri Gaztedi (People's Youth) played a similar role in educating young people around social and political issues.⁶ But in contrast to JOC and HOAC, which had a distinctively working-class, Spanish-speaking constituency, Herri Gaztedi was an inter-class organisation that worked primarily in *euskera*.⁷ By the mid-1960s, according to some narrators, Herri Gaztedi had become a focal point for nationalist consciousness-raising in rural and coastal communities and a recruiting ground and front for ETA.⁸

The central importance of nationalist priests and Catholic youth groups in providing a political education to a new generation of Basques is suggested in the life stories of several former female ETA activists and supporters who came of age in the 1960s. Even though all the narrators in this study eventually moved away from the Church, many recall that their Catholic education had endowed them with a keen sense of social justice – in the words of one narrator, a desire 'to defend the weak' (#4, b. 1936). Likewise, Dolores González Catarain (Yoyes), one of the first women to hold a leadership position in ETA, recorded in her teenage diary that religious dedication had been the first step toward political commitment.⁹ In addition to teaching on wider social issues, local churches sometimes provided a rare social space for bringing young women and men together. Several narrators recall, for instance, the innovation of Herri Gaztedi in breaking with gender-segregated social life through coed mountain excursions and other activities.

Thus in interviews with women who became politically active during the 1960s the Church figures prominently as an anti-Francoist and nationalist institution. They also describe it as a place of personal and social discovery, away from both the oppressive public sphere of the State and the often restrictive environment of the family home. But the Church also had its repressive side, a place where traditional sexual morals were taught and enforced and young women were encouraged to restrict their public movement. This ambivalence is reminiscent of narrators' attitudes to families and motherhood as discussed in the previous chapter. A parallel between Church and family is suggested in the language of some of the interviews. Words such as 'protection' and 'refuge' highlight an association of Church and home as places perceived as similarly separate from, and protective against, the forces of the State. One narrator, born into a Basque-speaking family in a small city in the province of Vizcaya, makes explicit this conceptual link between family and Church as privileged places where Basque culture was 'preserved', and where nationalism could be discussed openly:

> My brother also went to a seminary, to become a priest. They went to the seminary at about age 11 or around there . . . I think he was there for six years. Until 16 or thereabouts. And I think the movement, the culture in this country, has been very much preserved in monasteries, by priests, in

seminaries, in those places. They're the ones who've been able to dedicate themselves a bit more to it. It's like it was in some way the place where the State couldn't enter . . . Among them there were lots of learned nationalists from that period . . . As I said my brother was very nationalist . . . He learned that, apart from at home, he learned it through his education in those years. My brother's education was a religious education, but also a nationalist education. And not Francoist. Anti-Francoist in any case. And some people, from ETA, had emerged precisely from those circles. And it's no surprise that my brother would as well. (#1, b. 1947)

The Church, like the family, is 'the place where the State couldn't enter'. But, the narrator implies, the Church was also a place where *women* did not enter.

Many Basque parents, especially those from the nationalist middle class, sent their children to Church schools in an effort to avoid the Spanish nationalism promoted in state schools. But Catholic schools shared with state institutions a segregated and gender-specific education system. A prominent theme in interviews with women educated in religious colleges is the substantial gap between the popular image of a progressive and anti-Francoist Basque Church, and the harsh sociocultural climate of girls' schools run by nuns. While Basque priests are commonly identified as mentors to young male nationalists in seminaries, for many of the narrators raised in Church schools nuns represented cultural and sexual repression, unwavering piety and Francoist indoctrination. This distinction in turn reflected fundamental differences in the social role of priests and nuns. Whereas the former were often esteemed as intellectuals in their communities, the latter tended to lead more isolated lives dedicated to the service of others.

The following two narrators, who became involved in ETA in the 1960s and 1970s respectively, were born twenty years apart, but share remarkably similar memories of religious education:

I went to a nuns' school. Well, I don't think I hate anyone, but back then, I felt what hate was. I hated the nuns because they made me do everything: sing the national anthem, speak in Spanish, go to church, go to church every morning, go to church every afternoon, and if you didn't go you were punished the next day. I learned the entire holy story because of the punishments the nuns gave me. Later, lots of people said to me, 'But you, how? But you're a *borrokazale* [fighter], aren't you? You've worked for the cause and everything. How come you know all that?' And I tell them just that, for all the times I had to recite the holy story. (#4, b. 1936)

The typical ones that appear in *loads* of movies that there have been about the Spanish postwar. I mean, the typical nuns – let's say very Castilian. There they were very Castilian with castanets in their hands to hit you on the head if they passed you . . . Religion above all else, and teaching all the traditional values. It was really an education very much of the regime. (#14, b. 1956)[10]

Both these excerpts contain evidence of the popular stereotype of the nun as the incarnation of sexual repression and reactionary zeal. However, I want to read these memories not as true stories about fascist nuns, but as impassioned responses to the popular representation of the Basque Church as a unifying force against Francoism – an image that obscures these narrators' childhood memories of religious education. These and other interviews make clear that, in spite of the nationalist and left-wing leanings of many Basque priests, girls' religious education in the Basque country reflected, as in the rest of Spain, the sexual politics of the Franco regime. As Frances Lannon writes of the Church's reforms in the 1960s:

> [T]he Church was able to be much more radical in politics and questions of social justice, that primarily challenged the state and interest groups in Spanish society, than in matters concerning lay life and sexuality which threatened more nearly its own internal organization and values.[11]

The preservation of Basque tradition had long been associated with enforcing gender norms. During the early years of the Second Republic, when Church leaders all over Spain felt under siege from anticlerical legislation, Basque clergy responded to the assault on Church privileges by hailing the virtues of prescribed male–female roles, sexual purity, solid family relations and paternal authority.[12] Just as early Basque nationalists had feared the consequences of women marrying outside the national community, the Church hierarchy saw the protection of the sexual innocence of young women as key to upholding the moral standards of the entire community. In the Franco period as well, the preoccupation with chastity was directed largely at women as the guardians of society's morals, or, as one narrator succinctly phrased it, '[a] wall against man's conquest' (#22, b. 1961).

For some narrators the desire to break from the Church teachings is expressed as an urge to rebel. The narrator quoted below was raised in a small industrial city in Guipúzcoa and joined ETA in the 1970s:

> The whole thing about religion, I rebelled a lot, it was my first public protest, to stop going to mass . . . all that in my family was like a big bomb. My brothers, my sister was a catechism tutor, my older sister, and the next one too, so that was a bad example [*laughter*] as my father says, for the whole family. (#14, b. 1956)

Rebellion is frequently associated in the interviews with the desire to be modern – an identity that sits awkwardly with all that is Basque, which is in turn associated with the rural and the Catholic. This helps to illuminate an ambivalence expressed in many interviews towards Basque tradition. In the words of a narrator who was raised in the French Basque country and came into contact with ETA members in exile in the 1960s:

> The fact is I vacillated in being Basque, in identifying myself as Basque, because for me being Basque was *euskaldun fededun* [Basque-speaking person of faith] . . . I was a bit of a rebel and among other things I couldn't put up with were all the *contraintes sociales* [social constraints]. The thing about being *txintxo* [upright] – a good person, not going out with boys . . . not doing silly things, wearing a corset. We used to wear corsets in those days . . . giving the impression of a good person, rigid, moral, *etxekoandre txintxoa* [the upright housewife]. You know what I mean, don't you? What represents all those values, I'm not going to say conservative, but they were. And that's why I wanted so much to be French and modern. (#13, b. 1941)

In other interviews the drive to rebel is similarly portrayed through images of clothing. By the late 1950s and early 1960s outside cultural influences – whether Hollywood movies and television, magazines, or foreign tourists on Spanish beaches – increasingly made their ways into Basque and Spanish households and into the adolescent fantasies of a new generation.[13] With the rise of consumer culture the popular press became filled with advertising for beauty products and women's fashion.[14] As Aurora Morcillo points out, the influence of US and French fashion redefined and eroticised the female body in ways that created a distance from traditional images of motherhood, and sat awkwardly with Francoist ideals of 'true Catholic womanhood'. Several narrators who came of age in these years recall the dictates of the Church as a battle over the desire of teenage girls to assert their independence through, among other things, their choice of clothing. One woman raised in a Basque-speaking rural village in Guipúzcoa, who got involved in ETA in the mid-1960s through her local nationalist priest, recounts one particularly unpleasant encounter with him:

> I remember it was the local *fiesta* . . . so I wore a red T-shirt . . . and the sleeves like this [*gesture to show cap sleeves*]. This sleeve like this, falling down a tiny bit. A white pleated skirt, I remember perfectly, and a blue sweater. And I went to the *fiesta*. And then to come home . . . I fell. Pluf! I gave myself a horrible bump . . . And since my knees were bleeding, so you couldn't see them, I took off my sweater and tied it like this [*around her waist*], hanging down, and I set off home like that. And of course I passed by the church. And just then [the priest] was in the window . . . and he saw me go by. And I waved and left. And of course, well he saw me with the T-shirt, without sleeves. So, the grief he gave me! (#20, b. 1945)

These women's memories of childhood religious education at home and in convent schools, as well as later teenage experiences with mixed church groups and nationalist priests, highlight the need for a more careful documentation of the role of the Church in the formation of ETA, both in shaping the organisation's moral/ethical structure and in providing the early radical nationalist movement with a physical place to organise. The point is not that women experienced the Church as personally and sexually oppressive whereas men did not; interviews with early male ETA members would no doubt reveal painful memories of sexual repression and fanatical clergy. The crucial difference is that, in terms of future nationalist activism, for young men a seminary education was often enabling, but for women experiences of Catholic schools were often *disabling*.

The contradictory role of the Church in young women's political formation in the Basque country has interesting parallels with Latin America. In an essay about women intellectuals and social movements there, Jean Franco stresses the paradoxical position of the family and Church in relation to women's political consciousness and activism under conditions of military dictatorship. She argues that 'authoritarian regimes had the effect of enhancing the ethical value of private life, religion, literature and the arts as regions of refuge from the brutal reality of an oppressive state',[15] and many Latin American churches provided shelter for human rights groups. But the Church as an institution often proved a barrier to discussion about women's sexuality in particular, and to feminism in general.[16]

For several of the Basque women I interviewed who became active in radical Basque nationalism in the 1960s, memories of sexual repression were an important element in the decision to break with the Church:

> In concrete terms, it was as a result of coming into contact with nationalism . . . the movement around ETA, was when we women broke with the Church . . . For me it was like opening another set of doors, saying well, this isn't this closed world. Opening another set of doors for women. (#11a, b. 1946)

Although the Church is represented in this and many interviews as a 'closed world', a 'protective' space or 'refuge' out of which ETA itself emerged, this narrator, like others, recalls that the new radical nationalism offered a potentially more liberating space, 'opening another set of doors' personally as well as politically. What might be called a female cultural memory of the 1960s indicates that for many women ETA activism appealed not only to their sense of national identity, but also to a desire to create new, more modern gender identities.

Cuadrilla

In contrast to the proliferation of references to religion and the Church, few of the interviews contain explicit references to the *cuadrilla* or friendship group. Like the Church, the *cuadrilla* has sometimes been portrayed as a kind of mediator between the family and the State during the Franco years.[17] Although often cited as a traditional form of specifically Basque social organisation, the *cuadrilla*, like nationalism itself, is best understood in the context of twentieth-century industrialisation and urbanisation.[18] Originally formed exclusively by groups of men of similar age from the same town or neighbourhood,[19] *cuadrillas* claimed as their territory that public space – taverns and the town square – perceived physically and figuratively in opposition to the home.[20] This male occupation of the public sphere was put into practice on a daily basis through the *cuadrilla*'s basic activity, the *poteo*, in which groups went from bar to bar drinking *potes* (small glasses of wine).

Studies of ETA's origins have argued that the *cuadrilla*, like the Church and family, played a significant role in defining Basqueness in the face of change, especially from the 1950s to 1970s. In these years of simultaneous economic expansion and political repression, in many towns and neighbourhoods *cuadrillas* became a focal point of political organising. Like Church youth groups, *cuadrillas* provided a relatively protected arena for political discussion and organising. During the 1960s and 1970s *cuadrillas* constituted a major support network, and indeed a recruiting ground, for ETA.[21] Many accounts note the importance of *cuadrillas* in introducing individual male activists to ETA and radical nationalism.[22] One author even claims that in the 1970s it was not uncommon for entire *cuadrillas* to join the organisation.[23]

Beyond their practical role in providing ETA cadres, under Franco *cuadrillas* were instrumental in what Eugenia Ramírez Goicoechea calls the 'ethnic revitalization' of the Basque country. By celebrating the cultural symbols of 'Basqueness' (e.g. the *ikurriña* or Basque flag, Basque music and dancing) on social occasions such as local *fiestas* or sports events, *cuadrillas* politicised these symbols and Basque culture more generally.[24] But, like the Church and family, the focus on the ways in which the *cuadrilla* united the new radical nationalist community obscures the extent to which it divided that community along gender lines. The limited reference to *cuadrillas* in the interviews, in particular among those women who joined ETA in the 1960s and early 1970s, indicates that they had a very different function in young women's political development than in men's. Many of the traditional activities of young men's *cuadrillas*, such as mountaineering, which had been the focal point for the preservation of nationalist consciousness during the heavy repression of the 1920s, 1940s and 1950s, were generally closed to young women until the 1960s. The importance of such group activities in the formation of ETA is suggested by the mentor relationship developed within them between young men and their seniors, who sometimes initiated youth into the organisation.[25]

The predominantly male character of the *cuadrilla* and the *poteo* meant that women were largely excluded from an important place of political debate: the bar.[26] This circumstance was not unique to the Basque country. During the early years of the Troubles In Northern Ireland, for example, women had limited access to local pubs, which were focal points of Republican organising.[27] Kathy Peiss, in her study of gender and leisure among the New York working class at the turn of the last century, has argued that taverns could act as a space in which to reaffirm masculine modes of behaviour. 'Within this homosocial world,' she writes, 'rituals of aggression and competition – through card games, drinking, and gambling – were important mechanisms of male bonding.'[28] In many ways the male *cuadrilla* represented the 'homosocial world' par excellence, providing a place for the celebration of masculine activities and values outside the family, even after marriage.[29]

By the late 1970s young women increasingly participated alongside male friends in *poteos* and other activities of the *cuadrilla*. According to one narrator, mixed *cuadrillas* sometimes grew out of the Church organisations and mountaineering clubs of the 1960s (#12, b. 1947). But even if many young women welcomed the freedom of mixed socialising, during the 1960s all-male *cuadrillas* continued to offer envied opportunity for debate and political activity, as for this narrator, who joined ETA in the early 1970s:

> At 18, 19 years old when I start to get involved and to work in politics and everything, we were a really small group. They were all men . . . practically me alone, almost alone, as a woman, organised, going out. The girlfriends in my *cuadrilla* were really afraid . . . because a woman in politics was still really uncommon . . . Because of my father's ideas, I think that influenced me a lot . . . I always preferred to go out with guys, because with women I couldn't talk about that [politics], and I needed to. And so I always, even if I went out with my girlfriends, if I met some male friends in the street I stayed with them and I went with them. (#19, b. 1944)

As with the same narrator's memories of seeing her father as her main political role model at home (see chapter 1), this suggests that men could play an important role in introducing women to places of political activism from which they otherwise would have been excluded.

In stressing the segregated nature of the Church and *cuadrilla*, and the disabling effect this separation had on women's activism, I do not mean to suggest these institutions played an unambiguously liberating role in the lives of young Basque men.[30] The Basque anthropologist Juan Aranzadi has argued that the fixation of Basque men on their mothers as well as the proliferation of all-male institutions in the Basque country, such as *cuadrillas*, seminaries and sporting clubs, is related to a high level of repressed homosexuality among Basque men, and may even help to explain ETA's militarism.[31] Aranzadi's evidence seems to be largely anecdotal, and his conclusions are based on a reading of Freud's Oedipus complex which implies that homosexuality is deviant, and that mothers are largely responsible for this deviance. Nonetheless, Aranzadi's point – that, exclusively or predominantly male Basque institutions helped to create certain forms of masculinity and to validate certain identities and activities, including armed activism – is deserving of further study.[32]

The world of work

For the Franco dictatorship gender was an important tool in the construction of a social, political and economic hierarchy.[33] Under a regime committed to reversing all the liberal reforms of the Second Republic (1931–39), and to returning Spain to a mythic and glorious state united by 'National Catholicism', the legal and civil rights accorded women during the 1930s were symbols of the dangers and decadence of the republican period. Under Franco the ideal Spanish woman was to be first and foremost a wife and mother, whose primary sphere of activity was the family home. To this end the regime claimed, among other things, to 'liberate' women from the burden of paid work by barring married women from the labour force.[34]

In this as in many other areas, the aims of the regime were in conflict with the social and economic realities of the post-Civil War years. Labour legislation notwithstanding, many married women, especially those from the defeated urban working classes, continued to work outside the home throughout the 1940s and 1950s, often in semi-clandestine and highly exploitative conditions.[35] By the 1960s, with the instigation of controlled economic modernisation, the growing demands of the market prompted the regime to incorporate larger numbers of women into the labour market, and in 1961 the restrictions on women's paid work were partially reversed. This reform opened the way for increasing numbers of women to enter the labour force, especially in the expanding service sector. Even so, the pattern of women's work continued to vary greatly from region to region, and the percentage of working women remained well below the Western European average.[36]

The liberalisation of Francoist work legislation by no means signalled women's equality in Spanish society. It suggested, rather, that women were an important source of cheap labour in a rapidly expanding economy. The majority of Basque women in paid employment worked in jobs traditionally designated as feminine, including domestic service, health work and primary-school teaching.[37] This marginalisation of women in a largely female job sector had important consequences for political mobilisation, since very few women were employed in the factories that brought significant numbers of young nationalist men into contact with the Basque workers' movement, and in some cases with ETA, in these years. Women's incorporation into higher education was similarly well behind that of men.[38] This is another factor explaining women's lower numbers in ETA, since during the 1960s and 1970s universities provided many of the organisation's new recruits.[39]

The segregated nature of work and education during the 1950s and 1960s, and the ways in which these experiences shaped young women's experiences of political activism, are described in an interview with a narrator born into a Basque-speaking family in a small town in Vizcaya in the 1940s. Drawing a contrast between her own experiences of school and her brother's, and relating these in turn to her memories of the childhood rural family household, this narrator vividly evokes the gendered divisions in Basque society from the 1950s to 1970s. The interview is particularly valuable for its free-flowing narrative and suggestive associations. The narrator's reflections on women's changing roles in radical nationalism from the 1960s to the time of the interview in the 1990s were largely formed through comparison with the experiences of close family members: grandmother (see chapter 1), parents (especially her fraught relationship with her mother), and brother and husband (who had both been members of ETA).

In an excerpt cited above, the narrator distinguished between her politically conservative education at a nuns' school and her brother's years at the seminary, where the nationalist and religious education he received led him to ETA. A similar gender gap persisted in their post-secondary education. In the following two excerpts she contrasts her own training as a nurse, as well as her experience caring for her dying mother in hospital, with her brother's university years:

When I was 18 I came to Bilbao and began studying to be a nurse and we studied right in the hospital, and there wasn't much talk of politics. At least I don't remember, that first year. (#1, 1947)

> I took on the trips to the hospital myself. And at no point did it occur to me that my father should come. He did come to visit her. But not staying the night. But it wasn't just my father. I've seen that in the hospital . . . [It was] none of the men . . . I was already training to be a nurse, when I worked nights, I already saw. If I had seen that others came and he didn't come, I would have said, 'Hey! He doesn't love my mother.' But it didn't even occur to me.
>
> *Because it was the women who went to take care of –*
>
> Always. I don't know why it was like that. And what's more it didn't even occur to me that my brother would do it, and he's a year younger than I am. And he was in there with the most progressive, he was at university and he was in ETA, or, I don't know if he was in ETA or more or less in ETA. (#1, 1947)

These quotations, taken together with others in this and the previous chapter, show a series of gendered spheres that persisted through the period of social, political and economic change of the 1960s: home, Church, school, the hospital, the university. 'Spheres' should be understood here in both their literal and metaphorical senses, as actual physical spaces where women and men lived and worked and 'as a metaphor for complex power relations in social and economic contexts'.[40] The repeated claim that 'it didn't even occur to me' to question these divisions underlines the hegemony of Francoist and Basque nationalist gender ideologies, and the extent to which they were perceived at the time as natural. It also draws attention to the temporal and political distance between the events recalled and the time of the interview (mid-1990s), when the awareness of these differences had been shaped by a subsequent change in consciousness.

The link between a recollection of defined gender roles in the family, education, the Church and work, on one hand, and the relative invisibility of women in the history of Basque nationalism, on the other, is aptly summed up in a final memory of early childhood:

> It was the same in the public schools as in the private. The public schools were State-run, and there was the boys' school and the girls' school. And the majority of the private schools were religious – there were priests for the boys, and nuns for the girls . . . And, for years what's been recorded is the history of the boys. We women have always been more collaborators and maybe we've made a few decisions, but it was kind of the boys' war [*la guerra de los chicos*]. From the nationalist viewpoint and everything, even though there've been many nationalist women, I have no doubt about that. And in my house of course I think my mother was very nationalist, and my father, and my grandmother too. (#1, b. 1947)

The historical difference described by the narrator is not that men developed a nationalist consciousness at home while women did not. It was clear in chapter 1 that many narrators – at least those from nationalist families – did derive a sense of national identity and political awareness in their childhood families. But the form that consciousness took both inside and beyond the home was fundamentally shaped by wider socioeconomic and cultural forces.

In spite of the persistence of gender divisions in work and education, even limited access brought opportunities for women's activity outside the home. In the words of a narrator who left her rural home at the age of 15 to work in a bar in a neighbouring town, work offered the chance 'to get out, to discover new things' (#20, b. 1945).[41] The link between leaving home and the opportunities for political activism is highlighted in the following excerpt, in which three narrators discuss the different numbers of men and women at nationalist events in the mid-1960s:

> B: When I came to the *Aberri Eguna* (Day of the Basque Patria), it was mostly men who went. In the first years. It's as if, at least I speak for myself, to take those big steps, it was a real effort for me. It had to be something really positive – (#11b, b. 1944)
> A: Yes but maybe it wasn't only that. It was because of our upbringing – (#11a, b. 1946)
> B: Yes, yes.
> A: Not only because you were nationalist or not, but because –
> C: We were raised to be – (#11c, b. 1945)
> B: To be at home and –
> A: Yes, yes, yes.
> C: And with our mouths closed.
> A: And what's more to be housewives, you were raised like that. So to get out of that environment . . . As women join the world of work that also opens up a lot. But that's why I think there were more men, because none of the men considered staying at home without going to work. Paid work. So the men were *already* outside. *Already*. And I think the first women, who threw themselves into it [politics], were women who worked outside and that also has a lot to do with it. Breaking tradition a bit.

These narrators identify the beginning, in the 1960s, of what would be a longer process of change in gender relations. There is by no means a direct causal link between women's paid labour and nationalist activism; too many other factors were at play, including social class, ethnic background, family politics, and personal connections and choices. But entry into the workforce, as an act of 'breaking tradition a bit', could prove decisive for breaking traditions in other areas as well. Going out to work opened new spaces for women both in the physical sense of literally bringing them into contact with a wider range of people and experiences, and psychologically, by allowing them to imagine themselves entering new areas of activity previously associated predominantly with men.

It would be a mistake to argue that paid labour was only a liberating experience for young Basque women in the 1960s. Several narrators experienced their jobs – with their long hours and low pay – as exploitative. As one pointed out, while going out to work may have brought some women into direct contact with politics, it left them with precious little time for political activism (#12, b. 1947). Moreover, just as the division of paid labour tended to reproduce divisions of labour in the home, these same divisions persisted within activist circles, including ETA. In the words of one woman who joined the organisation in the 1960s:

> Women's professions were teachers and nurses. And all of a sudden you get involved in the struggle, and you don't renounce your thinking so quickly. You renounce your thinking with time. So we women accepted the role of little women in the struggle. But it's a totally ideological problem . . . And inside ETA too, inside ETA it was a total reflection of society . . . It was a photo. A photo of society . . . And *machista* a lot of the time, because it was a photo of society. (#15, b. 1946)

Importantly, while this narrator includes herself among those women who accepted the role of 'little women in the struggle', her own history runs counter to this narrative: she was a schoolteacher who went on to become one of the first women to carry a gun and take on a leadership role in ETA. But, while there is not necessarily a direct link between the jobs women held and their roles inside ETA, this excerpt does indicate awareness of a structure – an 'ideological problem' – that connects the gendered division of labour across a series of private and public spaces: home, workforce and the nationalist movement itself.

Studies of ETA's recruitment patterns and activist base during the 1960s have largely overlooked this pattern. There is general agreement among scholars that the economic, social and political crisis and changes of the post-war period had a particularly important impact on young people raised in Basque rural areas.[42] In particular, studies of early ETA have often drawn a direct link between the rapid economic development experienced by young men raised in rural farmsteads during the 1940s and 1950 and ETA's success in recruiting members and supporters in the rural areas of Vizcaya and Guipízcoa during the 1960s. Several academics have interpreted the organisation's popularity in these areas as the result of a conscious response by former peasants to cultural repression and economic exploitation.[43] Many future ETA members, it is argued, first experienced culture shock when they were transplanted from the Basque-speaking world of the family home to the state or Church school where *euskera* was forbidden.[44] Later, as young adults, they found themselves working not on the family farm, but in the new factories, where Spanish was the main language among the predominantly migrant working class. The alienation these young Basques experienced in an unfamiliar urban Spanish-speaking environment, and the 'traumatic' experience of rapid social and cultural change brought on by industrialisation, translated into a political commitment to nationalism and revolution.[45]

This story of alienation and political consciousness, the movement from farm to factory, basically represents men's work patterns in these years (even though a small number of women – including some narrators for this study – did become factory workers in the 1960s). Moreover, this analysis of how the proletarianisation of the Basque rural lower middle class became the impetus for nationalist activism tends to take for granted an idealised rural family home. But, in the words of Joseba Zulaika, the average ETA militant had 'a problem in distinguishing metaphoric and literal meanings when he dream[ed] of returning to the baserria'.[46] Moreover, it would appear that many women's dreams moved in the opposite direction, as indicated by the narrator in chapter 1 (#8a, b. 1948) who left her family farm to work in a Bilbao factory in the 1960s. In fact, by the 1960s and 1970s fewer women remained on the farm, leaving larger numbers of male farmers single, and putting into question the future of the *baserri*.[47] By the 1960s some observers familiar with *baserri* culture expressed concern about the daily conditions in which rural women worked and lived, and the consequent threat to rural culture as more and more young women left the countryside for the city.[48]

Histories of early ETA, therefore, provide only a partial explanation for the organisation's patterns of recruitment. But if women were largely excluded from ETA's key recruiting grounds (seminaries, *cuadrillas*, factories and universities), how did small numbers of women become involved in radical nationalist activism in the 1960s? A clue, I suggest, lies in another recollection from one ETA's first female armed activists:

> Basically there were guys. We'd already started to connect with the world of women [*el mundo femenino*], mostly in cultural things and the like. Mostly to look for houses to sleep in, and . . . In the structure, in ETA's armed structure, there still weren't any women. (#15, b. 1946)

In order to locate the origins of nationalist activism for many women, we have to focus our attention beyond the worlds of leisure, education, religion and work, towards the realm of culture.

Representations of culture and gender in early ETA

ETA's early theorists, like members of Ekin before them, were primarily concerned with Basque cultural and linguistic revival. They associated culture above all with language, identifying *euskera* as the defining principle of Basque identity and nationhood. Since the Basque language was spoken primarily by lower-middle-class ethnic Basques (as opposed to migrants or descendants of migrant families from other parts of Spain), its revival and survival required the formation of an inter-class 'national front' of ethnic Basques. Thus early ETA preoccupied itself relatively little with alliances with oppositional political movements outside the Basque country, and likewise had limited interest in forming coalitions with the largely Spanish-speaking Basque proletariat.[49] As the decade continued, other political ideas and claims would emerge inside ETA's membership to challenge, or at least to modify, this exclusionist definition of Basque nationhood, and in particular the conservative class politics of ETA's founders and early leaders.

Schematically, the political and strategic development of ETA can be understood as the gradual consolidation of power by the ethnic nationalist faction, which by the late 1960s was increasingly dominated by the military front. This faction was influenced to a certain extent by socialist ideas, but remained resistant to any ideology perceived as diluting the principal aim of national self-determination, or questioning the strategy of armed struggle. Historically nationalism and socialism had never been compatible movements in the Basque country. Indeed, the two movements had emerged in direct opposition to one another. Nationalists had traditionally suspected socialists, and migrant workers in general, of being irredeemably loyal to Spain, while the urban proletariat felt little affinity to a largely middle-class nationalist movement which, since the days of PNV founder Sabino Arana, had been openly hostile towards the 'Spanish' working class. This long-standing ideological conflict, acted out at the turn of the twentieth century as the hostility between the PNV and Partido Socialista Obrero Español (PSOE – Spanish Socialist Party), and in the tensions inside the Second Republic of the 1930s, repeated itself inside ETA during the 1960s.

Its first casualty came in 1966 when a group of left-wing students tried to initiate a move within ETA towards a broader-based movement incorporating both ethnic Basques and the largely migrant proletariat. The group's socialism was inspired by the writings of the European new left – made more widely available in these years due to the loosening of Francoist censorship laws – and by the mobilisation of an increasingly militant Basque working class. In the boom years of the early 1960s, the

Comisiones Obreras (CC.OO. – Workers' Commissions), clandestine labour organisations established by Catholic and communist activists, had made significant inroads into the regime's official unions, and workers at several Bilbao factories had initiated successful strike actions. During the most active decade of the revived Spanish workers' movement, from 1963 to 1974, the Basque provinces accounted for one third of all strikes in Spain.[50] When the socialist faction inside ETA managed to take over the organisation's political office in the mid-1960s, the 'old guard' (those supportive of the original ethnic nationalist principles of Ekin) reacted by dismissing their opponents as *españolistas* (pro-Spanish) and expelling them from the organisation. The ousted activists went on to form ETA-Berri (New ETA), which eventually moved away from nationalism to become a small Maoist party.[51]

Throughout this period, however, ETA's definition of Basque nationhood and culture remained effectively unchanged. The first articles published in the organisation's newsletter *Zutik* in the early 1960s presented a vision of a Basque Golden Age reminiscent of the rhetoric of Arana, promoting a return to a traditional Basque way of life, epitomised by the rural family home – or at least ETA's idealised version of it. The unifying feature of this pre-capitalist society would be the universal use of *euskera*.[52] The revival of *euskera* was described in life or death terms as the key to saving the Basque nation from extinction. The survival of both the language and the nation could only be guaranteed in a separate, sovereign Basque state.

To the extent that women are present at all in ETA's writings during the organisation's first two decades, it is primarily in relation to family and culture. In ETA documents of the early 1960s, women appear as the symbol of Basque cultural identity and marker of national difference. The following is from a 1961 issue of *Zutik* newsletter:

> Against such a general concept of Woman as a pleasant promise, against the 'Don Juan' mentality, against the concept of the 'Lady' – a beautiful and idealised, but depersonalised thing – the Basque opposes his transcendental conception of Woman as Mother and *Etxekoandre*, Lady of the House.[53]

Elsewhere, however, women are portrayed as dangerous to national identity and difference, as weak beings especially vulnerable to the seductions of a bourgeois and Spanish lifestyle.[54] As suggested in chapter 1, these images were typical of the dualist imagery of European middle-class nationalisms from the late nineteenth century onwards.

Yet ETA's representations of womanhood also reflected the newer ideological influences on radical nationalism during the 1960s, as well as the participation of small numbers of women in the organisation. From the mid-1960s there were increasing signs of awareness within ETA of women as a group, and as potential political agents. The first explicit mention of 'the woman question' appears in one of ETA's most important documents, the 'Letter to Basque intellectuals' written in 1964-65:

> With regard to the position of woman in Basque society, we think she should enjoy identical rights and possibilities to men in all areas of political, social, economic and cultural life. Nonetheless, conscious of the special function incumbent upon her in the home as wife and mother, society should pay due attention and facilitate the fulfillment of this function.[55]

The contents of this letter reveal the tensions in the gender politics of ETA's first decade. The discreet reference to equal rights is overshadowed by the glorification of women's primary role as wife and mother. Elsewhere in the same letter the Basque family is upheld as the 'basic cell' of the Basque people, and the demise of the traditional institution of marriage is lamented in the face of the atomised modern family. One of the suggestions for facilitating women's roles in the home is the provision of financial compensation for her 'work in the raising and education of future Basque citizens'.[56] Importantly, the document also contains some of ETA's first references to Marxism. At its Fourth Assembly in 1965, ETA adopted a revised version of the 'Letter to Basque intellectuals', in which the organisation reiterated its concern with the unequal position of women and men in Basque society, calling for a 'revolution' which would free women from the 'chains' which oppressed them.[57] In these months – the spring and summer of 1965 – *Zutik* dedicated several articles to the issue of women. A piece in the 1 May issue placed women's oppression firmly in the context of 'socialist objectives', and urged women's 'decolonisation'.[58] One historian of radical nationalism has suggested that this article represents the first reference in ETA to 'the new social movements born out of consumer society'.[59] But in 1965 it is much too soon to speak of feminism as a social movement. The Basque women's movement, like that elsewhere in Spain, would emerge later than the women's movements in the rest of Western Europe, not making an appearance until after the death of Franco a full decade later.

What this 1965 article does reflect is an interest in women as a social group or class. For ETA theorists in these years women's oppression was interpreted as a by-product of class and national oppression. Following a Marxist tradition going back to Engels, women's oppression was understood as a symptom of capitalism that would disappear with the establishment of an independent socialist Basque state. In fact, in the writings of ETA's socialist faction in the mid-1960s there is a discernible similarity in representations of women and workers. Both groups were addressed as an oppressed collective and as potential protagonists in the national revolution, while there was relatively little analysis of the material realities of their lives. In an article entitled 'Women's liberation', one ETA member drew a contrast between women's roles in the organisation – where they were apparently free to take part in any activities – and their position in the state-run women's organisation Sección Femenina de Falange.[60] The article claimed that the 'respect' and 'equality' Basque women found in ETA had led to a growing female presence in the organisation.[61] The work was signed with a Castilian name, possibly a pseudonym,[62] suggesting that ETA was eager in these years to give the impression that the organisation enjoyed support among the migrant worker population. In this light, it is interesting to note that the article presents the question of women's roles in ETA, not as a separate political problem but as one element of the wider ideological debate between traditionalist nationalists and left-wing dissidents within ETA. The organisation's written commitment to women's equality is best understood as part of its overall revolutionary project, rather than as a reflection of any real increase in the number of female ETA activists in 1965.

Throughout ETA's first decade, therefore, conflicting views of women formed part of a general ideological struggle within the organisation. But they also reflected the shifting social and cultural conditions in Basque and Spanish society. On one hand, debates about socialism and Third World national liberation movements introduced a discourse of gender equality and women's liberation, even if these did not translate into action.[63] On the other hand, the persistence of a traditionalist nationalist vision of nationhood and national identity, with its focus on cultural authenticity, contributed directly to an image of women as symbols of Basque national difference and reproducers of Basque culture and citizens. Yet it was precisely the enduring association of women with culture that provided some of the first spaces for women's radical nationalist activism. While most young men appear to have been introduced to nationalism in the 1960s via seminaries, *cuadrillas*, the workplace or university, evidence from the interviews and available biographies of former activists indicates that women were more likely to make their first contacts with the nationalist movement through activities such as dance, theatre or singing groups, nationalist celebrations and festivals, and language classes. In the highly charged atmosphere of late Franco Spain, these activities took on an explicitly political meaning which in turn shaped the consciousness of the new generation of activists.

Incorporating the feminine

Although the basic authoritarian structures of the Franco regime remained firmly in place, the mid-1950s onwards witnessed a certain relaxation of the cultural and linguistic restrictions that had been imposed on Catalonia and the Basque country in the immediate post-war period. Throughout the 1960s, choirs, dance groups, theatre and clandestine *euskera* classes were established in towns and neighbourhoods throughout the Basque country. Like paid work, cultural activities took young women outside the family home, and introduced them to new social networks and, in some cases, novel political ideas. These groups offered young women, in particular those who had grown up in Basque-speaking families with a history of nationalist activism, the chance to pursue interests and activities already initiated at home. More broadly, cultural groups provided opportunities for young people from a variety of backgrounds to socialise with their peers. Along with Church groups, cultural groups constituted the primary extra-familial social spaces for many teenage girls and young women. The mixed character of many such groups reflected the gradual shift in the cultural and social landscape of the 1960s.

Women's participation in teaching and learning *euskera*, dancing, singing and acting reinforced the traditional nationalist association between culture and the feminine, as with women in the EAB (Women's Patriotic League) earlier in the century. Yet the practice of this culture in public or semi-public spaces outside the home changed the political nature of this association. For young women raised in the conservative family and school environments described in the previous chapter, the very act of mixed socialising could in itself be experienced as personally and politically liberating. But a further factor contributed to the politicisation of Basque cultural activity in this period. Notwithstanding a certain superficial liberalisation, the Franco regime continued to view the public expression of Basque culture, including folklore activities, with suspicion, especially as it became clear that they were in many cases linked to a resurgent nationalist movement. This atmosphere of repression enforced an ongoing secrecy that had the effect of giving many cultural activities an explicitly political character, as well as radicalising those who partook in them.

In these years Basque cultural activities were typically held either under the protection of the Church, or clandestinely in the houses of PNV families, and were often monitored and interrupted by the security forces. Most of the narrators for this study remember incidents of heavy-handed police action during nationalist-sponsored events. In particular, stories of the annual Aberri Eguna (Day of the Basque Patria), held on Easter Sunday, feature prominently in the interviews as a landmark of individual and collective consciousness-raising. The case of Itziar Aizpurua, one of the three female defendants at the trial of sixteen accused ETA members in Burgos in 1970, and later a prominent radical nationalist politician, highlights the importance of cultural events in the politicisation process. Aizpurua's early activities promoting Basque culture were channelled through her leadership of the local festival committee that organised an annual Basque festival in the coastal town of Deba, with the usual demonstrations of folklore: dance, singing groups, Church masses in *euskera*, *txistulariak* (Basque flutists) and *bertsolariak* (singers of improvised verses in *euskera*). The regime's fear that such activities would breed political subversion led the civil governor to ban the celebrations in 1966. The Deba festival committee nevertheless went ahead with its events, prompting the intervention of the Civil Guard and the arrests of several participants and organisers, including Aizpurua herself.[64]

Cultural activities thus provided at least two ways into political thinking and acting for young Basque women in the 1960s. First, they expanded activities traditionally associated with the home into semipublic and public spaces, and linked them directly to a resurgent nationalist movement, thereby bringing many young women into direct contact with political activism. Second, because of ongoing Francoist repression of Basque cultural expression, the partaking in these activities often resulted in direct confrontation with the security forces – including in some cases injury or arrest – turning even the most innocuous folklore gathering into significant political events. Thus, while the home was associated in nationalist discourse with Basque culture and language, it was the attempt to expand cultural practices into public that gave them a more officially political status, as the following narrator from a small industrial city in Vizcaya expresses:

> Well in my house we spoke *euskera*, but I didn't speak much. For me of course it was after getting involved in the dance group, as if my eyes were opened, we started going to Basque *fiestas*, which at that time were held half-clandestinely or to the Aberri Eguna, which was held very clandestinely. (#11a, b.1946)

Even though the association of culture with 'the world of women' opened the way for some women into ETA activism, a number of narrators noted that it was subsequently difficult for women to move beyond such activities, or to combine them with other forms of activism. What they considered more 'serious' work in the political, workers' and military fronts was dominated by men.⁶⁵ In terms of grassroots activism, then, the old set of binaries (woman/man, culture/politics, private/public) remained stubbornly entrenched inside ETA. In fact, as the decade wore on, and as the repression of public expression of Basque culture became more intense, culture itself ceased to be associated primarily with women, and public cultural activities and events were increasingly led by men.

An important example of this shift from the association of culture with the private and the 'world of women' to the public sphere of politics and men is found in the case of the *ikastolas*, or Basque-language schools. The *ikastola* movement had its roots in the initiatives of the nationalist women's organisation EAB in the 1920s and 1930s, and in the clandestine *euskera* classes given in nationalist homes and churches under Franco.⁶⁶ One narrator who attended some of the earliest *ikastolas* formed in the 1960s, and later became a Basque language teacher herself, recalls that as the teaching of *euskera* and Basque culture became more formal in the 1970s and 1980s the visible leaders of the movement were increasingly male (#2, b. 1959). Likewise, Teresa del Valle and her colleagues note, 'as the development of *euskera* is institutionalised and gains importance in the political sphere, its direction is taken over by men'. ⁶⁷ Even when women were recognised as the primary transmitters of language and culture, this role was typically associated with the private sphere. As one group of feminist ETA supporters living in exile in the French Basque country in the mid-1970s expressed it: 'Women transmit the language . . . but don't have the right to speak.'⁶⁸

During the 1960s cultural, social and economic forces combined in the Basque country to provide new opportunities for women's and men's political activism. Women's entry into ETA in this period was prompted by a combination of factors. It was facilitated by the traditionalist nationalist association between culture and the feminine, and the explicitly political meaning given culture by the nationalist movement. At the same time, women's roles began to expand as a result of the wider changes under late Francoism, with its potent mixture of liberalising economic policy and enduring repression.

The language of the interviews cited in these first two chapters suggests that many narrators remember their lives in this period (from the 1950s to the early 1970s) as involving a constant negotiation of different spheres of activity: home, Church, school, work, politics. Their memories suggest a need to reconsider some of the assumptions about the relationships among institutions that shaped the development of early ETA, including families, the Church, the *cuadrilla* and the workplace, and the wider politics of the State, including sexual politics. If for several narrators the family and the Church represented sites of simultaneous freedom and repression, the new radical nationalist movement, in contrast, is remembered primarily as a place of unprecedented opportunity for young women's social and political activity. In the light of these associations it is important not to assume, looking back, that ETA and radical nationalism were largely negative forces for women. In the context of a reactionary military regime that had restricted women's rights and activities for decades, the new radical nationalism was experienced by many as liberating, even though it was still characterised by traditional gender associations and divisions. As the following chapters will argue, these divisions were exacerbated by ETA's increasingly violent conflict with the Spanish state, and above all through the organisation's militarisation.

3

Nationalism goes public

> You have to live through it . . . suddenly you've been silent for forty years . . . It's as if a son were buried, the prodigal son, and he reappears. You know he's there. But he has disappeared. (#12, b. 1947)

If the last chapter was concerned with the development of a new clandestine Basque nationalist resistance in the 1960s, the current one examines the ways in which this movement emerged into open conflict with the Spanish state at the end of that decade. Following other studies of gender and nationalism, I argue that nationalist movements are constructed in part through public performance and spectacle, and that these are themselves gendered acts. ETA's early forays into public consisted primarily of small-scale clandestine activities such as painting graffiti and flying the illegal Basque flag. Such actions aimed to mark the borders of the Basque nation, but they also operated to establish gendered boundaries within the radical nationalist movement. Moreover, despite claims to national difference, a striking feature of nationalist public performance was the way in which it mirrored the gendered performances and discourse of the Franco state.

As ETA's actions became more dangerous, in particular with its first assassination in 1968, its profile extended beyond the local to the national and international. Instrumental in this process was the role of the Basque and Spanish media. During the Burgos trial of 1970, in particular, media representations of ETA members helped to create an enduring image of the male armed militant as martyr and hero. Furthermore, women's narratives, including memories of male activists and leaders, help to construct a masculinised memory of early ETA, even while they sometimes challenge it.

Rituals of revenge and resistance

Several studies of Francoism have emphasised that the regime relied on public performance and display to promote its reactionary ideology of

National Catholicism and to impress upon the population its triumph in the Civil War.¹ In the media this ongoing celebration of victorious Francoism was managed through direct censorship, control of the state news agency, and the establishment of the government news and documentary (No-Do) and film companies (CIFESA). Another form of popular entertainment, football, became a forum for promoting nationalist sentiment, both through the regime's (ultimately futile) attempt to eliminate the association of Basque and Catalan teams with regional identities, and Spain's participation in international competitions.

The regime also endeavoured to fill public spaces (churches, universities, schools, government and other communal buildings, town squares, and so on) with the symbols of its victory, including photos of Franco and huge crosses. Even the style of architecture changed, with a rejection of modernism and an attempt to recreate the imperial aesthetic of the sixteenth and seventeenth centuries (epitomised by Philip II's monastery, El Escorial). The most notorious Francoist construction was the *Valle de los Caídos* (Valley of the Fallen), an enormous tomb and monument to the fallen of the Civil War, built largely by republican prisoners of war in the mountains outside Madrid.² The central role of the Church in Franco Spain was reinforced at open-air masses and regular religious celebrations throughout the year.³ In addition, the regime kept alive the memory of the Civil War (and a sinister reminder of its capacity for retributive violence),⁴ through military processions and parades, examples of what Paul Preston has called the regime's 'rituals of revenge'.⁵

In interviews with women active in Basque nationalist politics in the 1960s, the contrast between these public rituals of Francoism and the opposing political culture of family and local community is presented most starkly through childhood memories of school, as in this excerpt about a primary state school in Bilbao in the 1950s:

> [The teacher] talked about Spain and about the peninsula and about Spain . . . And I went home to study, and I said, 'Mama', and she said, 'What are you saying about Spain? This is not Spain!' And I said, '*Amatxo* [mummy], the teacher, Miss Dolores, says this is Spain.' 'Bring me the map,' she says, very practical. In Euskadi there are lots of women like my mother. And I think now [*laughter*] we women aren't like that, but I think that nationalist spirit in the homes has been transmitted by our mothers, who've been incredible. She says to me, 'Bring the map here! . . . What are you saying about the peninsula? Portugal, where is it? Isn't it in the peninsula, and is it Spain? Tell the teacher!' And I went, all clever, in the morning and said, 'My mother told me –' Well, what am I going to tell you about the problems she made for me?! [*laughter*]. (#3, b. 1944)

Another narrator, who in chapter 2 remembered the differences between her own education and that of her brother, recalls her early experience of school:

> When we started to go to school, it was the first time we heard talk about the Right, the Left, about the bad reds, the bad nationalists. We didn't know what those things were. We didn't know Spanish either . . . Some of the teachers talked, not all of them, but some talked. And since it wasn't exactly what we had heard at home, we went home and asked . . . What it seemed was that the public was everything to do with school, and the private was everything to do with home. (#1, b. 1947)

A particularly potent memory in this and other interviews with Basque-speaking narrators is the process of being silenced through being forced to speak Spanish. Given the importance of language to Basque nationalist claims to uniqueness and independence, the repression of *euskera* is a frequent theme in individual and collective stories about the Franco period. Because linguistic prohibition extended to the use of Basque names (a widely recounted story of the Franco years is that Basque names were Castilianised on gravestones), some narrators born in the post-war period literally had one name at home and another name at school and elsewhere in public. The extent to which the regime authorities and its supporters attempted to maintain the public sphere as 'Spanish' is highlighted by the story from a narrator whose name was translated into Spanish when it appeared in a newspaper obituary following the death of a relative as late as the mid-1960s (#2, 1959).

During the 1940s and 1950s open, collective opposition to Francoism was all but impossible. But as the regime shed some of its more authoritarian trappings during the 1960s Francoist cultural policies became more lenient, including the partial reversal of the prohibition of the Basque and Catalan languages. This set the stage in the Basque country for the movement of the Basque language schools, *ikastolas*, from private homes to public buildings. The *ikastolas* were funded by the parents of the children who attended them, and were only grudgingly tolerated by the regime.[6] As a narrator who attended one of the earliest legal *ikastolas* in Bilbao in the 1960s remembers, the Francoist authorities made life particularly difficult for teachers and students at these schools, and ensured that they would not be free from the daily public expressions of National Catholicism:

> There was the strange paradox that since the whole *ikastola* thing was so poorly accepted by the government, so controlled, that it was in the *ikastola* that I learned to sing the Spanish national anthem . . . and to salute the

flag every morning. There was an inspector from the Treasury, from Education, that I've never seen again, but if I see him I'll know him, for sure, I'm never going to forget his face. Who came *every* morning, to the *ikastola*, with a little moustache – typical, that. He came every morning and he was there until the Spanish flag was hung out on the balcony and all the children sang the national anthem. Which more than anyone the *andereño* [Basque female teacher] sang. And the rest of us moved our mouths. I'm saying there was also a consciousness about that. Of course you had to make it look like, but it was something that we obviously all felt as an imposition. That's why I tell you I'll never forget that man's face. (#2, b. 1959)

Like the portrayals of 'fascist nuns' in the previous chapter, the unforgettable image of the Francoist functionary, with his 'typical' moustache, owes itself to the archetypal nature of the image, and its repeated representation in popular culture. If the stereotypical Castilian civil servant served as an object of humour under Franco, in this story he serves not only as a trope for the dictatorship itself, but also of Spanishness more generally. This is in contrast to the quintessential Basqueness of the *ikastola*, which is in turn personified by the female teacher. Whereas in the excerpts cited above school was described as a public institution, juxtaposed with the relative cultural and political security of the home, here the *ikastola* becomes an extension of the home. Thus the male inspector quite literally invades the private, identified not only as the sphere of opposition to Francoism, but also as the domestic and the feminine.

If requiring Basque children to sing the Spanish national anthem and salute the Spanish flag in an *ikastola* were examples of localised Francoist 'rituals of revenge', the narrator's recollection of a small act of rebellion – mouthing the Spanish words and refusing to say them aloud – is presented in her narrative as a personal ritual of resistance. Several of the interviews contain similar stories. Before the rise of an organised anti-Franco movement in the Basque country during the 1960s, narrators remember that state repression was met with small rituals at home or with symbolic gestures in public. The same narrator recounts an example of how her nationalist family countered one Francoist ceremony:

One thing I remember really well every year on the 19th of June, which was the Day of the Liberation of Bilbao by the National troops, there was a parade that ended in the Plaza Moyua. A military parade . . . In my house the Day of the Liberation of Bilbao was always known as the Day of Occupation. So, they went by below the house, it was a huge parade, and they usually stopped there for a long time. I remember there were a couple of neighbors, who put the Spanish flag out, on the balcony . . . in my house, we pulled down the blinds, to the bottom, so as not to see that whole scene. (#2, b. 1959)

Another narrator from Bilbao has a similar memory of her family's attempt to extend small domestic acts of defiance to the street beyond:

> The day of the Aberri Eguna we used to go out to the window, we three nationalist families, and we made a signal with our hands, holding our hands as if we were saying, 'Here we are!' OK? And we're resisting.' And it was a ritual. (#3, b. 1944)

In both these examples the redrawing of boundaries between house and street was a symbol of the political border between Basque and Spanish, between political opposition and the State. In the first example the resistance takes the form of reinforcing the boundary between the two realms, literally shutting out the State, whereas in the second a private ritual of resistance is tentatively extended into public.

In the interviews as a whole the symbol that most commonly represents rituals of resistance and challenges to national borders is the Basque flag, the *ikurriña*. In the following excerpts three separate narrators tell strikingly similar tales about tiny *ikurriñas* hidden away in secret places:

> When I was 7 or something one day a friend of my father – I had never seen an *ikurriña*. My father explained it to us, but I'd never seen it. Because it was forbidden. And this man was from Azkoitia and he was a friend of my father and he was also *abertzale* [nationalist]. He had a wooden walking stick, and in the kitchen, hidden from everything, he opened the walking stick and inside he had a little *ikurriña*. The first time I saw an *ikurriña*. And hey! It was really exciting! (#19, b. 1944)

> They [my grandfather and mother] had a tiny *ikurriña*, that I've still kept, and well they put it in the house, hidden away, because it was very dangerous to show that in the village. (#3, b. 1944)

> I remember in my grandmother's house . . . there was a window that divided off the kitchen from the rest of the rooms in the house. And stuck on that window there were little *estampitas* [religious pictures] and things like that. There was a little picture of the Sacred Heart, I remember perfectly, that moved, and under the little picture of the Sacred Heart was a tiny *ikurriña*. From time to time we took out the tiny *ikurriña* to look at it. (#2, b. 1959)

In other interviews the *ikurriña* appears hidden in church prayer books or in the hems of schoolgirls' skirts. A symbol of the clandestine character of Basque identity under Franco, the *ikurriña* subsequently became a symbol of resistance when it was taken out of hiding into public. Thus one narrator recalls with laughter that she and her classmates at convent school in the early 1960s used to throw *ikurriñas* from the school windows, an act that was 'totally forbidden, and very punishable' (#12, b. 1947). More commonly, the *ikurriña* was taken by young people on weekend outings, and left to fly on a mountaintop. This act, as one narrator says, 'is a little absurd these days, but back then it wasn't absurd. Back then we did it because the mountains were full of police' (#4, b. 1936).

The *ikurriña* as these narrators describe it is an example of what Anne McClintock has called a national fetish object. In her study of gender and nationalism under the British Empire, she argues that 'nationalism inhabits the realm of fetishism . . . Far from being purely phallic icons, fetishes embody crises in social value, which are projected onto and embodied in, what can be called impassioned objects'.[7] The *ikurriña's* status as an 'impassioned object' is perceptible in the emotion and excitement in the voices of many narrators recounting the first time they saw the forbidden flag, sentiments apparent thirty or more years after the event. Precisely because of its enduring status as a symbol of resistance, the *ikurriña* is a good example, in McClintock's words, of 'the ways in which women consume, refuse or negotiate the male fetish rituals of national spectacle'.[8]

The *ikurriña* had been designed by Sabino Arana at the turn of the century, and adopted by the PNV as the Basque national flag in the 1930s. Under Franco its display was strictly prohibited. But the *ikurriña's* place in the history of Basque nationalism is also coloured by gender; historically, women from nationalist families had sewn *ikurriñas* in their homes. One narrator recalls her efforts to make an *ikurriña* as an example of women's work in the new nationalist movement of the 1960s:

> Women took on the role of . . . helpers. Of working on things like, an *ikurriña* had to be made, to be put up somewhere, and maybe that fell to us, to find the cloth. I remember I went out in a terrible state of fear, in one store I bought the green, in another I bought the red, because imagine if you bought the three colours in the same place. In those days for me that was awful, awful. And I used to sew it at home, and one time my father saw me and he got really worked up. He saw an *ikurriña*, and we had neighbours, and this was very secretive. (#11b, b. 1944)

The sight of the *ikurriña* in this story has an emotional impact that is not gender-specific. At the same time, however, the act of sewing the *ikurriña* encodes in memory the contrast between the narrator's nationalist activities and those of her boyfriend, who was an active member of the PNV youth organisation, EGI (Eusko Gaztedi del Interior). Thus the *ikurriña* represents, in McClintock's words, 'woman's relation to the nation as indirect, mediated through her social relation to men, her national identity lying in her unpaid services and sacrifices'.[9] This is not to suggest that the *ikurriña* is an enduring and static symbol of women's secondary position in Basque nationalism. In the 1960s it actually represented the fragility of the Basque nation as defined by nationalists. It was also a symbol of the division of women's and men's roles in the early radical nationalist movement. In the early 1960s, therefore, the *ikurriña* acted as a marker of both national and gender difference.

Another account of the secret sewing of an *ikurriña* demonstrates how boundaries of gender and nationality began to shift by the early 1970s:

> In the *Olentzero* [Basque Christmas celebration] an *ikurriña* was brought out. Incredible, because the *ikurriña* was forbidden. And at the junction there were always Civil Guards. They were doing checkpoints. And I remember for one, I was about 13 or something, at that *Olentzero*, we [*nosotros*] sewed an *ikurriña*. So each one [*cada uno*] went to Bilbao to buy one colour of the fabric because you couldn't, if you went to a store and asked for one red fabric, another green and another white, that was a bit much. So three of us from the *cuadrilla* went, like three teams, each one to buy one colour of the fabric. And later we sewed it in a friend's [*un amigo nuestro*] *txoko* [eating club] to take it out for the *Olentzero*. (#18, b. 1961)

The use of masculine nouns and pronouns in this excerpt (*nosotros, cada uno, amigo*) indicates that the narrator was part of a mixed friendship group or *cuadrilla*, and that teenage boys as well as girls were involved in going out to buy the fabric for the *ikurriña*, and sewing it in secret at the eating club of a male friend (*un amigo nuestro*).

That the *ikurriña* was symbolic of wider gender relations is further suggested by the 1977 prologue to a volume of early ETA documents. In it the editors state that 'women were incorporated as participants, in the capacity of activists, and transcending the old conception of *emakumes* who sew the *ikurriña* that the militants will hang at night'.[10] This claim of women's increased involvement in the organisation in the early to mid-1960s should not be taken at face value, since there is little empirical evidence to support it. What the quotation does suggest, however, is that, at least to the former ETA(p-m) members writing those words in the late 1970s, the breaking down of gender divisions signified an important ideological break with the traditional nationalism associated with the PNV. In the contrast between the first interview excerpt and the second, the displaying of the *ikurriña* by both women and men constitutes an important example of the ways in which, in McClintock's terms, women negotiated the 'male fetish rituals of national spectacle' in a move from indirect, unpaid servants of male nationalists to active national subjects.

While the public display of the *ikurriña* itself remains one of the more visible signs of the move of radical nationalism from private to public resistance, this story of the *ikurriña* undermines the characteristic nationalist reading of the flag as a symbol of a timeless Basque nation. In the nationalist tale the *ikurriña* is a marker of Basque unity and difference from the outside other (that is, Spain). But my interviews stress the historical power relations and negotiations *inside* the Basque country that have been equally significant in the construction of that nation, and of nationalism itself.

Projecting ETA into the public sphere

For most contemporary commentators on ETA, the date that marks the organisation's entry into history is not 1959 but 1968, the year of its first fatal armed actions. When remembered against the violence of the past thirty-five years, the public activities of ETA's first decade – destroying local memorials to fallen Francoist forces, painting Basque words and symbols on public buildings, distributing propaganda – may seem, in the words of one early ETA member, 'very simple things' (#15, b. 1946). Yet, as the stories of *ikurriñas* remind us, what in retrospect appear 'simple things' were, under the Francoist police state, potentially seditious acts – enough to warrant a lengthy prison sentence, and even put the activist's life in danger. But ETA's early actions were intended to do more than defy and taunt the Francoist authorities. They were also rituals that functioned to establish the boundaries of the new nationalist movement itself, and to construct and consolidate a new radical nationalist community.[11]

In her study of the Argentine military junta, Diana Taylor argues that '[p]ublic spectacles . . . are the locus of the construction of communal identity',[12] including nationalist identity, and that such spectacles are mediated by gender, class and nationality. Many of the examples Taylor offers of the gendered public spectacles of Argentine military nationalism are relevant to the Franco dictatorship: the historical construction of the *patria* as feminine, the exclusively male nature of the military, the discursive division by the regime of women into good (silent wives and mothers) and bad (left-wing activists, 'terrorists', prostitutes), and the feminisation of the enemy. Equally importantly, in her analysis of the rituals of the military regime and its opposition, Taylor notes the striking and disquieting similarities in their respective representations of nation and gender. While ostensibly challenging the violence upon which the military's power rested, critics of the Argentine junta sometimes eerily echoed the sexualised nature of that violence. In both cases, argues Taylor, 'national identity is predicated on female destruction'. Misogyny thus acts as 'a fundamental bridge or slash connecting the military/anti-military discourse. In the struggles for national identity, both groups of males were fighting to define and occupy the "masculine" position while emasculating, feminizing, and marginalizing the "other".'[13]

Taylor's study is also instructive about the gender politics of the Basque conflict in stressing the importance of spectacle and the media in building national communities. Below I explore how representations of the Basque conflict in the Basque and Spanish media placed women and the feminine on the margins and portrayed young male ETA members as the embodiment of the Basque cause. As in the case of Argentina, representations on both sides show similar constructions of gender premised on the celebration of the male hero and the positioning of women as outsiders or witnesses to the main performance, which is essentially presented as the competition between men. The oral history interviews provide testimony to the importance of spectacle and media in constructing the Basque conflict; they are replete with images reminiscent of cinema and television. Descriptions of certain archetypal characters in particular (like those of fascist nuns or Francoist functionaries, already discussed) indicate the importance of the moving image in shaping individual and group memories of the conflict, including representations of masculinity and femininity.

The emergence of radical nationalism into public, and the growing popular consciousness of ETA as a new, clandestine nationalist movement, occurred through the 1960s as the organisation engaged in increasingly daring and dangerous acts of sabotage and violence against state targets. Although its early actions had raised some awareness of the movement at the local level, widespread knowledge of ETA's activities came through stories of direct conflict between activists and the Francoist police, which were spread at first by word of mouth and later through the state media. The following stories, recounted by a narrator who joined ETA in the mid-1960s, emphasises the emotional and political impact of early ETA actions in one working-class neighbourhood near Bilbao:

> When all of a sudden, a bit of graffiti appeared in the town that there had never been before. The impact was amazing, and it was from people that had to be away [*fuera*]. People who were away [*fuera*] at that time. Of course, you knew who had done it! [*laughter*] (#12, b. 1947)

The original Spanish, with its emphasis on people who were *fuera* – literally 'out' or 'outside' – captures more vividly than the English translation the image of young activists leaving their local communities to go into hiding, only to return furtively to spread a message of active resistance. In the next passage (from which the chapter's epigraph is taken), this return is presented in symbolic terms as breaking the silence imposed on the vanquished by the Franco regime:

> When an *ikurriña* was thrown, at the town *fiesta*, well [*laughter*] there was an apotheosis. You revolutionised people. You revolutionised them with graffiti . . . You have to live through it . . . suddenly you've been silent for forty years . . . these things . . . even get forgotten. It's as if a son were buried, the prodigal son, and he reappears. You know he's there. But he has disappeared. (#12, b. 1947)

The biblical parable of the prodigal son evokes here the mystery and reverence surrounding early ETA, anticipating as well the martyr status later accorded ETA's fallen militants, who were sometimes portrayed as Christ figures.[14] This popular image of ETA members as heroic young men has endured despite women's widening participation in all aspects of radical nationalist politics, including armed activism. As a tale told thirty years later, this story of the prodigal son voices an enduring popular memory of the ETA activist as an eternally young man, an image imbued with Catholic imagery. Such memories continue to hold profound meaning years later, regardless of the significant social, economic and political changes in Basque society, including widespread secularisation and significant changes in gender roles.

Another narrator recalls that, following a particularly wide wave of arrests, people began to talk openly about ETA for the first time:

> I had already seen some kind of ETA pamphlet [at nurses' college] . . . One of the students showed it to me. But once I was here, in Bilbao, in '67, and then more in '68, there were loads of arrests, so people started to talk. With my schoolmates in the hospital . . . they weren't nationalist, but they talked about the arrests that had taken place. (#1, b. 1947)

This narrator pinpoints the beginning of an important series of events that brought ETA to the attention of the wider Basque and Spanish population from the late 1960s. This process began in the summer of 1968, during which ETA's military strategy was first put into practice with fatal results, and culminated in the military trial of sixteen ETA members in the Spanish city of Burgos in December 1970. During this two-and-a-half-year period ETA succeeded in posing a serious threat to the stability of the increasingly crisis-ridden Franco regime,[15] and also became the focus of national and international sympathy and support as the pre-eminent public face of struggle against the thirty-year-old military dictatorship.

Memories of male leaders

Throughout the early part of 1968 ETA waged a sustained campaign of violent actions, which, although designed primarily for propaganda effect, led frequently to clashes with police and arrests.[16] This period coincided with the hardening of measures against pro-democracy protesters throughout Spain. In April 1968, following strikes in and around Bilbao organised by the communist-led Workers' Commissions, a state of emergency was declared in the province of Vizcaya. During the summer of the same year, in the midst of heavy state repression against opposition protest, ETA committed its first unplanned killing, immediately followed by its own first casualty. When stopped by a Civil Guard roadblock, ETA leader Txabi Extebarrieta shot and killed one of the guards rather than risk arrest; within hours the Civil Guard tracked him down in his car and killed him.

In the weeks that followed, 'Txabi' was embraced as a kind of saviour. ETA hailed him as 'the first martyr of the Basque revolution',[17] and funerals and tributes were performed in his honour in villages and neighbourhoods all over the Basque country, including in some working-class urban areas where ETA had relatively little support. In addition to uniting different anti-regime groups across class and political divides, the wave of solidarity prompted by Etxebarrieta's death popularised ETA's cause and its commitment to armed struggle, especially among middle-class ethnic Basque youth. Equally importantly, it helped lay the ground for the network of practical and political support that would guarantee ETA's survival in the face of mounting state pressure in the years to come.

Although Spain, still under a dictatorship, did not experience directly the upheaval of the student and workers' movements that have given 1968 its name, narrators' memories of that fateful summer are nevertheless framed by the international context, with frequent references to the Paris events of May 1968 and the Third World liberation movements. The extent to which a transnational memory of May 1968 has been incorporated retrospectively into the popular narrative of opposition to Francoism is suggested by the ironic remark of one narrator: 'Today everyone was in Paris in May 1968!' (#12, b. 1947).

This narrator's interviews evokes many of the political and emotional associations of the events and movements of the late 1960s. Her personal history of activism in ETA runs parallel to some of the organisation's most important debates and schisms. She joined ETA in the mid-1960s, briefly moving to ETA-Berri, the first left-wing group to be expelled by the nationalist 'old guard' in 1966 (see chapter 2), before returning to ETA. In subsequent years she made the reverse move, from the militarist faction ETA-V to the more socialist ETA-VI in the early 1970s. The interview describes in detail the political debates surrounding such moves, in particular the ongoing conflict between nationalism and socialism, and the related debate over the armed vanguard versus mass mobilisation. But, more intriguingly, the narrator's memories of this period stress the emotional attachments associated with different political choices. In particular, in its references to different male political leaders – both Basque and international – the interview illuminates the importance of feeling, in particular affection and love, in the formation of political loyalties and identities.

In the first quotation below the narrator describes a meeting with Txabi Etxebarrieta in the mid-1960s, when the ETA leader came to speak to her and the other young women in her ETA cell to dissuade them from leaving his wing of the organisation:

> In one [of the meetings], I don't know if one of our contacts got a bit scared, and called Txabi Etxebarrieta. And he came to read us the riot act. Well, he convinced us. He came . . . I mean, think about it! [*laughter*] We were 18 years old, or 20. And the guy came and hell, he made a huge impression on us, and he explained everything to us really well, and how should I know what he said to us, how should I know what he said to us. Your guess is as good as mine. Well, the urban guerrilla, and well all this stuff . . . And, and he convinced us . . . He had a kind of, of humanity that made you believe him, sure [*laughter*]. He convinced us [*laughter*]. (#12, b. 1947)

Compare this description of Etxebarrieta, with his almost magical powers of seduction and persuasion, with two other memories of male political leaders associated with the student movements of the 1960s:

> I have a really strong memory of [Daniel] Cohn-Bendit, and it's because his presence was magisterial [*laughter*] . . . He was like a movie reel. It was something dazzling. (#12, b. 1947)

> Sure, we were all totally in love, in Madrid, they were in love with Fidel, with Cuba, with Cuba, and everything [*laughter*]. (#12, b. 1947)

When reading about the admiration and awe inspired by the above political leaders, through their persuasive speech and impressive physical appearance, the word that comes to mind is 'charisma'. In his seminal study of Hollywood stars, film critic Richard Dyer argues that Max Weber's theory of charisma and authority is helpful for an understanding of the ways in which charisma is attributed to certain film stars.[18] Although Dyer acknowledges some problems in transferring the theory of political charisma to the case of stars, the direct comparison above of Paris' 1968 student leader Daniel Cohn-Bendit with something out of a 'movie reel' suggests a connection between the two. Whereas Weber's theories of charisma form part of his investigation into the formation and legitimisation of modern political order and institutions, Dyer's theory is relevant to the study of popular political leaders who may or may not exercise institutional power but who are, like film stars, endowed with charisma through their appeal to a particular audience.

Dyer makes two arguments of special relevance to the relationship between film stars and popular political leaders. First, he notes, following S. N. Eisenstadt, that 'charismatic appeal is effective especially when the social order is uncertain, unstable and ambiguous and when the charismatic figure or group offers a value, order or stability to counterpoise this'.[19] Second, Dyer emphasises the importance of the audience as a historically, socially and culturally specific group, and its role in the construction of certain stars. In particular, he suggests that specific audiences – adolescents, women and gays – may have special relationships to the phenomenon of stardom and star charisma: 'These groups all share a peculiarly intense degree of role/identity conflict and pressure, and an (albeit partial) exclusion from the dominant articulacy of, respectively, adult, male, heterosexual culture'.[20]

If we move from the narrator's description of Daniel Cohn-Bendit and Fidel Castro back to her earlier memory of Txabi Etxebarrieta, Dyer's observations aid our analysis of the charismatic appeal of the young ETA leader. While Etxebarrieta's iconic status owes a great deal to his death and status as ETA's first 'martyr', I would argue that this representation is also shaped by his association with other popular leaders of the same generation. One of the female Burgos defendants claimed: 'Txabi was our Che Guevara'.[21] Etxebarrieta's eminence grew by virtue of the mythic narrative surrounding the 1960s – a narrative typically presented as transnational ('the 1960s', 'the generation of 1968') even through the social movements of the 1960s took different forms in different countries. If Txabi's popularity can be understood in terms of the star-like charisma of the popular political leader, this is in part because the period in which he lived and died was one of intense social, cultural and economic change in the Basque country, Spain and abroad. In the memories of narrators, and in radical nationalist discourse more broadly, Etxebarrieta represents both the young, untainted new generation of Basque activists opposed to everything associated with both the ageing, dictatorial Franco regime and the older generation of Basque nationalists and the ideals of Basque tradition and authenticity.

If Etxebarrieta was embraced as a hero by both the ethnic Basque communities where radical nationalism had its roots, and the largely Spanish-speaking, migrant working-class communities historically associated not with nationalism but with socialism, it was perhaps because he appeared to represent the merging of Basque identity and tradition with dreams associated with modernity: youth, democracy and the outside world. His popular appeal across political boundaries (appeal that did not, it must be noted, translate into significant sustained support for ETA or radical nationalism beyond its historical base in small and medium-sized ethnic Basque communities) can also be explained by Dyer's second observation: that specific groups excluded from dominant culture develop special relationships to stars. In practice Etxebarrieta represented a political position associated more with an exclusive ethnic nationalism than with the merging of national and class struggle (he was the leader of the nationalist faction in ETA that promoted the cross-class alliance of all ethnic Basques and the use of armed struggle). But his image may have held particular popular appeal to working-class communities doubly excluded by both Francoism and bourgeois Basque nationalism.

Dyer's theory may futher be helpful in explaining the particular representation of male political leaders in women's oral narratives, because women are one group Dyer identifies as having a particular relationship to stardom, owing to their relative exclusion from male culture. Yet the description of Extebarrieta in the interview cited above does not depart substantially from the images of him found in stories told by former male members of ETA. One such activist interviewed by anthropologist Miren Alcedo, for example, remembers 'idolising' Etxebarrieta as 'the greatest student leader there was' – 'a genius', 'enormously brilliant', above all in his capacity for public political debate: 'The guy was a god for all of us'.[22]

There is an interesting parallel here with Luisa Passerini's study of the Italian generation of 1968. Passerini notes that in interviews with former male student militants there is a homoerotic element in the feelings expressed for their leaders.[23] She contrasts the ease with which some men could acknowledge their love for male leaders with the difficulties faced by women activists in finding and accepting new female authority figures. Female leaders – relatively few in number – tended to evoke feelings of envy as well as admiration in other women: 'At the same time . . . they represented a model that was not wholly desirable because of its implicit rejection of traditional femininity'.[24] Passerini stresses the importance of language in the revolutionary 1968 movement, noting that a 'passion for the precision of language was extremely important for a leader'.[25] She argues that oral history interviews are particularly revealing in this regard because '[r]ecollections shed light on the nature of leadership as no other document does'.[26]

In my interviews with female Basque narrators there is little trace of the envy or resentment that some of Passerini's female narrators recall feeling towards other women in the Italian student movement.[27] For example, memories of the earliest female ETA members and the female Burgos defendants (discussed below) are expressed with admiration, and relationships with female comrades are generally remembered as supportive. But there is, as seen in previous chapters, a marked ambivalence in most of the interviews with regard to female role models, expressed above all in memories of mothers and women's traditional roles within the nationalist movement. In this context, it is perhaps not surprising that female narrators remember certain historical male leaders with an unreserved adulation that is more difficult to express for other women.

In this respect Dyer's analysis leaves unanswered one important question: To what extent is the very notion of charisma in the Western European and North American cultural traditions, to which both Weber's sociology and Hollywood belong, associated with masculinity? According to S. N. Eisenstadt, Weber himself defined charisma as:

> A certain quality of an individual personality by virtue of which he is set apart from ordinary men and treated as endowed with supernatural, superhuman or at least superficially exceptional qualities.[28]

For Dyer, Weber's concept of charisma is not exclusive to men; in fact, he cites Marilyn Monroe as an example of a star whose charisma owed itself in part to the moral flux of the 1950s. But other studies suggest that there may be a specific association between charisma and constructions of masculinity. In an article on gender and the rise of nation-states in Europe, John Horne notes that '(c)harismatic authority' – as defined by Weber – 'is not intrinsically masculine'.[29] 'But':

> its emergence through the breakdown of national values and identities that had partly been construed in terms of masculinity, and in crises dominated by war, enabled charismatic figures to fashion an unstable political authority in terms of a radically accentuated masculinity.[30]

Horne is particularly interested in those charismatic leaders who came to power during the upheavals of the European inter-war period. But his observations are relevant as well for later periods, and also for less powerful leaders. Horne claims that '[t]he role played by masculinity in charismatic leader cults in the twentieth century is a theme with major potential for the history of Fascism and Communism'.[31] I would argue that this is also an area that remains to be investigated in relation to the popular political and social movements of the 1960s, so closely associated with transnational iconic figures such as Che, Castro and Cohn-Bendit, as well as more local personalities like Txabi Etxeberrieta. To take the investigation a step further, and keeping in mind the interview excerpts above, one could also explore the ways in which women's memories of charismatic leaders contribute to, or perhaps challenge, a masculinised memory of the 1960s.

Dyer's study suggests a series of interesting connections between memory, charisma, media representation, gender and political identities. It is beyond the scope of this book to explore these relationships in detail, but it is worth elaborating on one or two points of special relevance to this study. Until now, most feminist oral histories have been preoccupied with constructions and representations of femininity in women's life stories. Yet the interview described above indicates that women's political identities, and their memories of activism, are equally made through memories of men and masculinity. Some of these memories may be obviously resistant – as in the recollections of the machismo of fathers in chapter 1. But the memories of Etxebarrieta expressed above, like those of male partners and prisoners explored in subsequent chapters, affirm and admire certain forms of masculinity. In particular, they celebrate what is represented as the merging of 'traditional' traits of the male political leader (sexual attractiveness, a penchant for verbal debate, toughness and even military prowess) with more androgynous characteristics associated with the 'modern' man (a commitment to community, more egalitarian gender relations, and so on). To return to Passerini, one could speculate that in the Basque country in the 1960s, as in Italy, it may have been easier for men to combine these attributes of old and new forms of masculinity than for women to discover new forms of female political identity. This imbalance is expressed in women's celebratory representations of male leaders as much as in their ambivalent attitudes towards their mothers and other female political activists.

These observations have wider implications for the study of gender and memory, indicating the need for further theoretical exploration of the ways in which women's memories are shaped by, and in turn help to shape, memories of masculinity as well as femininity – in other words, how women's memories are also made masculine. Given the importance of media images in contemporary imaginings of masculinity and femininity, and the proliferation of filmic images described in oral history interviews (as well as the historical fact that film and television became dominant cultural forms in the Basque country precisely during the 1960s), media and film theory may be particularly helpful in considering these questions.

ETA on trial: Burgos 1970

Having briefly considered the spectacle of Txabi Extebarrieta's death, in this final section I will look at another major event in which media coverage played an important role in constructing the image of male ETA activists as national and international heroes: the 1970 Burgos trial. In reprisal for Etxebarrieta's death, ETA planned its first assassination, choosing as its target Melitón Manzanas, a San Sebastián police inspector with a widespread reputation for torturing his detainees. It was this attack that prompted the wave of arrests remembered by many of the narrators in the summer and autumn of 1968. Until then, although ETA had been subjected to a series of detentions, media focus on the organisation had been limited. But this time the Francoist press vigorously applauded the heavy-handed actions of the state, decrying the threat of 'terrorism' and reporting arrests of members of a 'Basque separatist movement'. This attempt to portray young Basques as 'terrorists' and 'criminals' not surprisingly backfired, elevating ETA members to the status of heroes among large sections of the Basque – and Spanish – population. In turn, this widened the perception among Basque youth that armed resistance was the most effective weapon against the State, therefore prompting more of them to join ETA.[32]

With the arrest and subsequent trials of growing numbers of accused ETA activists and collaborators in the late 1960s, that which previously had been discussed behind closed doors increasingly became the topic of open conversation. People started talking about who had been arrested and what kind of sentences they had received (#2, b. 1959). But if individual incidents of repression – whether through direct encounters with the security forces or the arrest of someone known – were personal landmarks that signalled the end of years of silence, the first collective landmark, which went beyond the local to the national and even the international, was the military trial against the sixteen ETA members accused of the Manzanas killing. Of all the major events in the history of ETA, most narrators have an especially clear memory of the Burgos trial of December 1970, highlighting it as a defining moment in individual and collective political consciousness. According to Alfonso Pérez-Agote, the Burgos trial marked the end of the prohibition on public expressions of nationalism.[33] Before Burgos, ETA had been little more than an acronym. But during the trial the organisation acquired human faces and names for scores of Basque and Spanish citizens watching and reading coverage of the trial.

Burgos not only 'broke the silence' imposed by the regime on Basque nationalists and other opponents of Franco, it also allowed new ways of seeing both the regime and its enemies. Diana Taylor has argued for the case of Argentina under the military junta that specific '[s]igns indicated what the population was to see and not to see'.[34] She gives as an example photographs taken of groups of Argentines gathered outside newspaper kiosks, reading press coverage of the war in the Malvinas/Falkland Islands in the early 1980s. Such images, Taylor writes, 'indicate how communal identity is shaped and how public attention is controlled by the given-to-be-seen. The newspaper kiosks ... served as hubs from which people imbibed their national personality, the us vs them'.[35] Under a military dictatorship, where the press and media are carefully censored and effectively serve as propaganda tools for the regime, the population is given certain images that are 'meant to be seen', while they are supposed to be blind to others (in the case of Argentina, for example, police arrests and beatings on the street). As Taylor further notes, during Argentina's 'Dirty War' spectacles and spectators were positioned according to nationality, class, political affiliation and gender.

Extending Taylor's analysis to the Franco regime, I would argue that the regime promoted certain 'Spanish' symbols (flags, military processions, religious iconography, and so on) as 'given-to-be-seen' by the population, even as it prohibited and forced into hiding symbols of resistance and the 'anti-Spain', including the Basque flag and language. Another example of the way the regime endeavoured to unite the Spanish population through the witnessing of public spectacle is provided by press coverage of the events leading up to and during the Burgos trial. An editorial in the Bilbao daily *El Correo Español* following the killing of Manzanas illustrates how the male protagonist was positioned as an active political subject in the public sphere of duty, while female witnesses were placed as spectators, gazing out from the private sphere of the home:

> Because the real, incredible fact with all its brutal vestments, with its whole procession of aggravating circumstances, is that a member of the General Police Force, who was coming home after offering his services, fulfilling them as is his duty, has been brutally and vilely murdered before the eyes of his wife and his only daughter.[36]

The language of the editorial – with its militarist and religious references to 'vestments' and 'processions', and stress on the suspense of Manzanas's trip home after a day of heroic work – evokes the extravagant and melodramatic character of much Francoist public spectacle. The presence of the female witnesses heightens the sense of brutality of a crime that threatens to penetrate the sacred domestic sphere (home/land). In a common nationalist trope, the supposedly passive and helpless women viewers personify the Spanish *patria*, which is being threatened by outside attack. The female spectators provide unspoken testimony that Manzanas was a good 'family man', disassociating his (not-meant-to-be-seen) activities as a policeman notorious for torturing political dissidents from what was implied as his peaceful family life.

Two years after the killing of Manzanas, during the trial against those accused of his death, Spanish press accounts similarly presented a drama in which male protagonists (military judges and ETA activists) figured centre stage while women were presented either as spectators or as feminine adornments used to 'pretty up' the political show.[37] Coverage of the trial in the Madrid daily *ABC*, for instance, reads like a theatre review, complete with descriptions of the defendants' attire and performances.[38] The spectacular quality of the trial and the events surrounding it comes through as well in narrators' memories of the period. The following excerpt is from a narrator raised in an affluent middle-class nationalist family, who was not yet a teenager in 1970:

You spoke as well the other day about the period of '68 or '69 when there were a lot of arrests, the whole Burgos trial, and you would have been, I mean, you would have been 9 or 10 years old. But with memories –

With very vivid memories. I even remember once with a girlfriend who was a little older we went down to the demonstrations in San Antón [Bilbao]. Imagine, in those days instead of yelling, 'Izco Askatu', we yelled 'Izco Libertad' [Freedom for Izco!][39] . . . 'Izco Libertad', I remember [*laughter*] Izco was the most representative of the Burgos trial because he was the one they accused of being the actual killer of Melitón Manzanas. So, he was the most representative of the trial, even though there were others, there were up to 9 death sentences. And I remember once going down to a demonstration with a girlfriend a little older than I was, who would've been 13 or 14. We ran in front of the *grises*,[40] and it was an experience. But above all, the environment at home, of constant worrying, putting the television on the whole time, Radio Paris. Back then we listened to Radio Paris the whole time. And that sensation, of seeing every, my mother, my grandmother, my father's mother lived with us. And all the adults around, even the maids. My family was of a good – social status. All of them around Radio Paris, because it didn't come in well. And with feelings of – sadness and, bad blood. And I remember perfectly my grandmother, who didn't see well at all, she glued herself right to the television to see, and I remember her by the television crying, 'My God!' she used to say a lot, 'My God! He's going to kill *los chicos* [the boys]'. And ever since then they were *los chicos*. They've always been *los chicos*. (#2, b. 1959)

This interview excerpt captures many elements of the popular reaction to the Burgos trial, from the drama (a blend of excitement and fear) of young people running to escape the police in demonstrations, to the poignant image of an older woman weeping for the young men sentenced to death by Franco. The memories are recounted as if they were shots from a film – part action, part melodrama. The narration has a live action quality (the narrator herself refers to her memories of the time as being *vivos*, literally 'live' or 'vivid'), but also underscores the importance of the media – and above all the introduction of television to Spain – in constructing, extending and bringing together the new radical nationalist community. Though the family gathers together around the radio to listen to the news from Paris, the most powerful image is that of the grandmother watching events unfold before her eyes. As in the examples in chapter 1 of fathers commenting on the news, here radio and television are a link between private and public, and also a forum for both debate and resistance at home to the authoritarian state outside.

Thus the quotation shows the ways in which Basque spectators sympathetic to ETA refused the regime's representation of the Burgos defendants as 'terrorists'. The three female protagonists in these memories – the young narrator, her friend and her grandmother – claimed the ETA militants as heroes, affectionately referring to them individually by name and collectively as *los chicos*. It is a basic insight of contemporary cultural theory that, censorship notwithstanding, those who control the media can never guarantee an audience's reception and response. Not surprisingly, the national community that came together around these images was the exact opposite of that intended by the Franco regime; rather than reinforcing the authority of its own supporters, the regime's very public handling of the Burgos trial became a watershed moment in the construction of the pro-democracy movement. The visual images of the accused and demonstrators beamed all over Spain and the world created an increasingly absurd contrast between the crowds demanding justice and the archaic dictator handing down death sentences to a group of young self-professed freedom fighters. The regime's attempt to demonise the sixteen defendants backfired as *los chicos* became national – and international – heroes.

Although *los chicos* could be translated as 'the kids', the masculine term in Spanish conjures up an image of young men, as in the commentary of another narrator who noted that the history of Basque nationalism had been recorded as '*la guerra de los chicos*' – literally, 'the boys' war' (#1, b. 1947). The repeated naming in public of the sixteen Burgos defendants, symbolised here by 'Izco', was highly political in the context of a regime that had politicised not only spectacle, but also language and naming. Previously I discussed the regime's prohibition of the public use of Basque names and spellings. In addition, while republican figures were vilified, the names of leading rebels – including Franco himself, and the Falange leader Jose Antonio Primo de Rivera – were prominently displayed, painted in large letters on public buildings and churches.

The power of naming evoked by the story of the narrator above is corroborated by another recollection of the Burgos trial, recorded by former ETA members in the late 1970s:

> Some years ago, a Catalan journalist was amazed, during a visit to Euskadi, to note that children of 10 years or under recited the names of those condemned in the Burgos trial by memory, like we children twenty years ago recited non-stop the front line-up of Athlétic of Bilbao or Barça [football clubs]. What's more: with the same familial tone, of something that belongs to you, like children repeating the names of their older brothers.[41]

The comparison with football players is pertinent; like the discussion of charisma and film stars above, it suggests an association with different forms of charismatic masculinity that help to create, through repeated representation, the image of the popular male militant. The comparison also serves as a reminder that at the very moment when ETA itself became a household name the organisation was being imagined – visibly and verbally – as a collective of heroic young men. Indeed, those who would go down in history as 'the Burgos defendants' were the six men given death sentences (later commuted to life terms).[42] Even though the thwarted attempt to rescue from prison one of the female defendants, Arantza Arruti, had set off the events that led to the round-up of the other fifteen, she and the other two female defendants (Jone Dorronsoro and Itziar Aizpurua) were, and continue to be, largely overlooked in commentaries on Burgos. At other times they appear as the 'pretty faces' in the courtroom, or are recorded as the wives of other defendants.[43]

If shared memories are formed largely through public repetition of certain images, words and symbols, then the association of ETA members with other popular cultural figures is an important element in the masculinisation of the memory of radical nationalism. Women's memories are part of this process – not because women demonstrate a memorial 'false consciousness', but because their memories are shaped and expressed through cultural forms and associations, such as film and television, that are widely available in public discourse. As I will show in future chapters, the building of new forms of female political identity involves the construction of new models of femininity; crucially, these constructions were helped by the development of a popular discourse of feminism during the 1970s. The problem with the interpretation of the gender politics of ETA is not one of representation alone, nor solely due to the fundamental gap or contradiction between the organisation's masculine image and a 'real' move towards gender equality. Rather, we should read the internal development of ETA and its public representation as interrelated and interactive processes. In other words, the popular image of ETA, as projected by the organisation itself and as portrayed by the Franco regime, in turn shaped the gender roles and relations inside ETA. As the following chapter will argue, this process intensified during the 1970s with the increased militarisation of radical nationalism.

4

Constructing the male warrior and the homefront heroine[1]

> ETA, Socialist Revolutionary Basque National Liberation Organisation, assumes the political paternity of Andres Izagirre Gogorza 'Gogor' and Jose Jauregi Altube 'Josetxo', gunned down by forces of the Civil Guard and shot dead on the ground. (*Zuzen*, 14, November 1981)

> We are the clothes, we women are the clothes that make up the earth. But the men are the birds that go flying. And at some point they have to land, and you're always there to catch him. (#8b, b. 1947)

Defended by its supporters as a nationalist organisation seeking independence for the Basque country, for the vast majority of outside observers ETA's defining feature is its use of violence. Although in theory committed to military resistance to Francoism from its inception, it was not until the mid-1960s that ETA put in place concrete plans for the implementation of armed struggle.[2] The principal impetus for this development was the publication in 1963 of the book *Vasconia* by Federico Krutwig, a Basque of German descent.[3] *Vasconia* was a polemical cry against the colonisation of the Basque country, a call to arms that blended traditionalist Basque Golden Age myth with a utopian vision of a 'Greater Vasconia'. Following a series of arrests in the early 1960s that threatened ETA's infrastructure, the principles of revolutionary war as set out in *Vasconia* were officially made part of ETA's strategy.[4]

Krutwig and other supporters of armed action found their inspiration in the national liberation movements of Algeria, Cuba and Vietnam. By the end of the decade these so-called *tercermundistas* (literally 'third-worldists') had become the dominant faction within ETA.[5] In 1967 this group, led by Txabi Etxebarrieta, who the following year would become the organisation's first casualty, introduced the concept of the Pueblo Trabajador Vasco (PTV) the Basque Working People.[6] The theorisation of the PTV was an attempt to combine the principles of social and national revolution; the PTV was defined as an ethnic Basque unit whose members had become conscious of its dual national and economic oppression.⁷ The conviction that the Basque country was a colony of Spain was not original to ETA. PNV founder Sabino Arana had declared that the Basque country was occupied by the Spanish military, a claim with little basis in reality in his day, but which was prophetic about life under Franco.⁸ If the theory of military occupation bore some relation to the experience of ETA's founders, the economic aspect of the colonialism theory was less convincing when applied to the Basques, who enjoyed unprecedented economic prosperity in the 1960s. But the attempt to create a specifically Basque theory of colonial oppression was driven more by political pragmatism than historical analysis. In the face of what the *tercermundistas* called the *españolismo* (pro-Spanish sentiment) of left-wing factions within ETA, Third-World revolution, with its blend of guerrilla warfare and Marxist rhetoric, seemed to offer the ideal model for a modern, radical nationalism combining the class and national struggles. According to one narrator, early ETA theorists referred to the Basque country as the 'Cuba of Europe' (#13, b. 1941).

Through the 1960s and early 1970s there was increasing tension inside ETA between those who favoured an alignment with statewide pro-democracy forces and those who supported independence from Spanish politics. ETA members on the Left, who had made contacts with striking workers in greater Bilbao, envisioned the mobilised masses at the forefront of the movement for national liberation, aided, but not dominated, by the military front. The 'mili' faction, in contrast, increasingly defined ETA as an elite, armed vanguard that would lead the revolution against the Spanish state. In the words of one narrator, it was 'arms or Marxism' (#12, 1947). By 1970, tensions between the two groups would lead to the organisation's second major split between nationalist (ETA-V) and left-wing (ETA-VI) factions. While in theory the armed organisation would support popular political movements, ETA's history of schisms – culminating in 1974 with its division into two wings – ETA-militar (ETA[m]) and ETA-político-militar (ETA[pm]), suggests that those who carried the guns continued to 'call the shots' in policy terms as well.⁹ Following Franco's death in 1975, both wings actually stepped up their military campaigns, killing almost ninety people at the height of their activity in 1980.¹⁰ The apparent paradox that the militarisation of radical nationalism coincided with the years of Spain's transition to liberal democracy can be explained by two factors. First, radical nationalists were dissatisfied with the transition process because it focused on negotiations for Basque autonomy rather than independence. Second, during the 1970s ETA and its supporters, along with other left-wing activists, were subjected to ongoing police persecution.

It is in this context of escalating conflict between ETA and the Spanish security forces that women's roles in ETA during the 1970s must be understood. This chapter investigates the militarisation of radical nationalism during this decade, arguing that this process brought with it an intensification of gender divisions, in particular between male armed activists and female supporters whose roles tended to be associated with collaboration and defending the 'homefront'. This situation was particularly evident in the ETA exile community in the French Basque country. With the increased imprisonment and death of ETA activists – the vast majority of which were men – the association of the Basque hero with the young Basque martyr, a link already clear at the Burgos trial, was consolidated. Whereas the small number of female armed activists remained largely unseen, women became more visible as mothers of male activists. But, while radical nationalist rhetoric championed these women as the 'mothers of the nation', I argue that their political importance lay in their relationship to their sons, and their support for the radical nationalist cause, including ETA violence. Thus radical nationalist motherhood, like all forms of maternity, was an ideological construct rather than a natural role – one that served, moreover, to obscure the other roles of women in the movement.

Gender and militarism

Feminist studies of militarism have explored in detail the gendered division of labour underlying that supposedly most manly of pursuits: war. From military wives to prostitutes, nurses to factory workers, women have performed a whole range of work on the 'homefront' that has allowed armies, professional and clandestine, to function and fight.[11] Like feminist scholars of women and work generally, theorists of women and war stress the extent to which women's largely invisible, and typically unpaid or underpaid labour (associated in large part with the private sphere) sustains the highly visible public activity of male soldiers. To this extent, war is but one example of the ways in which work in the Western world has been structured around a gendered division between private and public. Yet precisely because fighting and, even more importantly, dying for one's country has typically been considered the ultimate symbol of membership in the modern nation-state, the gendered construction of war is of central relevance to ideas about citizenship and national belonging. For this reason some liberal feminists defend women's entry into state armies as a necessary step in the struggle for equal rights.[12]

Yet the gradual and increasingly widespread incorporation of women into state militaries – and unofficial insurgent organisations – in the late twentieth and early twenty-first century shows that the gendered nature of militaries and wars goes beyond the actual jobs of women and men, to concerns about selfhood, citizenship and even immortality. According to feminist philosopher Genevieve Lloyd, '[t]he masculinity of war is what it is precisely by leaving the feminine behind. It consists in the capacity to rise above what femaleness symbolically represents: attachment to private concerns, to "mere life".'[13] Comparative studies of masculinity and war have likewise argued that male soldiering symbolises the ultimate disavowal of the feminine. In his study of the fantasies of the men in the German Freikorps, for example, Klaus Theweleit argues that the urge to escape the private feminine world is part of the addiction of what he calls 'soldier males' to war.[14] Similarly, with reference to Irish Republicanism, Mary Condren proposes that the myth of male immortality through military heroism reflects a dream of a 'world without women', citing as an example men's attempt to usurp women's reproductive power through metaphors of men giving birth.[15] In a separate study, Nancy Huston argues that war and childbirth have been represented in Western thought as both analogous *and* mutually exclusive.[16]

According to these examples, the logic of the military division of labour cannot be justified in terms of the strong (men) protecting the weak (women and children). In fact, these studies suggest that the contrary is true: that men's direct participation in war protects men themselves from the perceived dangers of being held down and held back by women and the banalities of everyday existence. In this sense the military represents the opposition between the private and public both at its most false and its most extreme. On one hand, no army – large or small, official or unofficial – can function without women's emotional and physical work. On the other hand, the gendered discourse and practice of conflict highlight some of the entrenched beliefs about the physical and moral differences between women and men, and their respective relationships to the nation.

The militarisation of radical nationalism

From its origins ETA was understood as separate from home and family. The organisation's early codes of behaviour – many borrowed from other revolutionary groups such as the IRA – spelled out the ideals to which each activist was expected to aspire, giving up his personal needs in order to dedicate himself fully to the organisation.[17] Studies of ETA that include interviews with male activists indicate that many became largely dissociated from their families and friends, especially once they went into hiding.[18] This separation recalls both the tight-knit male group of friends or *cuadrilla* and the seminaries where many early ETA members had been educated.

The parallels between the seminary and the military organisation are particularly significant. As Sarah Benton notes in her study of the militarisation of Irish nationalist politics in the early twentieth century, the early IRA was akin to an 'armed priesthood': 'Like priests, the men who bore arms were special, and should not encumber their idealism with home lives.'[19] In an echo of this statement, one Basque narrator recalls hearing the following argument from a male ETA member in the early 1970s: 'Men have to choose between the Basque cause and women [because] men had to be like machines, and women touched the most sensitive vein.'[20] The military organisation, Benton stresses, is never just one among equals: 'Once a movement becomes militarized, the consequent military ethos and command structure subjugate or even annihilate other values and civic organizations.' While Benton notes that this militarisation does not, in and of itself, explain women's place in nationalist wars, she stresses that war 'creates, in actuality and in myth, potent forces for defining and enforcing gender divisions'.[21]

For Benton, the link between the militarisation of a nationalist movement and the 'disarming' of women is directly related to the 'myth of brotherhood':

> 'Brotherhood' is both myth and reality. In reality, it is an effective form of organization, stressing unity, selflessness, loyalty and secrecy. Where brotherhood rules, it shapes other social relations . . . It also separates an élite of brothers from ordinary men. The older men, who had exercised paternal authority, are displaced. The myth of brotherhood is a myth of male independence of women, it is a myth of human society with no women and no children, a myth of human life where death is always a chosen act of self-sacrifice for the common good. It is a myth about men who are free of base desires, of which the most base and the most possessing is sexual desire for women.[22]

There are significant parallels between ETA and the IRA in this and other respects. The Irish nationalist movement was an important model for Basque nationalism, and ETA in particular. Both nationalisms drew on strong traditions of Catholicism and had close links to the Church. The point to stress here is not that male ETA members, like priests, literally renounced sexual relations with women. As I will show below, heterosexual coupling, as well as fathering children, could be important sources of practical and emotional support for male activists. But the personal relationships and family lives of ETA members existed outside of, and were secondary to, their commitment to the military organisation, a closed and highly secretive world based largely on male bonding. Central to Benton's argument is the mythic nature of the armed brotherhood. Like Mary Condren's 'dream of a world without women', the importance of the 'myth of male independence of women . . . of human society with no women and no children' lies in its symbolic and cultural potency more than its literalness. Thus, in the case of ETA the 'myth of brotherhood' could persist even as small numbers of women entered ETA from the 1960s onwards. The power of the myth depended not so much on the gender exclusivity of the military organisation as on the creation and monitoring of the boundaries between that space – by definition masculine, as opposed to exclusively male – and the outside world, in particular the private domestic sphere associated with femininity. Hence the irony that during the same period, when greater numbers of women became directly involved in ETA during the 1970s, the radical nationalist community as a whole experienced a kind of entrenchment of conventional gender relations – relations more reminiscent of the pre-Civil War and early Franco periods than of the relative relaxation of social norms during the 1960s, when many narrators first became involved in ETA.

Political paternities

The idea of a brotherhood – that is, a group of men of one generation – more aptly describes ETA than the model of the traditional army. One aspect of the paramilitary brotherhood according to Benton is its construction in opposition to 'ordinary men', and specifically the displacement of 'older men, who had exercised paternal authority'.[23] In chapter 1 I showed that one myth about the founding of ETA is that the younger generation had to avenge the loss of the Civil War in the face of the weakness of their fathers' generation, including the older men of the PNV (Basque Nationalist Party). Although the split that brought about the founding of ETA has often been presented as a generation gap, following Condren we could interpret it as an example of the male reproduction of nationalism. The militarist rhetoric of ETA as it developed through the 1970s and into the 1980s is compelling in this regard. Since the older generation of male nationalists was tainted with the loss of the Civil War, the military organisation itself – conceived and constructed in opposition to the home and mothers – came symbolically to represent the father. Thus in its communiqués of the early 1980s, such as that cited in the first epigraph to this chapter, ETA(m) claimed the 'political paternity' of its fallen militants.

The development of masculinity in ETA and Basque nationalism remain to be studied in more detail, but some sense of these can be gleaned from female narrators who lived with or close to male activists. I follow here the example of Penny Summerfield, who shows in her oral history of British women workers during the Second World War how women's discussions of masculinity draw on images popular both at the time being recalled and subsequently, including the time of the interview.[24] Similarly, women's memories of male ETA members can be understood as examples of the ways in which gender relations were negotiated in the radical nationalist community during the period in which that community was becoming increasingly militarised. Remembering dead or exiled male activists is also a way of insisting that they are loving human beings and freedom fighters as opposed to 'terrorists'.

While written nationalist sources often betray an excessive interest in women's relationship to their children, and in particular to their sons, my interviews with radical nationalist women indicate the need to consider the importance of fatherhood for male ETA members, and more generally its role in the reproduction of nationalist community and violence.[25] The memories of two narrators married to ETA activists in the 1970s and 1980s underscore this preoccupation with paternity, related in turn to the constant threat of death with which ETA activists lived:

> He also had a lot of needs . . . with respect to his paternity. Remember he lost a lot of blood when he was wounded, and so at that point he felt the fact of not having children. And that he wasn't going to go on, I mean that everything would be left there. And now he thinks that – he thought and he thinks that it would continue. (#21, b. 1945)

> He asked himself why we had children. He says at heart I think it's the extension of oneself, that's why we have them. We fool ourselves and that's the reason. I mean, there's something of me that remains here. (#17, b. 1958)

In the second excerpt above, the activist in question did not survive to see his two children grow up; he was killed by the state-sponsored 'anti-terrorist' organisation GAL in the mid-1980s.[26] The anthropologist Miren Alcedo has observed that at the time the GAL began to target suspected ETA members and their family members in exile in the French Basque country there was 'an extraordinary fertility rate' among ETA members because of their intensified fears of death.[27] This image of the male ETA member rushing – in the words of one of Alcedo's narrators – to 'leave behind a seed' appears on the surface to contradict the stories above of priests and ETA leaders cautioning male fighters against the temptations of the flesh. Yet we could interpret these contrasting images as corresponding to different phases in the cycle of armed activism, and to the different spheres in which this activism was carried out. Military actions and fathering children belonged to different aspects of activist life, yet both involved in their own way the reproduction of radical nationalism and nationalist violence.

These competing yet ultimately complementary forms of masculinity appear with particular persistence in the memories of the second narrator (#17) above. This interview communicates more than any other the emotional and political intensities of life of the exile community in France during the late 1970s and early 1980s. Since I conducted the interview in the narrator's kitchen on a Saturday afternoon, with her three daughters wandering in and out regularly, the interview captures the significance of family to radical nationalist memories and identities. This interview is also compelling for its central paradox. The relationship it presents between the narrator and her dead partner on the surface resembles a conventional heterosexual union between a male armed activist and a woman who followed him into hiding and stayed home to raise his children. But in her reflections upon both their relationship and the situation of her partner's death, the narrator offers cogent criticisms of the sexual double standards and the insularity of the radical nationalist community.

If the presence of the daughters provides the frame for the interview, the protagonist is the dead partner, in what can be understood as an individual example of the collective construction of radical nationalist history around ETA's 'martyrs'. The partner is a constant, ghostly presence, and the narrator's memories of his words and advice to her, and his relationship with her and with their young daughters, brings into relief her identity as mother and widow of an ETA activist. In response to my questions about how she and her partner had managed in the face of the risks his activism posed to his life, the narrator recounted the events surrounding his killing. During this passage, the periodic interruption of the daughters – one of who was also present, at a very young age, when her father was killed by GAL gunmen – works to link the family together over the period between the events and the recounting of them fifteen years later:

In the end the moment arrived . . . Was it like you, was it something you had expected but was nonetheless unexpected? Or, how did you experience it?

The thing is it's very difficult to say. I think it's a good thing I knew. Or that I had considered it a few times. [*Interruption as narrator speaks to her youngest daughter*] I don't know how to tell you. Let's see. It was very hard. Even though you've thought about it. But a good thing, because . . . I wouldn't have been able to live my life and I wouldn't have gone on and, my children were well and . . . But it's very hard. I don't know. I'm trying to tell you that many times I thought about it. Because they killed him when he was coming home with me. One night. I thought – I wished I had died there too. I thought about it many times. It was much easier. You don't have to face anything. Understand? But more than anything, I remember [*interruption as narrator calls out to her older daughter*] that at the time [*mumbled words*] someone said to me [*younger daughter again*], 'The most important isn't the one who's left behind. It's that that person can't live anymore.' (#17, b. 1958)

Her partner's death and the events surrounding it are the occasion for reflection about her own and her family's place within the radical nationalist community, as well as about her relationship to her partner and their respective roles. Although she took solace in the solidarity provided by the radical nationalist community after the killing, she does not describe a harmonious community, but talks of a world which she often experienced as closed and even stifling. The dead partner, in contrast, is portrayed as an ideal figure, combining traits of traditional masculinity (bravery in the face of danger, commitment to his family) with a more modern egalitarian model of sharing domestic responsibilities, and in particular of caring for his daughters. This sensitive image is extended to his relationship with the narrator. When she asked him what she would do after his death, she recalls the following response: 'Don't worry, you'll go on ahead. If not, I wouldn't be with you. If not, if I knew you were someone who was going to collapse, I wouldn't be with you' (#17, b. 1958). Here the narrator's partner seems to be evoking the archetypal image of the strong Basque mother as a figure his future widow could imagine herself as after his death. If men's stories of military activity are often formed around male comradeship and bonding, memories that draw on stereotypes of the male solider as national hero, women's memories can similarly be traced to popular representations of women in Basque culture. In this interview, the male partner is remembered as someone who supported the model of 'complementary roles' by recognising and validating the narrator's chosen parts as wife and mother. Recalling the aftermath of his death, she says:

> Everyone said to me, 'Hey, well one day your daughters will be really proud of their father.' And I said to them, 'But I think they also have to be proud of their mother.' That's a mistake, to think proud of their father. Yes. And their mother? . . . In reality the woman has supported the home economically, emotionally and she's supported him, as well as the children. She was the one who brought balance, the one who managed the situation, every day. I think without women there wouldn't have been this kind of movement; things wouldn't have been managed in such a way . . . I remember a poem he wrote, I think it says, 'You help me hold up the gun. But you don't touch any guns.' But you help that person at a certain point . . . And for

me one thing is just as important as the other. And one thing is just as good as the other. (#17, b. 1958)

This excerpt contains one of the few direct references in the interviews to the arms used by an individual ETA activist. In this memory the gun symbolises both the masculinity of military action and the separate but complementary roles of women and men in times of conflict. Like the *ikurriña* in the previous chapter, the gun is a gendered boundary marker. The poem written by the male ETA activist to his female partner underscores the necessary, if indirect, participation of women in reproducing nationalist violence. The narrator celebrates this role, validating the gendered division of roles, and the nationalist tradition of celebrating women as mothers. At the same time, she challenges what she perceives as a double standard behind this model, made manifest in the public honouring of men's armed activism in a way that obscures women's roles in supporting the nationalist movement materially and emotionally. Through the remembered words of her dead partner, contrasted with the less generous attitude from some others in their own community, the narrator also constructs a specific model of masculine militancy; one that stresses respect and compassion, and represses any trace of the aggression or cold-bloodedness normally associated with 'terrorists'.

The memories of this and other narrators suggest that paternity and family were important elements in the formation of radical nationalist masculinities, and underscore the extent to which such constructions were made against ideals of nationalist femininity. These representations in turn rested on an ideological separation of spheres of activism. While preparing and carrying out armed actions, the activist's duty demanded of him total dedication to ETA and complete removal from family life, but when the activist was 'offduty' at home – his 'refuge', as some narrators called it – his limited time there increased the pressure to fulfil what had been demarcated as his natural male role of procreation.

Against radical nationalists' justification of ETA violence as necessary for the protection of the Basque country, the anthropologist Juan Aranzadi argues that ETA violence actually creates the very community it pretends to defend.[28] In this analysis, ETA itself acts as an ethnic boundary marker, reproducing the radical nationalist community through its use of violence, and through the emotional and ideological identification of its supporters with ETA members and with the violence itself. I am largely in sympathy with this argument, but I would expand it to say that in the 1970s ETA violence also reinforced boundaries *inside* the radical nationalist community, making more rigid the lines between women's and men's roles. While nationalist movements are often associated with traditionalist gender politics, I posit that in the case of ETA the hardening of conventional gender roles came largely through the process of militarisation. As we saw in previous chapters, during the 1960s the new radical nationalism, with its focus on the recuperation of Basque culture, actually opened up new opportunities for women's political activism. But, whereas narrators' stories of the 1960s often express excitement at new possibilities – of the flowering of cultural and national identity, and modern gender roles – stories told about the 1970s often express claustrophobia, with their focus on a community under constant threat. Such memories are expressed with particular force in reference to the radical nationalist community in the French Basque country.

Back to family values: ETA in exile

Since the early 1960s ETA leaders and members had found relative safety from Spanish police persecution by escaping across the border into France. By the end of that decade a small community of activists and their families had settled in and around the French Basque towns of St Jean de Luz and Bayonne.[29] From the outset gender structured this exile community's activities and relationships. According to several narrators, it was typically male activists who went into exile, sometimes followed by female partners. Many activists spent the majority of the year living clandestinely in ETA commandos inside Spain, where they carried out sporadic armed actions, returning to France when they were off duty. Female narrators who lived in exile, or visited others in the French Basque country, observed that the roles of male ETA activists (whom one described as 'very traditional' in their attitudes) and their female partners were 'clearly defined': the men were the activists and the women their 'companions'.[30] In a minority of cases these women were also activists, but the female partner's activism was often ranked as secondary to that of her husband, especially if the couple had children. Even those women who were known activists were sometimes referred to in nationalist circles and documents as the 'girlfriends' or 'wives' of high-profile male ETA members.[31] The small number of women activists who went into exile of their own accord often found themselves performing the role of 'companion' to the wider community.[32]

In an article entitled 'Exodus', Benedict Anderson discusses the central role of exiles in shaping national identities across the globe, arguing that for those who left their homeland attachment to nationalist sentiment was intensified by the experience of exile. In the new land, 'home as it emerged was less experienced than imagined through a complex set of mediations and representations' (including flags, maps and ceremonies).[33] In other words, nationalism was transmitted in exile by those same 'fetish objects' that, according to Anne McClintock, are central to the communication of all nationalisms. What Anderson does not mention – and what McClintock, in contrast, makes the centre of her analysis – is the importance of gender in these nationalist 'mediations and representations'. As argued in chapter 2 with reference to the Church, the patrolling of gender relations and roles is one of the common concerns of institutions and regimes determined to impose social order in the face of real or perceived threats to stability. Nira Yuval-Davis argues that the control of women's behaviour is one of many facets of the 'freezing' of cultures commonly encountered in diasporic communities.[34] While she offers examples of beatings and even murder of women in some such communities, less violent impositions of 'tradition' (such as the return to what are considered 'natural' gender roles in the home) are equally part of this process of 'freezing'.

The stories of narrators who lived in or visited the French Basque country from the late 1960s to the early 1980s are filled with references to family and gender relations, and to the importance of these in establishing a sense of 'normality' in exile. In the words of one narrator, in the French Basque country (*Iparralde*) during the 1970s and 1980s,

> [y]ou could lead a 'normal', in inverted commas, life. By that I mean that families as a cell, as a nucleus, could remain in a space, a physical space, which was *Iparralde*. (#18, 1961)

Many of the narrators from this period reflect upon the ways in which customs from 'home' were imported into exile. Narrators recall that a familiar (and familial) space was recreated through the organisation and daily activities of the community. Thus exiles lived in close proximity to one another, gathering for meals and parties on weekends, when family members and friends came to visit from 'the other side' (the Spanish Basque country), bringing with them food and supplies. Although they lived among and developed friendships with French Basques, ETA exiles and their families imported customs from their own Spanish Basque areas. One former ETA activist, who visited friends and family in exile during the 1970s, was struck by the importance of the formation of new *cuadrillas* and the daily ritual of the *poteo* to the emotional survival of the exile community:

> There were people who got to the other side and they collapsed because they didn't have a group to hold on to . . . Until they formed a new *cuadrilla* in exile, and they could go drinking.

Were these mixed cuadrillas, or were they more likely male activists?

It was more likely the men . . . *Here* there were more mixed relations than on the other side. (#14, b. 1956)

As the same narrator notes elsewhere in her interview, the social norms of exile not only relegated female partners to traditional roles; it also isolated the handful of female activists:

I didn't experience exile. I only know from friends, but the other day I was talking here to one of them and she told me that she had been reproached because . . . she talked about machismo. And she said, 'Imagine. After all that, they say to me, "How can she say that about our boys?" That would be *your* boys – I had a really bad time of it in exile,' she said . . . It was the *men* who went drinking. The women were the lesser. The women were the wives of refugees, or the girls who went to visit, who went to take food to the refugees, and to flirt with them in many cases. The warrior's repose, we called it back then. (#14, b. 1956)

Such memories offer an alternative to the popular image of 'our boys', that collective of male activists who made their way into the hearts of ETA supporters during the Burgos trial. They also provide an example of the 'freezing' of culture in exile. In the Spanish Basque country, even under Franco, by the 1960s mixed church and cultural groups, as well as *cuadrillas*, were already being formed, and socialising among young people of both sexes was becoming more common. But in these interviews arrival in exile is associated with a retreat into tradition. Other narrators remember that women and men led more separate lives in exile in France during the 1970s than they had in the Spanish Basque country a decade earlier. In an untaped conversation, another former female ETA member recalled the shock she received when she went to the French Basque country to live in the late 1960s. Whereas she remembered ETA's cultural front in Vizcaya as a mixed environment where women and men worked together, reading Simone de Beauvoir and Frantz Fanon, she called the ETA she encountered in the French Basque country 'a world of men', dominated by the military front (#22, b. 1943).[35]

If exile is represented as a world in which gendered spheres became more regulated, in temporal terms it is remembered as a step backwards in time. Other narrators recall that, while they had gone into exile as part of a commitment to building a different future for themselves and their children, they found there a society reminiscent of their parents' generation. The following narrator spent some time in prison in Spain in the early 1970s before going to France to join her husband, who was also an ETA activist:

The machismo was unmistakable.

And had you experienced this type of machismo here [the Spanish Basque country] *in* –

No.

Why was there this change?

Well because I think, in reality men show their worst face at home. It's where they take least care. Their machismo reaches such a level, that in front of *their* wives, they don't have to prove themselves. (#21, b. 1945)

This description of some homes in exile echoes the criticism of 'our boys' voiced by the narrator cited above (#14). For these women the construction of a community based around a series of nuclear families in the French Basque country was perceived as a regression to the restrictive, even 'bourgeois', values of their own childhood homes. Another narrator, who visited friends in exile in the 1970s, recalls that eventually some of the male activists themselves began to recognise this irony:

So I think it was the women themselves who start to make the men understand that, 'Hey, this can't be like this!' . . . And the ETA activists themselves start to say, 'Hell, exactly, we're a bunch of retrogrades, in this respect. I'm the same as my father!' (#5, b. 1949)

The metaphor of moving backwards in time is precisely that, and should not be interpreted as a literal repetition of parents' roles. Through such metaphors narrators evoke a sense of the importance of personal relations and family in assessing the radical nationalist project. Exile itself prompted a series of comparisons with home. In the interviews these are expressed both in terms of time – references to different generations – and space. Narrators' memories of exile are filled with descriptions of geographical and symbolic places: the French Basque country as a physical location where families could reproduce a 'normal' home life; exile as a 'world of men'; the importance of the formation of *cuadrillas* and the ritual of the *poteo* that allowed male activists to recreate the occupation of public space which had been central to their identity 'back home' in the Spanish Basque country. In the phrase of the narrator cited above whose partner was killed by the GAL,

You spend the whole day with your eyes fixed here [on the Spanish Basque country] . . . It seems like there's no space for anything else. (#17, b. 1958)[36]

These words echo Julia Kristeva, who interprets this kind of nostalgia as a form of melancholia: 'We all know the foreigner who survives with a tearful face turned toward the lost homeland. Melancholy lover of a vanished space, he cannot, in fact, get over his having abandoned a period of time.'[37] In the case of ETA exiles in France, the mourned 'vanished space' and 'lost time' belonged to a place and past beyond personal experience, before the 'invasion' of Franco's forces and the mythic 'occupation' by Spain. Even though many did return to the Spanish Basque country following the death of Franco and the general amnesty of 1977, a core group has remained away through the years. There are obvious strategic reasons for this, but the chosen and enforced exile of ETA members in France and in some cases Latin America confirms the conviction among radical nationalists that the Basques remain a people without a home. The 'refugees' thus become symbols of the exile of the entire Basque population, living in an occupied homeland. Paul Preston has argued that, following its victory in the Civil War, Franco's army ruled Spain as if it were a victorious army occupying a foreign country.[38] This military occupation positioned entire republican communities as outsiders in their own country. This experience of a kind of internal deportation under Franco is expressed by a narrator who remembers her mother's embittered words, uttered during the 1940s or 1950s when people whispered about the PNV in exile: 'We're the ones living in exile, here with Franco' (#3, b. 1944).

The creation of a familiar environment in exile depended upon the establishment of a specific *familial* environment, which was based upon a conventionally gendered division of labour. If the exile community as a whole constituted a kind of 'warrior's repose', individual family homes were specific locations of 'refuge'. Yet, if Western discourse makes the home the epitome of the 'private' (a sphere whose very meaning derives from its opposition to the 'public' realm of work, politics and leisure), the home in this case was a refuge from an equally contained space – the military organisation. In the interviews, the family home in exile, inhabited by the female partner and children of male activists, is often constructed as ETA's 'other'. Central to this conceptual opposition between home and ETA is the construction of 'complementary roles'. The following excerpt comes from a narrator who had been active in ETA herself before marrying another activist and having two children:

> He also depended on me. He led his whole [activist] life but of course he depended, at the family level, on it working without him. I had to forge ahead without him. And in practice it worked without him. He was an activist. I knew he was an activist but I didn't have to know any more. And it worked well. He could count on me, in exchange I fulfilled my role at home to the maximum. He didn't have to worry about anything. The house was covered, and in the street as well I worked as a political woman. On one level. (#6, b. 1946)

ETA is never named directly here – an example of the persisting secrecy that often surrounds ETA membership, even in describing the dead. The claim that the narrator knew her husband was an activist, but 'didn't have to know any more' contributes to the imaging of a clandestine space of armed activism. The family and ETA are conceived as separate, but highly dependent, spheres of activity. Both are described in contrast to the 'public' space of the street, where different rules applied. Both institutions were essential to the survival and future of the radical nationalist community (and by extension, to the nation itself), but were necessarily mutually exclusive. However, while the military organisation was carefully policed against intrusion of outsiders, and depended upon the ignorance or at least silence of even its staunchest supporters, ETA activists did of course come home when they were not engaged directly in military activity. Home and ETA were equally essential to the reproduction of the radical nationalist community and violence, but they were not equal. The needs of the family typically came second to those of the military organisation.

Mothering militants

The theme of complementary roles runs through several interviews. In the following quotation, from which the second epigraph to this chapter is taken, a supporter of ETA explains why she believes so few women were directly active in commandos based in the French Basque country in the 1970s:

> Maybe because the conditions of the life they have to lead are very hard and they think maybe not all women are prepared to take it on . . . you have to keep in mind that you might have to live in the mountains for days on end, you have to learn how to survive in the mountains, and we're not prepared, we weren't raised for [that]. And maybe we don't have such an adventurous spirit. We are certainly supportive, and we're, how can I put it? We are the clothes, we women are the clothes that make up the earth. But the men are the birds that go flying. And at some point they have to land, and you're always there to catch him . . . Each one has his or her duty. You're the one in the shelter, when they need you. And they're the ones who go to prepare the actions. So they wouldn't prepare those actions if they didn't have the security of knowing that the shelter is there, waiting for when they need it. They couldn't, or they would be more limited. They count on having that unconditional support *always*. (#8b, b. 1947)

Here complementarity is expressed through a series of gendered oppositions: mountain/shelter, sky/earth, adventurous/supportive, action/waiting. While there is nothing particularly Basque about this set of terms, it is consistent with the nationalist emphasis on nature as an essential element of eternal Basque identity. Thus in this quotation the narrator paints a picture of the male ETA activist returning to an idealised Basque past, epitomised by the mountains. (In Basque and Spanish, 'to go to the mountains' is a general expression for making an excursion; in radical nationalist terminology it also refers to an ETA activist going into hiding.) The protection provided by the mountain is complemented by that of the woman who waits to 'catch' the activist when he arrives home.

During the 1970s the symbolic connection between the nation, the land and the mother found its most potent expression through the representation of the mothers of male ETA activists, and in particular mothers of the 'fallen'. In September 1975, shortly before his death, Franco ordered the execution of two young accused ETA members, Angel Otaegi and Jon Paredes Manot, alongside three activists from the Spanish left-wing armed organisation FRAP (Patriotic Revolutionary Anti-Fascist Front). The popular protest against the executions, in the Spanish and French Basque countries and throughout Spain, was reminiscent of reaction to the Burgos trial five years before, and the event is similarly recalled by several narrators as a landmark memory. In tributes to the dead activists, the mother of Otaegi in particular figured prominently. One radical nationalist journal, for instance, featured a photograph of her standing alone at his grave, which was covered with an *ikurriña* (Basque flag) and flowers. The accompanying caption read: 'A mother's pain. Angel rests in Nuarbe. The *ikurriña* he so loved protects him. A new sapling will be born from this piece of Euskadi.'[39] These words associated the activist's mother with both the *ikurriña* and the nation/motherearth who gives birth to a new activist ('sapling').

In the years to come, Otaegi's mother would often be presented as a symbol of the radical nationalist cause, and in particular the movement for the amnesty of ETA exiles and prisoners. She was portrayed as the essence of goodness and resistance to oppression.[40] When the military campaigns of both wings of ETA were at their height in the late 1970s and early 1980s, the association of maternity with giving and caring for life was a rhetorical device that drew attention away from the death and destruction caused by ETA's armed actions. It also helped to dissociate individual activists from these actions. A common element in tributes to fallen ETA activists in these years was the character report of the mother, who painted a portrait of the male activist as peaceful, loving and generous to his friends and enemies alike. In these portrayals maternal devotion to, and knowledge of, the activist son were presented as natural, unconditional and irrefutable.[41] The legitimacy accorded to armed activists by their association with a mother figure is seen clearly in one example: the killing of two male activists and a female bystander in a shootout with police in 1978. In radical nationalist posters calling for justice for the three deaths, the older woman – who had not known the men in life – was placed between the young activists, evoking a familial relationship of mother with sons.[42]

But what benefit did the mothers of activists derive in sacrificing the very thing they supposedly held most dear (their male children), and even celebrating that sacrifice? In her analysis of Hegel's *Phenomenology of the Spirit*, Genevieve Lloyd explores the meaning behind the construction of 'patriotic motherhood'. In particular she looks at the paradox between women's nurturing roles and their seeming willingness to sacrifice their sons 'to provide the nation's cannon fodder':

> In giving up their sons, women are supposed to allow them to become real men and immortal selves. Surrendering sons to significant deaths becomes a higher mode of giving birth. Socially constructed motherhood, no less than socially constructed masculinity, is at the service of an ideal of citizenship that finds its fullest expression in war.[43]

In the Basque country this version of women's nurturance and of motherhood did not go entirely unchallenged. Some women resisted the use of their sons as 'the nation's cannon fodder'. They did so by supporting their sons in a way that contradicted or confronted other nationalist politicians or community members. A striking example is the story of the mother and aunt of Eduardo Moreno Bergaretxe, 'Pertur', the ETA(pm) leader who disappeared in 1976 following a dispute with rivals inside his organisation. When he was still missing over a year later (he has never been found, alive or dead), Pertur's aunt revealed that before his disappearance he had been critical of certain members of ETA(pm), naming at least two whom he suspected of plotting against him. When the family went public with this information, supporters of ETA(m) (to which Pertur's rivals had defected shortly after his disappearance) accused Pertur's mother and aunt of treachery. This treatment in the nationalist press was in complete contrast to the image of the silent and patient mother of one of the defectors, Miguel Angel Apalategi, 'Apala', who was widely suspected of being involved in Pertur's disappearance, and who was himself threatened with expulsion from France.[44]

There is an abiding tension in nationalist rhetoric and imagery, then, between the representation of maternal devotion as natural and unconditional, and an explicitly political concept of 'patriotic motherhood'. Women were actively encouraged to be visible, interviewed and photographed in public as mothers, as long as they were seen to be supportive of radical nationalism, and of ETA violence. Thus the nationalist movement exalted not motherhood *per se*, but a very specific maternal relationship to the activist son. However, the stories of those mothers who chose a different relationship to their sons and to ETA demonstrate that family relationships could, and sometimes did, clash directly with the demands of the nationalist movement.

Any assumption of a common national and familial interest is further undermined by the fact that those women who supported their sons' political activism played a media role very similar to that of the mothers and widows of ETA's victims, who were widely featured in the Spanish press in these years.[45] Images of mothers and widows of both ETA members and their victims idealised women's strength in the face of suffering, thereby reducing women's personal and political choices to the stereotype of maternal sacrifice.[46] Since at this time women were rarely direct protagonists in the struggle (whether as ETA members, police or targets),[47] such representations created the impression of an environment in which male fighters clashed while women watched from the sidelines, in a way similar to coverage of the Burgos trial in 1970. As these examples indicate, the entrenchment of gender roles within the radical nationalist community was not an entirely internal process. It was also the outcome of actions by the security forces and divisions in wider Spanish society.

Negotiating patriotic motherhood

But if 'patriotic motherhood' was an ideological construct, it is equally true that many women were committed to, and derived a sense of personal and political purpose from, that role.[48] Several narrators reflect on the value accorded to 'patriotic motherhood'. One woman born to a working-class family in the industrial belt around Bilbao, who joined ETA in the mid-1960s, remembers the admiration she felt for her mother (aged 83 and living with the narrator at the time of the interview) when she came to visit the French Basque country in the early 1970s:

> They say this is a matriarchy . . . I don't know if it's a matriarchy or not, I don't even ask myself that, I don't even consider it [*laughter*]. Because a lot of the time it's just opportunism, said to put on a show. In my house, this one has been . . . at 83. She's the one who's helped me do tons of things at home. She went to Baiona [Bayonne], with the mother of another friend of mine, and they came to the border, soaked in *bags* of propaganda . . . And they told us that in the bus, the two of them went along, 'Ta, da, ta,' talking, when the cops came to ask for their passports, they talked more, they both talked at the same time, they didn't know what they were saying. They saw these little old ladies. These women have passed on propaganda . . . they've had people in their houses, people with serious charges against them. And

they've had, and on their own initiative . . . Women have participated, they've participated loads. (#12, b. 1947)

This story echoes those of other narrators cited in chapter 1, recalling that during the Franco regime women could often pass unnoticed as they carried out illegal political activities, such as prison visits. To this extent the story is archetypal, and depends on the clichéd image of the stupid Spanish police officers who assume 'old ladies' cannot be political. But the triumphant tone of the story is offset by the opening scepticism expressed about the matriarchy theory. The laughter recalls a similar observation from a narrator in chapter 1 in reference to her father's machismo, which similarly showed awareness of the irony of women's position.

Although radical nationalism offered, through its symbolic and practical incorporation of the family into the political sphere, a space for the politicisation of motherhood, this blurring of boundaries did not extend to the military organisation itself. In other words, patriotic or politicised motherhood – like the home itself – existed in relation to, but outside, ETA. In the majority of cases women either had to sacrifice motherhood in order to become ETA activists, or to sacrifice activism once they became mothers. While male activists were often fathers, and some may have seen paternity as a way of leaving behind a part of themselves in the event of an early death, during ETA's first two decades there were few cases of women combining armed activism and motherhood. In the few known exceptions, women's sacrifice took the form of being separated from their children during activism and imprisonment.[49] In radical nationalist terms, a man's sacrifice involved giving up his own life, but a women's sacrifice was typically seen in relationship to her children. The division of labour, whereby women cared for children while men engaged in military action, was one important obstacle to women who wished to combine activism with child-rearing. But there were also important symbolic barriers to the incorporation of mothers into the military organisation. ETA itself had developed largely as a masculine arena in opposition to the supposedly feminine world of the home as represented by the figure of the mother. The blurring of the boundaries between home and battlefront posed a threat to that basic structure. While this framework could be temporarily and ritualistically subverted, as Mary Condren suggests, by the 'spurious' inclusion of women in war,[50] the 'feminine' world represented by the mother was almost entirely excluded from the space of the military organisation. In fact, if we examine the organisation closely, we see that the absent figures are not women, but specifically mothers.

In the light of these observations an understanding of the gender politics of radical nationalism must go beyond a description of the day-to-day activities of male and female activists, to an analysis of the ways in which relationships and roles were negotiated and reworked. Nationalist discourse celebrated the family and its constituent members as enduring and natural, but the 'nationalist family' was a construction that frequently required substitutes and even role reversals. The radical nationalist narrative of the family endured precisely through its adjustment to new social parameters, including the incorporation of a small number of women into the military organisation. But to suggest that roles were negotiable is not to claim that anyone could take on any role at any time. Men were often able to perform more than one part at a time, whereas for women role reversals usually involved substituting one identity for another. While motherhood was flexible, and could be taken on by many women ('real' mothers or not) in relation to any number of children (their own or those of others), the ubiquity of the maternal figure served to overshadow other possible female activities and identities. To put it another way, the celebration in radical nationalism of the role of the mother of the male ETA activist tended not only to simplify women's experiences of motherhood; it also had the effect of marginalising, and to a large extent making invisible, those women who chose to enter ETA not as reproducers of male activists, but as activists themselves.

5

From the domestic front to armed struggle

[T]he young woman, girlfriend of an individual who is in Soria prison as a member of the Basque separatist organisation ETA . . . was, it is believed, coerced into taking part in the attack because the organisers thought that the presence of a woman would facilitate the action and would not raise suspicions. (*El Correo Español*, 1 August 1970)

Just imagine . . . if I told my life story to any old person in the PNV, [they] would say, 'They used that girl.' In fact I was never used. I was already with them, and I did the things they sent me to do. But it also coincided with the things I wanted to do. (#13, b. 1941)

Early ETA documents make little mention of women, in contrast to women's prominent symbolic position as mothers and housewives and markers of national and cultural difference. The first written record of women involved directly in the organisation is dated 1963, when two are listed as participants in ETA's Second Assembly.[1] Between the mid-1960s and 1970 small numbers of women joined the organisation, the majority active in cultural activities or support roles. By the late 1960s there was a small number of female armed activists, as well as three women members of ETA's executive.[2] In addition, three women were among the sixteen accused at the Burgos trial in 1970.

During the 1970s there was a gradual rise in the percentage of female recruits. Moreover, there was a growth in the number of women accused of direct involvement in armed actions and of holding leadership positions. By the early 1980s a few female ETA members were serving lengthy prison sentences for violent crimes including murder. Moreover, by the late 1970s at least one woman, Dolores González Catarain, popularly known as Yoyes, had become a member of ETA's executive committee.[3] Overall, however, the numbers of female activists in the period under study (1960s to 1982) remained small, probably never more than about 12 or 13 per cent. The significant majority of these women were active as collaborators. Thus in spite of the rise in numbers of female armed activists and leaders, the gendered division of labour inside ETA persisted.

This chapter focuses on those women who were directly active in ETA, including in the military front, from the mid-1960s to the early 1980s. It opens with an examination of academic interpretations and popular representations of women's armed activism, and moves on to women's own memories of their experiences in ETA, based on interview and written evidence. I argue that, while external observers typically interpret women's activism as motivated by personal factors – in particular, romantic relationships with male activists and sexuality more generally – women's own accounts stress their political commitment and agency. Finally, through examination of two female activists from different generations, I conclude with an analysis of the ways in which these activists constructed personal and political identities within a set of ideas in which militarism was associated with masculinity and pacifism with maternity.

Constructing 'couple terrorism'

In the existing literature on ETA membership, the small number of women in the organisation has been explained primarily in terms of wider social and cultural factors, such as the gendered nature of Basque cultural traditions, including sports and games,[4] or the patriarchal nature of Basque and Spanish societies more generally.[5] Thus by and large studies of ETA have been concerned to explain women's relative absence from the organisation, rather than the participation, and experiences, of those women who did take part.[6] One exception is the work of Fernando Reinares, who, drawing on interviews with ETA activists from the 1970s to the 1990s, concludes that women tended to join the organisation via contacts with a man who was already a member, and with whom the woman had a close emotional relationship.[7] Reinares thus claims that his evidence corroborates the work of American radical feminist Robin Morgan, who argues that '[f]emale terrorists are rare, almost always "tokens" . . . and invariably involved because of their love of a particular man, a personal demon lover who draws them in'.[8]

According to Morgan, women can only be involved in an armed organisation through what she calls 'couple terrorism',[9] and this thesis forms the basis of Reinares's conclusions as well. Reinares acknowledges (in contrast to Morgan) that the female armed activists he interviewed had an ideological commitment to their cause prior to recruitment into ETA, but he sees this as secondary to their more personal and emotional motivation.[10] While Reinares believes that emotional factors motivate male activists as well, his analysis implies a division of affect among activists: whereas men are motivated by their hatred of Spain, women are driven by their love of a Basque man. Thus he echoes Morgan's assertion that the male 'terrorist' is a 'demon lover' who seduces women towards the 'false liberation of death'.[11]

The works of Reinares and Morgan do not so much invent as simplify and make natural the concept of the 'terrorist couple'. A more detailed analysis of gender roles inside ETA demonstrates that, although there is evidence of heterosexual coupling, this phenomenon is both more complicated and more contradictory than the 'couple terrorism' model suggests. As formulated by Morgan and applied by Reinares, 'couple terrorism' is an undifferentiated and inadequate model through which to answer important questions about women's participation in armed organisations: What are the popular representations of women armed activists? How do normative gender relations reproduce themselves inside armed organisations, including when these are consciously exploited for 'strategic' purposes. What are women's relationships with male comrades inside an organisation? And, finally, how and why do women enter an armed organisation in the first place? These questions, and the need for a more complete framework for understanding gender relationships in violent movements, are the basis for the remainder of this chapter.

From innocent victims to 'dangerous elements'

In the conservative social context of late Franco Spain, media and police reports portrayed most female ETA members as girlfriends of male activists, lured into criminal activity against their will or knowledge. This is demonstrated in the following report of the arrest of a woman in the course of an attempted armed robbery in 1970:

> [T]he young woman, girlfriend of an individual who is in Soria prison as a member of the Basque separatist organisation ETA . . . was, it is believed, coerced into taking part in the attack because the organisers thought that the presence of a woman would facilitate the action and would not raise suspicions.[12]

Five years later, reports of the detention of a nineteen-member ETA commando named three men as full-time armed activists, while the remaining (nine men and seven women) were charged with lesser actions and collaboration. One report described some of the women as 'housewives' accused of lodging ETA members in their homes, and others as 'girlfriends'.[13]

But what was generally represented in the Basque and Spanish press in the early 1970s as fact – that women were active in ETA as part of a heterosexual couple – hid a much more complex set of personal and political practices among both female and male ETA members. For one thing, the prejudices of the security forces and legal system during the late Franco and transition periods offered considerable strategic advantages to individual female activists and to ETA. Accused female activists were sometimes absolved or given lighter sentences by judges who accepted the defence that women were merely following orders or were ignorant of the nature of their partners' activities.[14] During the 1970s there were several reported cases of lawyers attempting – sometimes successfully – to reduce or eliminate charges against women by arguing that they were unknowing girlfriends or wives of male militants,[15] or simply 'by reason of their sex'.[16]

Indeed, as in the examples of women in other armed movements, such as the *moudjahadites* of the Algerian war recorded by Frantz Fanon,[17] both male and female activists sometimes used popular stereotypes to avoid raising suspicion. Some female activists stressed that women were less likely than men to be detected by police, because a woman, alone or with a man, could provide cover for preparations, armed actions, escapes, and so on.[18] As one woman narrator put it, 'Two men and the police are always there . . . But when it's a couple it's OK' (#8b, b. 1947). Another noted wryly:

> The good thing when you're a woman is that . . . the police didn't go looking for you, because they were the most *machista* . . . With feminism, now that we're all equal to men, the police look for women just as much as men. (#13, b. 1941)

These excerpts suggest that the 'terrorist couple' in public is best understood as an act, a deliberate strategy on the activists' part, rather than a reflection of actual male–female roles inside the organisation. But this is not to say that ETA members and supporters did not share ideas about normative female and heterosexual behaviour. As described in chapter 2, writings produced by ETA and radical nationalists reveal a tension between a belief in complementary gender roles and a commitment to gender equality, influenced by feminism. These competing models co-exist with an awareness of the malleable nature of both gender and heterosexuality. Such tensions are clear in a passage published in the radical nationalist newspaper *Egin* about the escape of two members of ETA's Madrid commando during a massive police search for a kidnap victim in early 1983:

> [A] police force was set up around Pilar Nieva's house. At 10 p.m. numerous 'Geos' [Special Operations Group of the Spanish police] were present

at the scene. Shortly thereafter, María Belén González and José Luis Urrusolo, both with false identification, arrived at the door of number 5 Federico Rubio Street. A lieutenant of the Geo comes out to meet them and asks the couple where they're going. 'We live here,' they answer, by this point unable to turn back. Their ID is checked and the Geo official comments to them, 'Get inside the house because we're going to have a tangle with some *etarras* [members of ETA].' María Belén, without losing her calm, embraces her companion while she says to him: 'Let's get out of here, let's go to Mom's house. I'm really scared of weapons.' And they left the place . . . According to police sources, the couple's capture would have led to the immediate localisation of the place where Diego Prado is still being held hostage.[19]

This report about a prominent female ETA activist underlines the extent to which gender stereotypes crossed ideological divides. But it also demonstrates the move by the 1980s away from the idea of women as unwitting participants. The new view was of female activists as coldhearted killers: from innocent victims to activists who were more dangerous than their male comrades. In contrast to reports of the early 1970s in which some women were portrayed as the unknowing girlfriends of male activists, here innocence is revealed as a cover. There is an implied contrast between González's naive facade and the hardened – and implicitly masculine – activist underneath. (Other versions of the same story claim that González was carrying a gun and explosives in her bag at the time of the exchange with the officer.)[20]

Cameron Watson has argued that in representations of ETA, both in the Spanish press and in ETA propaganda, the threat posed by ETA is conveyed by the image of the militant's hood or mask. 'Facelessness', he claims, 'both empowers ETA and disempowers the onlooker.'[21] Watson also argues that, when they are portrayed with their masks removed, 'all ETA members represented in the Spanish media are male, unshaven, and unsavory-looking'[22] (note the similarity with the radical nationalist representation of the Spanish police). Watson's conclusion that this portrayal 'obscures . . . the role that women play in ETA'[23] can be taken a step further. I would argue that in the case of the female activist the 'mask' is actually the activist herself.[24] That is, her female body and specifically 'feminine' markers – clothes, accessories, hair, make-up, and so on – are represented as a kind of drag covering the presumed masculine activist underneath, making her doubly dangerous for her duplicity.

The image of the female ETA member as deceitful and dangerous fits within the idea of the 'terrorist couple', but reverses the woman's position from good girl to bad. This kind of portrayal appeared in the

Spanish media as early as 1969, with the detention of one of the future Burgos defendants:

> María Aranzazu Arruti Odriozola [was] recently arrested and officially considered a dangerous activist of the terrorist separatist organisation E.T.A., with a special mission to establish contacts for this organisation's subsequent sections in Navarra. The detainee had managed, according to official statements at the time of her arrest, to attract to these ends one Gregorio Vicente López Irasuegui of Bilbao, to whom she was married secretly in Guipúzcoa last November 5.[25]

This description presaged the more sensationalist images common in the Basque and Spanish press as increasing numbers of women were arrested and accused of political violence.[26] By the late 1970s, the Spanish press quoted police sources saying female ETA militants were 'dangerous elements'.[27] Media representations betrayed a particular fascination with the fact that these women had been accused of committing *armed* actions. In an interview with five female ETA(pm) prisoners in 1982 in *Cambio 16*, the women are described as 'hardened activists'; one in particular is portrayed as 'tall, gorgeous, a whirlwind of energy and convictions'. A photograph accompanying the article shows a figure with long hair, standing on a mountain, holding a rifle, silhouetted against an empty sky, while the caption beneath the photo reads: 'ETA women shoot too: white hands that kill.'[28] Such imagery and language highlights the supposed contrast between feminine purity (represented by the Basque landscape, as well as the long-haired figure) with the virility associated in popular discourse with the rifle (an obvious phallic symbol). Some months later, the same magazine ran a photograph of another accused female ETA activist topless on the beach. In a reference to the popular idea of women as 'the repose of the warrior' (see chapter 4), the caption reads, 'the [female] *etarra's* repose'.[29] Again, such representations were not necessarily restricted to ETA's enemies: in their interviews with anthropologist Miren Alcedo some male activists claimed that women acted more 'coldly' in armed actions, and were more 'bloodthirsty' and 'dangerous' than their male comrades.[30]

Popular representations of female ETA activists are strikingly similar to those identified in academic literature on women and 'terrorism' elsewhere. To date the analysis of women armed activists has been largely the domain of journalists and criminologists, many with little or no engagement with feminism or gender theory.[31] As one group of critics of this literature noted in the mid-1980s, 'The majority of the explanations of female involvement in political violence tend to be highly individualistic, emphasizing personality factors, social problems, boredom and so on.'[32] Such studies, like the 'terrorist couple' model and press images of female ETA members, offer generalisations based on gender and sexual stereotypes. They assume that women join armed movements for personal reasons, related to their relationships and sexuality, and that these same private motivations continue to determine their relationships, activities and participation in armed actions. Moreover, in such interpretations the female activist is either lacking in agency (a victim of a boyfriend) or overly independent (a 'dangerous element'). Such representations say more about gender ideology and public fantasies about armed women than about the actual lived experience of female activists. Evidence from ETA and other illegal armed organisations indicates that female activists enter armed movements for a variety of reasons, political and personal, which overlap substantially with men's motivations. Moreover, in the Basque and other cases, many female activists roundly deny that they were coerced or even encouraged to join by male partners.[33] As the next section shows, women formerly active in ETA whom I interviewed stress instead their political and personal commitment to radical nationalism and to the strategy of armed struggle.

Activism and agency

It was another decision. It was one more step. You don't dramatise it, and all of a sudden, 'Ay! I was thinking about it for six months and then I picked up a gun.' No, no. A lot more, more natural, like life itself. Another step, it was so obvious. I picked it up because I wanted to. No one forced me to. If I picked it up it's because I decided to pick it up. And if I put it down because I, because it's no longer my turn. What I want to say is, I chose this life. I like it. At that moment I picked it up as well because I felt like it. I could give it up in any moment. Instead of all these stories that whoever enters ETA can never get out. It's all a damn lie. I got involved because I wanted to, and you leave when you want. And you don't have to blame anyone else, or go around like a martyr or a victim in this whole story. (#15, b. 1946)

There is a tension in the oral sources between the appeal of a collective story of sacrifice, and a desire to establish an individual identity, that can be threatened by the competing discourses of victimhood and demonisation found in both pro- and anti-ETA propaganda. The recounting of a life story can therefore become a chance for narrators to assert their independence and to voice their rejection of gendered social norms within and outside their community.

Another narrator, fifteen years younger than the one cited above, describes the personal and political motivations which led her to nationalist activism during the 1970s:

When, at what moment did the national question begin to have more focus, going from something you saw around you to something that had importance for you?

I don't think there's any special moment. I think it's a bit like the course of history. Elements or incidents or events that begin to interlace. And you start getting involved . . . I remember when I was in the eighth year of EGB [primary school] when I was 13, at school we chose one theme a month and we worked on it. And we chose ETA. Why? Well now I don't remember . . . At home as well my parents were very simple but they always taught us what dignity was. What it was not to lower your head in the face of serious situations. I think in an objective way, in the *mili* [military service] my *aita* [father] had met friends who'd been in prison. With ETA. So in our milieu there were people who'd participated in ETA as well. Who'd been arrested. Who'd been tortured. So those things, and I don't think it's *one* determining moment. They're things that are told in people's houses. Our grandfather was in prison at the time of the war. He wasn't a Basque nationalist. He was a commu, he was a red. So I think at home we've always experienced on one hand that need to reaffirm ourselves as, not in a very clear ideological way, as working class, for any man or woman. I had a very strange family because my father always helped with the housework. He's always worked. I had a brother . . . but there weren't tasks for me and not for him. My house is very special. Why? I don't know. Because that's the way it is. So there are many elements that mean that when I get to high school, I'm not someone who keeps her arms crossed. I'm class delegate. And little by little you start to get involved in more things and everything that seemed like an injustice, I rejected it, and we could say that I was a rebellious woman. That's all. (#18, b. 1961)

In spite of the generational difference, this second excerpt recalls many of the personal and political elements within the childhood and adolescent stories of the generation of women born in the 1940s. History operates on multiple levels in this story. On one hand, there is a recognition of the wider structural factors that shaped activists' lives – family, repression, class, community. Memories of a 'simple' family in which children were nevertheless taught to be 'dignified' and to stand up for justice are common in the interviews. On the other hand, the narrator repeats the conviction that joining ETA was something that 'just happened'. The idea that membership in ETA is something more than an individual choice, that it falls to certain people (that is, those most capable of carrying the burden), is another common theme in the interviews. Some of the narrators cited in the last chapter, for example, remember dead partners as having met their fate. In these stories ETA members are represented as eminent and exceptional members of their community.

Oral history can be valuable in providing an alternative or complementary view to that represented in dominant representations of the Basque conflict. But, as Ronald Grele reminds us, the reverse side to this is that interviews can encourage narrators to individualise their stories, to locate themselves outside or above the collective, or to present themselves as exceptional.[34] In one important sense, of course, these ETA narrators *are* exceptional: they constitute a tiny minority of women who became armed activists. Yet, if their stories are to be of value for an analysis of the gender politics of the Basque conflict, their individual actions and choices must be read in the context of wider circumstances and structures that shaped the lives of their peers. The choices these activists made were exceptional, but the circumstances in which those choices were forged were not.

Both the interviews cited above emphasise the theme of rebellion: the first, older narrator proclaims at the opening of her interview – 'I've always been, I'm a rebel' (#15, b. 1946). The rebel identity is by definition an individualist one. Yet if we resist the temptation to take tales of rebellion literally, and look instead for the common threads in them, we can find in them a collective meaning, or a set of references to the social conditions that shaped the rebel identity. In chapter 2 I explored cases of women born in the 1940s who expressed their sense of revolt against the Church and the attitudes it fostered. A link can be made in some of the interviews between the tone used to describe rebelling against the Church and the emphasis on the individual choice involved in joining ETA. A narrator raised in the French Basque country explained:

> Just imagine . . . if I told my life story to any old person in the PNV [they] would say they used that girl. In fact, I was never used. I was already with them, and I did the things they sent me to do. But it also coincided with the things I wanted to do. (#13, b. 1941)

I am not suggesting a causal link between religious rebellion and ETA membership; I am pointing, rather, to a common emphasis on independence and individual choice, one clearly linked to gender. Being 'rebellious' is associated with acting out against the roles traditionally designated to women – at home, at church, in the wider community, and later inside ETA itself. This connection between religious, social and political rebellion can be seen in an early memory of imprisonment:

> I was arrested for the first time . . . with tons of propaganda. And some detonators and some cartridges and the like. And I spent a few months in

prison in Martutene. And of course, I was the first girl they picked up, imagine that, what a commotion! Teacher in a nuns' school, and I was in ETA, imagine that. A girl in ETA, imagine that! (#15, b. 1946)

In this story there is a kind of double life associated with clandestine activism. The effectiveness of the religious school as a cover for illegal political activity (see chapter 2) is enhanced by the gender of the activist. When she is caught, she is doubly 'unmasked' in this sense. The story also displays an acute awareness of – and even a certain pride in – the element of surprise in going public, being 'the first girl they picked up'. In another story of the 'double life' of an activist, a different narrator recalls the importance of clothing in establishing different social and political identities:

> I was just as likely to put on stockings and shoes and go I don't know where with my girlfriends as to put on boots and a knapsack and go with other kind of people to a different place. (#20, b. 1945)

Clothes appear in several of the interviews in relation to women's identity and claims to independence. In some cases dress becomes an expression of independence and female sexuality, typically in defiance of the modest norms associated with the Church (see chapter 2). In others, clothes are props associated with moving between everyday life and the secret world of activism. The younger narrator above remembers that, when she was arrested after years in hiding, she was carrying 'a pair of stockings, two pairs of underwear, and a pair of shoes' in her bag (#18, b. 1961). In her analysis of the oral life stories of female political prisoners in Italy, Luisa Passerini suggests that women activists were alert to the importance of their appearance as part of what she calls 'the accentuated sensibility to the spectacular, cultivated by the media'.[35] Clothing is only one element of this increased sensibility. Passerini also draws attention to how a consciousness of the power of spectacle shapes memories of activism. Commenting on her interviewee's tendency to interweave tales of everyday life with accounts of small robberies, Passerini notes that '[t]he way in which these robberies are experienced and imagined owes much to stereotypes of cinema and television'.[36] In other words, not only do media representations construct stereotypes of the female activist; these activists' own memories and identities are shaped by images from popular culture.

In chapter 3 I described an example of how a memory of an illegal demonstration during the Burgos trial was recounted as if it were an action film. But even moments lived in utmost secrecy, where the safety of the organisation and its members depended on *not* being in the public eye, can be remembered as if they were played out in front of the camera. Such is the case with a story of two female activists arriving to a clandestine meeting of ETA's leadership at a farmhouse following the killing of Melitón Manzanas in 1968:

> We arrived four or five hours later. It was already night. Everything was turned off. We went into the farmhouse and we said, 'It's us. Nothing's happened. No one's following us. So turn on the light and you can come out.' We were there for more than a half hour saying, 'Nothing's wrong. Look, it's been a half hour since we arrived.' Of course they didn't know if we'd come with the police. And after a long time, well we said, 'They must be here. Would they have gone up the mountain?' Because on top of it there was no light . . . And at the end of a bit of time, a voice came out. The silence was broken, in the darkened door, a voice that said, 'We trust the women, and the same thing always happens. And they're going to catch us all here because of these imbeciles.' And I didn't recognise that voice. But I knew the rest of them, all the voices. And in Spanish too. And I said, in Spanish as well I said, 'I don't know who's talking because I don't know that voice. Turn on the light and say it to my face because I'm going to kill you,' I said to him. (#15, b. 1946)

Although the isolation of the two women could set the scene for a drama or even a tragedy, here it provides the backdrop for a tale of proud female defiance. The activist's ability to dodge the police is compared to her confidence in standing up to the machismo of one of her own comrades, whose crudeness is highlighted by the fact that he speaks in Spanish instead of Basque. The anecdote takes a comic turn when the narrator remarks later that she is speaking of her first meeting with her future husband (an example of a couple who met inside the organisation). The story helps to create the narrator's public identity as a rebel, a woman who knows how to defend herself and is not afraid to stand up to men in her own community. With a history of solid activist credentials, this woman was more open than most in speaking about what she saw as the weaknesses of the radical nationalist movement, including its double standards for women. Yet she also made such criticism in the context of support for the movement's aims and methods. Repeated affirmation of commitment to radical nationalism can act as a strategy that permits a certain degree of dissent. Here, however, the familiar finale of marriage allows for the containment of rebel female identity; the 'happy ending' of heterosexual union forecloses the possibility of more fundamental gender or sexual subversion.

In her interviews with Italian women who lived through the Fascist period in Italy, Passerini has found many similar stories of female rebellion. The importance of such narratives, she argues, lies not in the evidence they provide about women's actions, but in their symbolic and inspirational nature:

> The rebel stereotype, recurrent in many women's autobiographies, does not primarily aim to describe facts and actual behaviour, but serves a markedly allegorical purpose, which changes continually through contact with different life experiences. It is a means of expressing problems of identity in the context of a social order oppressive of women, but also of transmitting awareness of oppression and a sense of otherness, and hence of directing oneself to current and future change.[37]

The rebel identity may be read as sustaining a sense of self through a series of challenging 'life experiences', providing a bridge between different moments in a narrator's past and, as Passerini suggests, offering the possibility of change in the future. This identity, in other words, is both political and personal. In contrast to Robin Morgan, who says of the woman 'terrorist', '(t)o rebel on his terms is only to rebel against the challenge of living on your own terms',[38] I argue that women's ETA activism is an example of rebellion as agency. And precisely because it represented both a site of male privilege *and* a direct challenge to the authority of the Spanish state, ETA provided a particularly appealing site for revolt against social norms.[39]

Proving themselves

Women's activism in ETA signalled both political consciousness and choice, but, as the story of the farmhouse indicates, this does not mean that women avoided facing discrimination. Such tales do not always have a 'happy ending'. Sometimes they are represented as attitudes or incidents that were not overcome or accommodated. The following excerpt, taken from an interview with a narrator who was the lone woman in an ETA cell of five or six people in Bilbao in the early 1970s, provides a counter to the farmhouse story:

> I realised I was being followed. The police were following me. What's more I realise perfectly that I was being watched, and so, I inform the organisation. 'Look, I'm being watched by the police' . . . At the beginning they said to me, 'Ah! Women always see the police everywhere!' They took me as a bit of a joke (#19, b. 1944)

Taken together these two accounts of police surveillance suggest that female activists often found themselves in a double bind. In narrators' memories such experiences, and the realisation that some male comrades believed women physically and psychologically incapable of holding positions of responsibility, actually increased their sense of discipline. For instance, the narrator who recounted the tale above of the late-night confrontation at the farmhouse describes the ways she acted in order not to undermine her authority as a young female ETA leader during the 1960s:

> I knew I was a young woman, very young, that I was a woman, and that I was the boss. The boss – I want you to understand in what sense. Not because I went around like a boss. But I was in charge. So that the guys would see me as an activist and not try to play around with me because I was a woman. That the fact of being a woman would be totally extraneous. When I was with them I acted in a certain way, a way in which the fact that I was a woman didn't have too much influence on them. And to be disciplined, much more austere, because I was a woman, and in fact it did have an influence. (#15, b. 1946)

This story is echoed in interviews with other female activists. The theme of 'proving themselves' runs, like that of female rebellion, through many of the life stories. It also resonates with similar comments in recorded sources, including this description of the roles of women in ETA during the Franco years provided by a group of ETA(pm) activists:

> At that time there were very few women activists. Before, women who managed to become activists were entirely within their rights, but to get to that category they had to prove they could do a ton of things. And if the man had to measure up to ten, the woman had to get to fifty.[40]

Even many years later women still had to 'prove' themselves, according to this narrator, who went into exile in the early 1980s:

> Well, I think we women did have to demonstrate that we were militants . . . once you're active eh, you have to prove that, in certain moments that, that you're good. That as a woman you're good . . . But I think that's disappearing. I'm saying that we, I think there were mostly, different social and cultural experiences, in the generations. (#18, b. 1961)

Memories of having to 'measure up' are common in the interviews, especially among the small number of narrators who had direct involvement in ETA's military front. These are most commonly associated with the use of weapons. For example, the same narrator who was accused of 'see[ing] the police everywhere' recalls facing resistance from male comrades when she wanted to learn how to handle a gun:

> I remember once we were asked to go to a mountain, to learn at least how to use a gun. And they were all men in that meeting except me . . . And I was really scared, but my female pride said, 'I have to learn too.' They said to me, 'You're not going.' 'Why am I not going? Because I'm a woman?' I said

to them. And they all shut up. 'No. It's just that –' And I say, 'I'm going too.' They didn't say anything. In the end we didn't do it, because there were problems. But machismo? Of course there was. And a lot. (#19, b. 1944)

Again, this story is similar to that told by a group of female ETA(pm) prisoners published a decade later, in 1982:

> I think we're all activists, but sometimes it's cost us; we've had to demonstrate a greater ability in certain areas in order to be accepted. I remember when I decided to take up *la pipa* [gun].[41] There were incredible debates about women's role in the organisation. They saw us as part of the infrastructure, but when it came to picking up a gun, they had a paternalistic feeling that is inherent in the male and which is proven in all areas. You have to prove yourself; but in the end they see you as just another.[42]

In these examples the gun represents the perfect ETA weapon. This is in part historical. During the time under study, guns were still ETA's weapon of choice – the car bombs which have subsequently made the organisation notorious came into more widespread use in the 1980s. But the prominent symbolic status accorded the gun also reflects its stereotypical phallic connotations. When asked about the relationships between women and men in ETA in the early to mid-1970s, one narrator summed up: 'Women cleaned the house and men cleaned the guns, and never the other way around' (#14, b. 1956). For this narrator, even inside a safe house the gun represents in her memory the separation of the military realm from the domestic sphere. As described in the previous chapter, in which the gun appears in a narrator's story of a male ETA activist, here it functions as a gendered boundary marker between ETA and the family or the home, which was associated with women.

The gender politics of political violence

As a symbol that links militarism and masculinity, when held by a woman the gun can have a particularly unsettling impact on perceptions of gender. This is suggested in Gilda Zwerman's description of the 'female guerrilla' as:

> a woman with a rifle slung over one confident shoulder and a baby cuddled in her protective arms. This image has an appeal that was not [sic] entirely political. The female guerrilla symbolizes the stereotypical extremes of gender identity. It permits the traditional character and dichotomy between masculinity and femininity to remain intact, while giving the women access – albeit temporary and highly supervised – to the male realm of power and aggression.[43]

In her research on women imprisoned for their participation in clandestine armed organisations in the United States, Zwerman stresses the need to take seriously women's participation in such movements as an expression of their political consciousness. She rejects the work of some feminist scholars – including Robin Morgan – who assume that women who participate in armed activism must be coerced into it or are merely 'tokens'.[44] She also challenges the 'pacifist mother' model that assumes women have a special relationship with peace.[45] With reference to activists in US armed organisations, she stresses that 'women's role in reproduction does not entirely direct and dominate her [sic] consciousness'.[46]

Yet Zwerman's work still implies that there is some relationship between women's roles as mothers and their attitudes towards violence. From her interviews with women imprisoned for political violence in the United States, she concludes that those women never initiated violence, and that when they did participate directly in armed actions they were uncomfortable with this active role.[47] Moreover, she argues that these women used motherhood and their relationships to their children to mediate their conflicting feelings around violence and underground life.[48]

Zwerman's conclusions that women are more likely to be active in support roles than as direct participants in armed actions is paralleled by my own findings about women in ETA. But my interview evidence does not corroborate her thesis that women's relationship to violence was or is conditioned by maternity. These different conclusions are in part due to the context of the two studies. Unlike women in small underground left-wing and anti-imperialist US organisations, very few women who were active in ETA from the 1960s to the 1980s were mothers. As I argued in the last chapter, motherhood and armed militancy were considered incompatible roles and identities in the Basque radical nationalist movement.[49] But there is more at stake here than the question of the compatibility of motherhood and armed activism. The idea that motherhood determines women's views of, and participation in, armed actions has implications for our understanding of the wider gender politics of political violence.

My interviews with female armed activists do confirm that armed activism holds a particular appeal related to fantasies of gender subversion. But in contrast to Zwerman's narrators, most of the women I interviewed emphatically reject the idea that women's capacity to be mothers in any way shaped their relationship to political violence, as supporters or direct participants. In this final section I will focus in particular on interviews with two female ETA activists from different generations, chosen for their similarities as well as their differences. Both became prominent members of ETA, the first in the 1960s and the second in the

1980s, both were arrested and imprisoned for several years, and both remained active in the radical nationalist community at the time of the interviews in the mid-1990s. Read together, the interviews – and in particular the memories of women's roles and gender politics in ETA – highlight the continuities as well as the changes from the 1960s to the 1980s. Yet the interviews are also remarkably different in tone, reflecting in part a more general discrepancy between my interviews with younger narrators and those who were fifteen years or more older than I. Whereas interviews with the latter group were on the whole lively and engaged conversations, suggesting that older narrators enjoyed the opportunity to recount their stories to a younger woman, many of my interviews with younger narrators were rather more difficult, in spite of supposed shared ground of age and, in several cases, commitments to a form of feminism.

The passages below form part of ongoing discussion throughout each interview about the roles and relationships of women and men in ETA, and the relationship of each to ETA violence. These narrators have been cited previously in relation to the motif of the rebel. If stories of rebellion represent a rejection of traditional and restrictive gender roles, even a desire to 'overturn' these roles,[50] this is in contrast to parts in the same interviews in which narrators defend women's and men's roles as necessarily different but 'complementary'. In these interviews complementarity functions to maintain the narrator's sense of a boundary between 'men' and 'women', just like the trope of the baby in Zwerman's description above of the 'female guerrilla' as 'a woman with a rifle slung over one confident shoulder and a baby cuddled in her protective arms'.[51]

> When I talk about equality, I'm not talking about – If I become like a man, and I take on men's values, and I screw and I smoke like them, are we equal? I don't want to be a man. I don't want to be a man . . . I want to be fundamentally different from men in the ways we're different, and then at a social level, be equal. But I don't want to become a man.
>
> . . .
>
> *But, what is that difference? Is there an essential, a fundamental difference, do you think, between men and women?*
>
> Yes.
>
> *What is it?*
>
> Well, women, we have another kind of energy . . . Men have a different type of energy, and they're very good for certain types of things, and we for others. We complement each other. (#15, b. 1946)

I don't like the thing about saying, 'I want to be the same as you.' I think equality between women and men; I don't like to contain it in that respect. I think we're two different genders, and we do have the same capacity and above all the same opportunities to contribute. But then each one is as she or he is. And each one contributes. And I think we complement one another. (#18, b. 1961)

These speakers express a version of a familiar 'different but equal' model of gender relations. The first woman's repeated insistence that 'I don't want to be a man' may be understood as a response to the popular perception that female armed activists are 'masculine', women who 'imitate' or take on certain male characteristics.[52] There is evidence in some of the other interviews of a conviction that physical differences between women and men made the former less suitable for armed activity. But these two women, who had participated directly in ETA, disavowed any association of physical and sexual difference with the capacity for using arms for political aims.

In response to my questions about whether women had a different relationship to political violence than men, the narrators gave the following responses:

ETA violence is absolutely political. It has nothing to do with a person's violent character. That's something you have to be clear about. ETA violence is absolutely political. It's not about testicles. It's not about ovaries. It's not aggression. It's a front of struggle. You take up arms not because you're violent, and because you like violence. No. It's a way of fighting because unfortunately there are moments when the enemy doesn't understand any other . . . Violence has nothing to do, absolutely nothing to do, with the feminine sex, or with the masculine . . . Because there's machismo so the important things are done by men. And the women. . . It's an ideological issue. It's not maternity. (#15, b. 1946)

I am very opposed to women in mourning. Or to women for peace. Because it seems to me that's taking women back to the role we've always been given. Because we create life we're more sensitive. Because we can be mothers. And I think that's absurd. If not there wouldn't be women who kill. And we all know that isn't true. And I can tell you what I've told you before. I have male comrades who I've talked to, and who're in prison. For whom there's no fun, nor joy, in going to kill someone. But they kill because they believe in the struggle, for liberation. (#18, b. 1961)

The adamant and defiant tone of these narrations can be read as a radical rejection of two different representations of ETA and its members in dominant discourse: first, the assumption that military activity is 'masculine', and second, that ETA members are criminals whose use of violence derives from personal pathology. If much in the oral narratives – including many other passages in these two particular interviews – can be read as testimony to the overlap between the personal and the political, the passages above draw a clear boundary between the two. Interestingly, it is precisely the example of women's capacity for armed activism that serves to politicise and depersonalise ETA violence. Against the popular perception that violent action is a male domain, and that women who participate in armed movements either become masculinised or are drawn to the movement through their love of a man, the first narrator (#15) argues that women's participation offers proof that such activity itself is unrelated to sex ('It's not about testicles. It's not about ovaries'). The excerpts are linked as well by the reverse side of the equation: both narrators are particularly resistant to any connection between maternity and peace.

I would argue that the statements above are not so much claims to basic differences between women and men as strategies for creating new – individual and collective – female activist identities. It is essential to understand these statements in the wider context of the popular perceptions of the Basque conflict: the widespread association of militarism with masculinity, the association of motherhood with pacifism, both described in chapter 4, and the representations of female armed activists as 'dangerous elements', as outlined above.

If we return to Zwerman's description of the 'female guerrilla' above, and understand the baby as a symbol of sexual difference and not just a literal product of maternity and biological difference, we can see that the appeal of the role of the 'female guerrilla' for women active in clandestine movements in the US has some similarities to that of the female ETA activists in this study. But, whereas in Zwerman's image of the female guerrilla there is an opposition between one cluster of terms (masculinity/gun/public/political) and another (femininity/baby/private/personal), my narrators perform a different kind of gender subversion. They 'de-gender' violence (represented by the gun) and reject the baby as a symbol of femininity. If traditional nationalism offers motherhood as the only model for strong womanhood, these narrators assert an alternative form of feminine strength.

Comparative studies of female armed activists and soldiers indicate that, for some of these women, there is a certain appeal in performing a 'man's job' while retaining, and displaying, a particular 'feminine' identity.[53] I am not suggesting that we should assume this is the case with all armed activists, nor much less that all women who participate in military activity share similar gender identities and understandings of femininity and masculinity. My argument, rather, is that what Zwerman calls 'gender fantasies'[54] may play a role in some women's decisions to enter an armed organisation, even if these fantasies vary greatly from woman to woman. Moreover, a consideration of the 'gender fantasies' of male activists would also contribute to understandings of the gender politics of political violence.

As both my study and Zwerman's make clear, in spite of women's fantasies of overturning gender norms, roles within armed organisations often remained divided by gender.[55] Yet the tone and language of the interviews cited above suggest that the ideal of the 'female guerrilla' who expresses the extremes of gender identitiy while retaining her own idea of femininity, forms an important part in some narrators' identities. Like the rebel identity, the importance of the 'female guerrilla' lies not in its proximity to real life, but in the notion of constructing an alternative reality, one that draws both on traditions of women's irreverent behaviour and fantasies of gender subversion.

Evidence of the patterns of women's entry into ETA indicates that on the whole women's motivations for participating in armed activism did not differ substantially from those of men – that is, they had a personal and political commitment to the radical Basque nationalist community and to attaining independence for the Basque country through the use of violence. Contrary to popular myth, there is little evidence that women were lured into activism by men, or that their activism was an expression of their sexuality. What *did* differ historically were the social conditions and opportunities for women's and men's activism, and the deeply entrenched association between militarism and masculinity, both in wider society and inside ETA.

The participation of small numbers of women in political violence in the Basque country raises difficult questions for feminist scholars and activists, who have contributed to the development both of important critiques of the gender politics of militarism, and vibrant anti-militarist movements. By arguing that women who have participated in ETA are neither tokens nor victims, I am not suggesting we should celebrate these women's choices. An obvious problem with the argument made by one of the narrators above – that ETA violence is political and has nothing to do with the individual activist – is that it distances the activist from her responsibility for the consequences of that violence, and particularly the suffering of ETA's victims. As the examples cited in this chapter show, analyses of the choices of armed activists must take into account a broad range of factors. The passages above suggest that, contrary to widely held assumptions that violence is the prerogative of men, political violence may hold specific appeal for some women. A continuing challenge for feminist theories of violence is to incorporate an analysis of some women's commitment to violence into critiques of the gender politics of political violence.

6

The final front: arrest and prison

> At first they talked about *presos* [male prisoners]. And when we arrived [we said] 'What do you mean, *presos*? *Presos y presas* [Male and female prisoners]' . . . At the end of the day it wasn't just changing vocabulary. It was trying to make them recognise that we women were there, in different spaces, in the struggle. (#10, b. 1957)

Prison inhabits a special, separate space in the iconography of radical nationalism. To fall prisoner is, after falling dead at the hands of the police, the most prestigious act of an ETA activist. Through being arrested, spending several days in the police station, possibly undergoing torture as well as interrogation, appearing in court, and forfeiting their personal freedom in the name of freedom for the Basque people, ETA prisoners represent in the eyes of many in their community the strongest and worthiest of the living members of the movement. In the words of anthropologist Miren Alcedo, 'Prison constitutes the *etarra* [of ETA] space par excellence.'[1] Here the ETA activist, after months or years in hiding, can be fully recognised publicly by all – family, friends, the state justice system, police, politicians, prison wardens, the Basque and Spanish media and wider public – as a 'member of ETA'. Prison is also the place where the prisoner returns to the community, through regular visits from family, friends and supporters, after a lengthy clandestine existence. Finally, as the space in which the prisoner lives on a daily basis alongside 'the enemy', in the form of prison guards, prison is often represented in radical nationalist rhetoric as the final front of struggle.[2]

Importantly, however, in the nationalist imagination prison is defined not only by what it is, but also by what it is not. As enemy territory and the place where ETA members are locked away from their families and friends, prison represents the antithesis of the home, both in its literal and symbolic senses. One of the oldest mottoes of the campaign for the amnesty of ETA prisoners is *Presoak etxera* (Prisoners [to] home). The prison/home dichotomy also figures in the words of the song that became the virtual anthem of the pro-amnesty movement in the 1970s, 'Hator,

hator mutil etxera' ('Come home, boy, come home').[3] In these words and images the idea of the ETA activist as a 'son of the people' is reinforced through stressing the relationship to the mother.

This chapter examines the construction of prison as a gendered space in Spain in the 1960s and 1970s. It also explores the gender politics of the radical nationalist amnesty movement, including the participation of the mothers of prisoners and the manner in which female prisoners were marginalised within the ETA prisoner community. Here I consider women's testimonies of arrest and torture, arguing against celebrations of women's bravery in the face of suffering in favour of an analysis of how state violence constructed gendered and sexual subjects through the actions of police and torturers. Finally, the chapter examines narrators' memories of prison, focusing on the tension between memories of isolation and violence and positive feelings about the formation of new female communities and activist identities.

Prison as gendered space

In the 1970s Spanish prisons were male domains in almost every sense. They were designed to be occupied by a male prison population, while female prisoners were assigned to special wings of men's prisons or to smaller prisons that were often makeshift in character. (For example, Yeserías, the Madrid women's prison where most ETA women prisoners were held between the mid-1970s and mid-1980s, was a converted convent.)[4] During the turbulent years of the transition, inmate rioting, usually led by 'social prisoners' (so-called to distinguish them from political prisoners) kept many of the big men's prisons in the public eye. At the end of 1978, as part of the Spanish interior ministry's 'anti-terrorist' campaign, the majority of male inmates from the two wings of ETA were transferred from various institutions in the Basque country to the high-security prison at Soria in Castile, a move met with massive protests from radical nationalists and far-left Basque political groups. Soria became popularly known as an 'extermination prison', said by ETA supporters to be modelled on the maximum-security units created for members of the West German Red Army Faction in the early 1970s.[5]

In contrast to the frequent references to the actions, hunger strikes, and general plight of male inmates, the situation of female ETA prisoners, concentrated in Yeserías, rarely made the front pages.[6] Nor did it capture the full attention of amnesty groups such as the radical nationalist Gestoras pro-amnistía. Prisoners' rights campaigns did make some references to the specific circumstances of Yeserías – cramped living spaces, limited visiting hours, censorship, harassment by guards and officials[7] – but the fundamental problem identified by female inmates themselves, their feeling of being isolated from the rest of the radical nationalist community, was rarely addressed.

In part this isolation was a consequence of the small proportion of female ETA prisoners (around 10% of imprisoned ETA members).[8] Moreover, the typically gendered division of labour within ETA commandos meant that women were more likely to be members of 'legal' information and support units than action commandos, and were therefore given lighter sentences. Consequently, although many women were arrested in the 1970s under anti-terrorism legislation and charged with collaborating with ETA,[9] the majority of women tried and convicted as members of ETA remained faceless to the public, unlike the many high-profile male militants.

Furthermore, while in theory the amnesty movement campaigned on behalf of the collective of ETA prisoners regardless of gender or position within the organisation, in practice many of its activities served to reinforce women's anonymity. During the transition period one of the primary roles of groups such as Gestoras pro-amnistía was to remind the populace about prisoners through actions such as protests, marches and poster campaigns. The names of arrested, imprisoned, exiled or dead activists appeared in 'repression dossiers', in pamphlets distributed at demonstrations and on banners hung in towns and neighbourhoods all over the Basque country. In their most visible form in town squares or bars, such lists placed the heroism and martyrdom of male fighters at the centre of a popular history of the Basque resistance movement. As when the names of the Burgos defendants were chanted in the streets and repeated in people's homes in the early 1970s, the process of naming reinforced the public association of ETA activism with men. This gendered imagery mirrored that of the mainstream Basque and Spanish press in a manner also reminiscent of the Burgos trial. Political cartoons throughout the 1970s and 1980s portrayed nationalist politicians and activists wearing the Basque beret or *txapela*, an image that fused national identity, political activism and masculinity.[10]

The most prominent public image of women in radical Basque nationalism during these years was that of the mother of the male ETA prisoner. This representation fit with the cultural construction of the strong Basque maternal figure, and was also grounded in the historical practices of Basque nationalism throughout the twentieth century. Several of the interview narrators recall their own mothers taking food and clothes to inmates in the years following the Civil War. Like the figure of the prisoner, the image of the prisoner's mother serves in many of the interviews to create a sense of continuity over several generations:

> My boyfriend was 3 when he met his father . . . His mother was pregnant when they put him in Puerto de Santa María, and they gave him a death sentence there . . . They took him from Santoña, at the time of the war . . . and my boyfriend didn't meet his father until he was 3 years old.[11]

So his mother had lived through the imprisonment of her husband, then her son.

> She was a very strong woman. She was one of the women who was always involved, and she went to visit her son *a lot, a lot*. And the siblings too. His father went, but much less. (#7, b. 1943)

As this last sentence suggests, during the Franco years voluntary work in aid of ETA prisoners was largely sustained by coalitions of female relatives and friends.[12] During the dictatorship this support work was performed largely in informal networks. But by the 1970s more formal prisoners' rights organisations were established, in which women were particularly active. Even if their motivation for getting involved in the amnesty movement was based on personal and familial relationships, women's work had significant political and practical value: networking, raising money for and making trips to prisons, preparing food and clothing packages, providing support during visits and in letters, writing to politicians to protest against the treatment of prisoners, participating in hunger strikes and marching at the front in pro-amnesty demonstrations, where older women often came into close contact with armed members of the Spanish security forces. Among the most striking images of the amnesty campaigns of the 1970s were those of middle-aged women chained together in public protest, shouting '¡Amnistía!' while being dragged away by heavily armed police.[13]

The impact of such images lies precisely in the tension between a popular perception of mothers as apolitical, by definition associated with the private sphere, and their political performance in public. But as scholars of 'militant motherhood' in Latin America have argued, motherhood as activism is always open to a variety of political interpretations and is never the prerogative of any particular political faction.[14] While the public protest of women as mothers could provide a high-profile role for women in the largely male world of public politics, an emphasis on political motherhood could simultaneously have the effect of obscuring other forms of female activism.[15] In Northern Ireland, for example, where women were instrumental in establishing the relatives' support committees for prisoners during the hunger strikes of IRA prisoners in 1980–81, media focus on the mothers of dying male prisoners held in the H-blocks eclipsed the protest actions of IRA women in Armagh.[16] A similar observation was made by the radical nationalist organisation KAS Emakumeak

(KAS Women) in the Basque context:

> [E]veryone knows the central role mothers, sisters and wives have had in various acts of 'aid' in support of political prisoners and refugees: and the fathers, brothers and husbands? Their lesser presence in this kind of struggle is justified because it is assumed that their participation is DIRECT, reproducing in this way once again the division of roles based on sex. If for society women's place is in the family, the same occurs in the revolutionary struggle, without questioning the fact that women can and should have other forms of political participation.[17]

Prison in memory

Prison figures prominently in almost all my interviews – as lived experience, as stories recounted by parents and grandparents, as visits to and correspondence with prisoners, as activism in solidarity with those inside. Moreover, prison memories typically stand apart from other recollections, both temporally and spatially. It is as if the words and images in which prison is remembered are sectioned off from other memories, in a symbolic reconstruction of the physical structure of the institution itself and of the time marked out by inmates' sentences. In this sense, prison memories have some parallels with the memories of exile discussed in chapter 4; both are remembered as a time and space of enforced separation from home. But if exile is described by narrators as a place where a sense of home could be, to a certain extent, recreated, prison is typically described as an alien space, totally removed from domestic life and any previously known place. The two sets of memories also vary in temporal terms. Years of exile are frequently recounted at an accelerated pace, whereas in memories of incarceration time seems to expand. In the words of one narrator imprisoned in the late 1960s and early 1970s, 'three years in prison are three centuries of life' (#21, b. 1945). Where the two sets of memories converge, however, is in their shared association with the Civil War and post-war period, and with political repression generally. In the chronology of nationalist resistance, prison and exile are remembered as constant evidence of an oppression that is unchanging and ongoing, extending back to a time before memory, and forward to an unseen future.

Like stories of the war and of state violence generally, then, prison tales form part of a narrative of continuity in the interviews, one that emphasises links with the past above historical change. The repetition of prison stories indicates the centrality of the fate of ETA prisoners to radical nationalist commitment. In chapter 1, I explored the interview with narrator #3, born in 1944, whose father had died when she was two years old. Through memories the speaker inherited from her mother, she describes a father locked in time, a perpetual inmate, as suggested by the frequent repetition of the words 'prisoner' and 'prison' in the introduction to her life story. In this interview, as in several others, the theme of the nationalist prisoner links family and community history over several generations. Later in the same interview political prisoners appear in the form of friends and children of friends:

> Unfortunately, I've had friends in prison. And now it's the children of friends . . . And the profile – the strategy has changed for whatever reason, because life has changed. But the boys' profile . . . I remember my friends' children, friends of my daughter, and it's very similar. They're children of the people, normal, everyday children of the people. (#3, b. 1944)

As in other intergenerational stories of arrest or imprisonment, there is a contrast here between an acute awareness of historical and personal change and the sense of the static profile and position of the political prisoner. An objective historical analysis would conclude that the profile of ETA's detainees, as well as the political circumstances in which they act, *has* indeed changed over the years. However, such memories are valuable not for their historical accuracy but rather for the emotional evidence they provide. Although by the time of the interview in the mid-1990s this narrator had distanced herself from, and become critical of, ETA's armed actions, she shared with several other narrators a feeling of being stuck in a never-ending struggle, in which she and others shared a collective responsibility for the fate of ETA prisoners. In this sense, the prisoners in these stories are more than real-life characters. They are also archetypes, hero figures central to radical nationalist myth. An appreciation of the status accorded to 'the Basque political prisoner' by the radical nationalist community is necessary for understanding the place of female ETA prisoners within this community, and also for women's memories of prison.

Perhaps the most noteworthy – and surprising – aspect of narrators' memories of imprisonment is the extent to which they focus on positive experiences of relationships and community, rather than on the punitive regime. This imbalance in the interviews is not necessarily reflective of the feelings and experiences of the narrators during their actual incarceration. The cluster of positive memories associated with prison may be explained by a variety of factors, including an overall emphasis in the interviews on narrators' experiences 'as women' within the radical nationalist community. This may have encouraged narrators to focus on their relationships with other women in prison. There was also the fact that most of the narrators were imprisoned for relatively short periods of time (six years or less), and in most cases one to two decades prior to the interviews, allowing for significant distancing and a period of assimilation and reflection of the prison experience. Finally, these women were also imprisoned during a relatively lighter prison regime than that experienced by republican prisoners of the 1940s and 1950s[18] or the one imposed later on ETA inmates, in particular after 1986, when members of the organisation were 'dispersed' to penal institutions throughout Spain. During the 1970s and early 1980s, female ETA prisoners lived in 'communes' and most shared cells with and had daily contact with others of similar class, gender, national and political backgrounds.

It is important to avoid jumping to conclusions about the emotional meanings of these memories; in particular, one should resist the temptation to assume that negative or traumatic memories of prison have been repressed. Such an interpretation risks mimicking a popular melodramatic narrative of prison as a space in which repression (in both senses of the term) gives rise to uncontrollable passions. The stories in these interviews in fact often stress the banality and repetition of everyday prison existence. But, while narrators often remember imprisonment as a challenge, and at times an excruciating one, for some it is also recalled as a time in which they could analyse, discuss, learn about and reflect upon the ways in which women had experienced radical nationalist activism. So the fact that prison stories often emphasise a sense of community above alienation, and sometimes contain happy tales and humorous anecdotes, underscores precisely the fact that these are *memories* – that is, highly mediated representations of past experiences.

Arrest and torture

Memories and testimonies of arrest and torture are among the most challenging of personal narratives to analyse. Like all memories, they raise important questions about subjectivity and reliability. Like testimonies of violence generally, they have been the focus of fierce debates about memory and truth. Revelations of early childhood memories of sexual abuse have sparked accusations of so-called 'false memory syndrome'.[19] In situations of war and conflict, the apparently conflicting accounts found in some eyewitness testimonies of genocide and torture have prompted some commentators to question the trustworthiness of such stories.[20] The highly political nature of both sets of debates about memory underscores, once again, the difficulty of drawing a simple division of violence into 'personal' and 'private' or 'political' and 'public'.

This section on women's memories of arrest and torture explores the ways in which such experiences were shaped by gender relations. In it

I am more interested in the meanings of women's personal memories than in determining the objective truth of the individual stories. In the context of a highly charged political conflict, some readers may be sceptical of narrators' accounts of torture, believing they could be exaggerated or even deliberately falsified. But the written evidence of torture against suspected ETA activists generally corroborates the oral evidence in the interviews. For the period under study (the late Franco and transition periods) there is significant recorded proof of the torture of political prisoners in Spain.[21]

To say that the details of the narrators' accounts of torture are broadly consistent with those found in written documents is not to suggest that these memories are pure or unmediated. Because torture testimonies are accorded a privileged place in the historical narrative of radical nationalism, several of the narrators had spoken of their experiences prior to the interviews. In addition, it is likely that all the narrators – regardless of whether they themselves had experienced torture – were familiar with the public denouncements of police abuse made by others accused of ETA membership. In fact, such statements may lend themselves particularly to a narrative formula. This is not only because the act of torture is often highly staged, and even choreographed by the torturers themselves, using a set of common acts. It is also because, as Elaine Scarry stresses, the intense physical pain associated with torture is 'language destroying', rendering direct testimony of personal experience particularly difficult.[22]

By the late 1970s and early 1980s several women detained under anti-terrorist legislation as suspected ETA activists or collaborators had reported police abuse with a component of sexual violence – either in the form of taunts, threats of rape or actual sexual assault.[23] Among the cases that received significant media attention was that of a young woman raped with a broom handle after being forced to change her tampon in front of police officers in Pamplona.[24] In another example, a female ETA(pm) activist reported being taken up the mountain in the rain by Civil Guard officers in San Sebastián, where she was undressed and sexually assaulted.[25] A few years later, another ETA(pm) member recounted being threatened with the same treatment as her comrade in San Sebastián,[26] suggesting that the perpetrators may have intended that the attacks be reported, in order to instil fear in other activists.

Female detainees were not the only ones to attest to the sexual nature of the treatment of women held by the security forces. One group of male ETA(pm) prisoners reported the following behaviour of the police to a Spanish journalist in 1980:

We want to make clear how obsessed they are with sex . . . they didn't talk about anything else but how the French woman [a female activist] had syphilis, how they'd put their fingers in her vagina to get papers out, let's see how many times we'd slept together, etc., etc.[27]

Generally speaking, however, reports of the torture of ETA prisoners in the Spanish and Basque press, or in the dossiers of prisoners' rights groups, did not highlight instances of sexual abuse (including, in some cases, against men). It was only with the development of a small radical nationalist feminist movement that such cases were placed in the spotlight. During the 1980s and 1990s, the organisations Aizan (and later Egizan) produced a number of documents recounting the experiences of women arrested for ETA-related offences.[28] Another example was the work of Eva Forest, a former communist activist from Barcelona with connections to radical nationalist politics for many years. Forest had herself been a prisoner under Franco and later collected numerous testimonies of women arrested and imprisoned for political offences during the 1970s.[29] She described in detail some of the typical experiences of these women, based on twenty statements from women suspected of connections to ETA, most of whom were released without charges after being held for several days in the police station. These included:

- mothers forced to abandon their children at the time of arrest;
- threats of rape during transportation to the police station;
- women arrested during the night and forced to dress in front of police or taken away naked;
- women arrested as 'hostages' if the man the police were seeking was not home;
- women being forced to urinate in front of police, and to clean it up ('women's work');
- constant sexual jokes and insults;
- officers making sexual gestures using weapons;
- women accused of making 'hysterical' complaints about officers' behaviour;
- threats to the women's children;
- physical torture directed especially at breasts, genitals and bottoms;
- women told to leave their activist boyfriend, get married to someone 'nice' and have children;
- threats of rape or rape with various objects (e.g. broom handle);
- taunts about lesbians in prison and about women's sex lives generally.[30]

In documenting the treatment of women activists, Forest's work highlighted the importance of sexuality and sexual difference in the acts and experiences of arrest and torture. But in her analysis she sometimes implied that women's and men's emotional relationship to politics and to pain – emotional as well as physical – were inherently different:

> [W]omen, especially when they are conscious of what is happening and they have a commitment to the struggle, which is the case with so many of the testimonies, have magnificent means of resisting and a great imaginative and creative capacity to exploit and turn around the great shadow of patriarchal culture which hangs over them.[31]

Similar beliefs about women's supposed special ability to withstand arrest, torture and prison are expressed in some of my interviews:

> I remember, a girl once told me, and it made me think because I think she's right. She said to me, 'Look, I don't think a woman in prison and a man in prison is the same. A woman will tolerate a lot of things. And a man will need socks and this and that. And everything for himself.' She talked about a couple, I don't even know who they are, 'Wow! He needs all kinds of things and she never asks for anything!' . . . I think women's spirit is very strong. (#17, b. 1958)

In 1996 former Burgos defendant and longtime radical nationalist leader Itziar Aizpurua was asked to send a message to other female activists from prison, where she was serving a sentence as a member of the national executive of the radical nationalist political party Herri Batasuna. She said:

> Keep fighting, keep fighting. We women have an innate sensitivity. We aren't better or worse, we're different and that means we experience prison in a tremendously intense way, with a strong philosophy; without giving up our smiles for the future, but always living in the present.[32]

The wording used in the excerpts above implies that women have a special capacity for withstanding suffering. All three women attribute this to their 'innate sensitivity' and difference from men. It is a language that resonates with the belief common in Catholicism that women have a different relationship to suffering than men, and that women should 'offer up' their suffering to God. It is also reminiscent of cross-cultural beliefs that women bear pain better because of their experiences of childbirth.[33] In the rhetoric of radical nationalism male activists were also expected to sacrifice themselves to the cause, but their relationship to pain was constructed as different than that of women. As Begoña Aretxaga has argued in the case of Irish Republicanism, men's suffering is perceived as direct, encountered through violent conflict with an unjust system, while women's is imagined as indirect, experienced through the bodies of others, primarily male relatives. Women's socially recognised suffering is therefore associated with motherhood, and with silence.[34] In this gendered binary of pain the dominant model for women who experience direct violence on their own bodies is to endure pain in a way similar to that of mothers of male prisoners.

An alternative model for explaining women's 'different' experience of police abuse and imprisonment takes into account wider power relations and the historically constructed nature of gender. In her analysis of torture under the Latin American military dictatorships of the 1970s and 1980s, Nancy Caro Hollander argues that

> The capacity to sustain oneself in the face of the acute torture situation on the basis of love for others, as well as or instead of the commitment to a set of abstract political principles, seems to resonate particularly with the gendered attributes of women in patriarchal society.[35]

A similar argument is made by one of my narrators:

> A man in prison always has a woman. Always. Whether it's at the level of help or affection. Women in prison, we have our mothers, we have our female friends. And male friends. But it's different. I think we're more self-sufficient. Why? Because in the system we were raised in, women, in order to get something, have to prove and they've had to fight and struggle. For men it's almost innate, because that's the way the system's been. (#18, b. 1961)

While this second set of interpretations moves away from the claim that women are inherently different from men, and recognises the process of socialisation, it still attributes women's special ability to survive torture and imprisonment to their identity and experiences *before* arrest. But I would argue that it is equally important to consider the ways in which the very process of arrest and torture constructs sexual difference through the actions of the *torturers*. In recounting their experiences of police abuse, several of my narrators attributed the specificity of their experience 'as women' not to their own prior gender identities or biological difference, but to the words and actions of the officers. By accusing female activists of being the 'girlfriends' of male activists, targeting certain parts of their bodies (for example, breasts and bottoms), using explicitly sexual language, taunts and threats, and even accusing arrestees of undermining conventional gender roles through their activism in ETA, the police emphasised the femaleness of detainees from the outset.

Although the procedures and forms of arrest, torture and imprisonment changed between the 1960s and the 1980s, all the narrators who passed through a police station recall being treated and targeted in some way 'as women'.[36] The following two accounts come from narrators arrested and imprisoned fifteen years apart: the first was detained in the late 1960s as one of ETA's earliest armed activists; the second was arrested and charged with collaborating with the organisation in the early 1980s.

> In my case they didn't do attempted rape and that kind of thing to me. Hit me in the breasts and that, yes. And I've heard many female comrades who've been tortured, physically and sexually. I'm not conscious of that. I mean they tortured me a lot, I pissed, I felt horrible. I pissed my pants. More than anything they hit your breasts a lot, because it hurts a lot. But there were no attempted rapes. No. Not yet . . . And on top of it I was always in the station with the Civil Guard, the 'greens', they always caught me. Since they knew my story they were thrilled. I was like a trophy for them. (#15, b. 1946)

> I went through it. In the Civil Guard . . . Torture in all cases is torture. But . . . women have a special torture. Because the state apparatus, what we women haven't been forgiven is that we've gone beyond being housewives, women who in some way have maintained the political system as it was, to being women who turn the system upside down. (#8a, b. 1948)

I am not arguing – as the last narrator implies – that these testimonies provide evidence of a deliberate and conscious change in state policy towards women arrested for political violence. But the self-representation in both cases above of the female activist as rebel against the system ('a trophy' for the police, 'women who turn the system upside down'), a motif explored in chapter 5, may have helped the narrators to maintain dignity in the face of a situation of severe pain. Most of the narrators who recounted stories of torture, like many of the testimonies contained in written records, indicate that much of the physical and psychological violence involved depended upon popular – and often misogynist – constructions of female sexuality. Burgos defendant Jone Dorronsoro, for instance, who received serious physical injuries while in detention, recalled in an interview shortly afterwards: 'I was treated like a "whore". You know the language those men use . . . they also spoke a lot about my husband.'[37] Several of my narrators also recalled that, along with physical assault, they were submitted to psychological abuse aimed at breaking them by hitting their 'weak spots'; that is, their personal relationships. Each of the following narrators, for example, was arrested for ETA collaboration in the early 1980s:[38]

When I talk about specific torture, I remember for me the *hardest* was that suddenly, you're nothing. You become a rag. Anyone can shake you. But more than that, they make your level of self-esteem fall, it falls through your shoes. Like you're shit, that you've been used, because look what you'll do for a guy. On top of that, you're young. It's the first tough experience you've had. And I remember for me it was really hard, it was really hard to feel like shit. Like shit because on top of it I was a woman. (#16, b. 1958)

More than anything it was insults. Insults for your condition as a woman and above all the whole thing about sexual relations, specifically between [my partner] and me. They always use that. The issue of sexual relations between the people arrested. If they're girlfriend and boyfriend and whatever. They use that tons – the issue of sex, and the issue of sexual relations – threats of rape, those things . . . At the end of the day torture is the *same* everywhere. And since it's about attacking someone where it hurts the most, to a woman, where will they attack? Well they attack the women that way. (#10, b. 1957)

Women were not the only ones to experience sexual torture; there were also cases in which it was performed against male activists (for example, the burning of the area around the genitals with cigarettes).[39] In both instances what was at stake was an explicitly political imposition of power in which gender was a key referent. As Diana Taylor argues in the case of the Argentine junta, the torture scenario often includes motifs associated with a sexual encounter (foreplay, coupling, penetration). In particular, threats or actual acts of rape – against women or men – are aimed at feminising the victim, 'in the cultural understanding of the feminine as penetrable'.[40] Such acts occur in – and concur with – a wider political culture in which the enemies of the State are constructed as 'feminine', in contrast to the virility of the militarist nation, a case comparable to that of Franco Spain.

In suggesting an interpretation of torture testimonies that stresses the construction of sexual difference through the torture act itself, I am not arguing against taking seriously the pain of torture, nor women's and men's strategies for coping with that pain. Rather, I am making the case that women's experiences of torture are always already informed by wider power relations, including those of gender and sexuality. As such, my narrators' stories resonate with contemporary feminist theories that stress the construction of gender and sexual difference through language and through competing social discourses, and which understand gender as a social relation and as a process, rather than as a fixed identity. Torture testimonies can be an important way of contesting the power of the torturers and, in Temma Kaplan's words, 'reversing the shame'.[41] Moreover, in these passages the self-identity as a female rebel against the system, and the narrators' analysis of the sexist behaviour of the torturers, challenges the label of 'victim'. Using Taylor's theorisation of torture as a gendered and sexualised performance, it is possible to move away from the common association of femininity with victimisation, towards an understanding of torture as a set of acts that involve the violent feminisation of the victim.

Memories of prison

The first place in which narrators and others arrested as suspected ETA activists had the opportunity to tell their experiences of torture was inside prison. Several of the narrators recall that prison provided a space in which painful recent memories of torture could be shared and compared with one another. Exchanging such stories can be seen as an example of what Jean Franco has called the 'creative "remaking" of the world' following what Elaine Scarry describes as the 'unmaking of the world' through the intense pain inflicted during torture.[42] This sharing may well have had the effect of shaping the memories themselves, of prompting women to recount their stories using similar, though not necessarily uniform, language. Equally importantly, however, the collective recounting of tales of torture, like other exchanges of experiences among women prisoners, involved a process of political analysis and awareness. In this, as in their careful attention to the physical details of acts of abuse in detention, women's testimonies are similar to those of men. But these narratives contain an additional awareness and analysis of the role of gender and sexuality in this power relationship.

From the first stages of arrest, usually carried out by an all-male group of police officers, several narrators remember being conscious of the extent to which gender relations shaped their experiences. For women, the police station, described by Alcedo as representing for the ETA member 'the incarnation of enemy space',[43] was also an indisputably *male* space. As one narrator arrested in 1974 recalls, 'there wasn't a single woman police officer in those days'.[44] If, as Alcedo further notes, some ETA members experienced the arrival at prison almost as a relief after several days of torture,[45] for the female narrators interviewed here this relief was accentuated by the contrast between the predominantly male world of the police station and the all-women's prison. One narrator even recalls the women with her in the police van singing all the way to prison – and shouting, 'Women! Finally!'[46]

Memories of being united with other women are perhaps the first positive memories of arrest and prison, but they are frequently followed in the interviews with recollections of feeling excluded from the wider community of ETA prisoners, and the frustration and anger that stemmed from this. The following narrator was arrested in the Basque country in the late 1960s, and tried and sentenced by a military tribunal. She was later transferred to the women's wing of the prison at Alcalá de Henares outside Madrid, where many female political prisoners were held during the final years of the Franco regime:

> It was really hard for us . . . The lawyers seldom came to see us. It was obvious that we were girls. And . . . in the beginning I was alone, completely alone in prison, there wasn't a single Basque prisoner. I was alone for a long time. But later there were people from the PCE, from the Communist Party. And then people from ETA came in, with lighter sentences than us . . . At some point I was with groups of fifteen Basque prisoners. They [the lawyers] came, but very little. The guys were always informed. And we had nothing. Nothing. And I'm not talking about people's bad intentions. I'm talking in political terms. (#15, b. 1946)

For radical nationalists imprisonment was not considered a period of recess from political activism. Rather, it was a place from which ETA members would continue to engage directly with the political processes of the organisation. When ETA underwent major schisms in 1971 and 1974, male prisoners were key contributors to discussions over the organisation's future. Given their high profile and status, prisoners' loyalties were important to establishing the legitimacy of competing factions. But political debate and decision-making required access to information, and female narrators imprisoned in Alcalá during this period recall that this rarely reached them:

> And we talked about that in prison too. Because the men got all the information and we didn't . . . We were totally uninformed . . . I remember perfectly, because we protested. We *never* had information. In this respect [we were] discriminated against. Totally. And later they did start to send things. But very little. (#19, b. 1944)

This last narrator was in a particularly privileged position from which to assess the levels of debate and discussion among the female prison population in Alcalá in the early 1970s. She entered prison in 1971, in the middle of the split between ETA-V and ETA-VI. These resulted from differences over ideology and strategy between traditionalist nationalist proponents of the military front (ETA-V) and the left-wing faction that favoured mass mobilisation (ETA-VI). Upon her arrival at Alcalá, the narrator – who had been active in these debates as a member of an ETA cell in Bilbao – remembers being struck by the lack of informed debate among the ETA inmates. Other narrators imprisoned in Alcalá during this period similarly recall the confusion and lack of information surrounding the split between ETA-V and ETA-VI.[47] Eventually, many of the women in Alcalá switched over to the more strictly nationalist and militarist ETA-V. Two lengthy articles in a 1973 newsletter, dedicated to the experiences of male ETA prisoners in Soria and Carabanchel, included a brief footnote indicating that the *chicas* (girls) in Alcalá had left ETA-VI.[48] Otherwise, the political choices made by female prisoners drew little attention.

Published sources suggest that the marginalisation of female prisoners continued through the 1970s and into the 1980s, even as larger numbers of women activists were incarcerated including, increasingly, for participation in armed actions.[49] By 1977, all the 'historical' ETA women (that is, the Burgos defendants and their generation) had been released under the terms of government-decreed amnesties. But with the escalation of ETA(m) and ETA(pm) violence in the late 1970s, and the application of the new anti-terrorist legislation, dozens of women were arrested and imprisoned after 1977.[50] Still, in August 1982 women from ETA(m) in Yeserías sent a letter to Gestoras pro-amnistía complaining of 'the situation of isolation in which we find ourselves with respect to the outside and to the rest of the prisons'.[51]

In retrospectively constructing their own activist lives and identities, several narrators remember that the collective recognition and discussion of such forms of discrimination marked the first stage of a broader analysis of their roles as women in wider society and in ETA itself. As one member of the earlier generation of prisoners recalls:

> You start to question, and then later you start to read and, to discuss with other people, and with the women in the PCE [Spanish Communist Party], and with the Trotskyists. I plunged in . . . and I became a convinced feminist. That was a process as well. Another step. Steps that have arrived one by one. And that's how, in that period, I came to feminism, above all through the everyday contradictions. (#15, b. 1946)

In this excerpt the metaphor of the step identifies a memorable moment in the process of recognising and addressing the 'everyday contradictions' of female ETA activists, a moment associated with coming into contact with other female political prisoners. These included women from elsewhere in Spain, and from political parties or movements with longer histories of women's direct activism. Bearing in mind both the traditional gender division of roles within radical nationalism, and the lack of any organised women's movement in Spain before the mid-1970s, prison became in the minds of several narrators a place of political education about the different traditions of women's activism in Spain.

In earlier chapters I showed that a cultural memory of the 'strong Basque mother' provided a political model for women's participation in nationalist politics from the early days of the PNV in the 1920s and 1930s. During the Civil War, for example, Basque nationalist women played significant roles on the 'homefront', but did not participate directly in political decision-making at party and government level, much less fight on the front lines of battle. Women who joined ETA in the 1960s therefore did not inherit a history of women's direct activism from within their own political tradition. Female political prisoners on the Left, in contrast, had much more varied histories of activism, which formed part of their own sense of tradition and identities as political prisoners under Franco. Thus one narrator imprisoned in the mid-1970s remembers communist inmates singing songs celebrating the roles of women during the Civil War.[52] Women in the Communist Party in particular were likely to have been involved in early forms of feminist organising in 1960s Spain.

More generally, for Basque women raised in the conservative Catholic environment of Franco Spain, prison meant contact with groups of women rarely encountered on the outside. One narrator imprisoned in Alcalá in 1971 recalls:

> [The women's movement] hadn't emerged in Euskadi yet. I did have a certain consciousness, because of course I saw myself almost always alone and always [surrounded by] men. And of course little by little you start to notice that there's a problem. Why are the women and men separated? I had a certain consciousness, but I wasn't sure about it. I don't know how to put it. The feminist movement hadn't emerged here yet . . . In prison in Basauri,[53] I saw lesbians. But they were prostitutes. And I had heard about them, but it gave me a great shock when I saw them. I go to Alcalá prison and I see two political prisoners. And that really shocked me. But you start to think it over. Since you know them, they're left-wing political prisoners, and you live, and talk, we didn't talk much about that, but we did a few times. So lots of things start to change. Later, I leave prison with a lot more feminist consciousness. Not because we talked there, but because you have a lot of things to think about. (#19, b. 1944)

Other narrators imprisoned during the late 1960s and early 1970s also recall that it was through direct observation and contact, rather than open discussion, that they began to change their ideas and views about women's roles in politics, and in society generally. The following is another excerpt from an interview with an narrator imprisoned in Alcalá in this period:

> There were two, two. I think she was there for stealing too. They were friends, intimate friends, they were lesbians. And well she was the one who

kept the prison alive [*laughter*]. Because they had some terrible arguments! Suddenly you saw, pluf! a plate over here, a plate over there. Carmen and Carmencita. They had been in prison for years. They stole things. I think that was it. And well, they were a couple . . . And then we had films, we watched television. And then we political prisoners had study groups, I don't remember what we studied. But well. (#20, b. 1945).

There is a compelling contrast here between the vivid, comic memory of the lesbian 'social prisoners', and the final comment, almost an afterthought, about forgetting what the political prisoners studied in their study groups. The description of 'Carmen and Carmencita' – whose names seem an ironic play on the extreme, folkloric Castilian nationalism of Francoism, while at the same time evoking a stereotyped butch–femme relationship between 'big Carmen' and 'little Carmen' – parodies the excesses of both the Franco regime and the regime of a women's prison. At the same time, however, the narrator's story highlights the social and material marginalisation of working-class lesbians under Franco, and suggests the existence of an urban working-class culture completely foreign both to the supporters of the regime and to these Basque political prisoners.

In these narrators' memories it was not so much the content of the specific study or discussion as the experience of community, daily life and interpersonal relations that made prison a site for political and social education. Prison is reconstructed retrospectively as a space of learning, and in some cases as a feminist space as well as a female one. These memories of the shock and pleasure at discovering new worlds reflect the specific class and cultural background of ETA's membership in the 1960s. The majority of early female ETA prisoners had been raised in traditionally Catholic, rural or small-town, lower-middle-class communities during the height of the Franco regime in the 1940s and 1950s. Few of these women would have had any regular contact with the urban working-class communities from which many Spanish 'social prisoners' had come. In addition, the particularly strict religious education most of the narrators had received at home and school meant that seeing prostitutes and lesbians for the first time came as a 'shock'. In a society in which women had been actively discouraged from talking about intimate relationships and sexuality, imprisonment also provided an opportunity for discussion and even experiment.

In this regard there is a noticeable gap between the experiences of those women who entered prison in the late 1960s and early 1970s, and those who followed a decade later. The younger group had already been exposed outside prison to the early impact of the 'sexual revolution'. Although the consequences were felt almost a decade later in Spain and the Basque country than in much of Western Europe, by the late 1970s Spain had seen the legalisation of contraceptives and the emergence of active women's liberation and gay rights movements.[54] Just as feminists in wider society were arguing about women's control over their own bodies, some narrators remember that for women inside prison sexuality was a frequent topic of discussion. In many narrators' memories prison is associated with, among other things, a sense of emotional expansion. Thus sexuality becomes one of the points around which other memories of discovery, conflict or personal and political growth cluster. In some ways the conversations these women held while imprisoned are reminiscent of the 'consciousness-raising' groups of early second-wave feminism. In other ways, though, discussions about female sexuality were specific both to the prison environment and to questions about women's roles in the radical nationalist movement, and particularly in an illegal armed organisation. The relationship between women's sexuality and political activism was thrown into relief, for example, by the contrast between the political ideas and experiences of women in ETA, and those in another Spanish insurgence movement, GRAPO.[55] One narrator from the period recalls:

> We used the issue of sexual relations between us, to scandalise the GRAPO women. [For them] on top of feminists we were dykes . . . [They were] so puritan! They went around in stockings, with those winter stockings, leotards, in summer. In summer. And in summer we sunbathed nude on the patio. We had certain attitudes towards our own bodies, to accept your own body between us all. And those ones? Not wearing a bra, was – it wasn't revolutionary in the sense that it wasn't clandestine. Because it attracts attention. A woman without a bra attracts attention in the street. And so from the point of view of the armed struggle, that's dangerous . . . They went around like nuns . . . the typical small-town woman from the forties. (#10, b. 1957)

As suggested in the previous chapter, for the female activist dressing could be part of a dual strategy – a security against identification and arrest, and also against the perceived threat of losing her identity as a woman in a male-dominated movement. For the GRAPO women, in a far-left organisation that saw feminism and sexuality as 'bourgeois' issues, dressing like 'nuns' or '[women] from the forties' reflected as well a sense of ideological purity. Another narrator noted that, while women ETA inmates discussed a range of social, cultural and political topics, the GRAPO women devoted most of their time to studying the 'classical' Marxist texts (#16, b. 1958).[56] In the words of the narrator cited above:

It was another type of woman. Another way to be a woman, to understand activism, to understand life, to understand the struggle. It was a totally different world. So, of course, we clashed. (#10, b. 1957)

These perceived differences – in lifestyle and personal relationships as well as political views – between the prisoners from the two wings of ETA and those from GRAPO, undermine claims by 'anti-terrorism' experts about the similar profiles of all women in armed, underground organisations.[57] But they also highlight a difference between the roles played by women in the two movements. Whereas a substantial majority of women imprisoned for ETA-related offences had been arrested for collaboration with ETA, most of the female GRAPO prisoners had been full members of their organisation and consequently had a different relationship to it.[58]

Although prison was a space in which women were defined as a single, unified collective of 'female ETA prisoners', the narrators themselves remember the differences among them as much as their commonalities. Positive memories emphasise prison as a place in which shared memories of activism and torture gave women a sense of common experience. But the recollection of being together in confinement also accentuated memories of different political views, life choices and power relations among women. As one narrator recalls of the early 1980s:

It was a bit mixed in there. The majority were wives with husbands . . . and in other cases, like me, *mujeres libres* [free women] who had been a bit more committed . . . And had gone in of their own account. Freely. Not for a man, but for themselves, because of their own experience among the people. There were two types. And living together was difficult, when it came to thinking about how to construct a future society, with people who were totally reactionary, because they hadn't evolved as people, because they were the 'wives of'. (#8a, b. 1948)

The tension between the pull to unity and the recognition of difference is stressed by another narrator – young, unmarried and childless at the time of her arrest – who was taken into custody following the detention of her male partner, an ETA activist. Before and after her time in prison she had been active in radical nationalist feminist organisations, and at the time of the interview continued to support feminism and ETA. By then she was also the mother of a small child, and hers is one of the interviews that best voices the tensions and challenges of women's roles in radical nationalism. It was also one of the interviews in which the emotions of activism were expressed most openly: the intensities and difficulties of activist life, but also the joy and humour. Although the narrator had spent a relatively short time in prison (about a year in the early 1980s), her memories of relationships with other women there seem to have been life-shaping, as the excerpt about women in GRAPO suggests. She stressed the experience of meeting both women her own age who had been directly active in armed commandos, and middle-aged women engaged in more traditional 'support' roles:

> We had a woman who we called the mother . . . A woman who didn't speak Spanish perfectly, who learned Spanish in prison. And who had had a farmhouse, and her farmhouse was en route for lots of commandos, action commandos. And so they caught her red-handed. She had been and was the *etxekoandre*. She was the lady of the house. And she said, 'but I didn't do anything other than make dinner and wash underwear'. That's all she'd done. And she was in prison with pretty heavy charges. Later she got out, because the whole thing about married couples still works here, the woman is supposed to obey the husband, and do what the husband orders, and they were able to get her out . . . Because she didn't know how to drive, the lawyers used all kinds of arguments.(#10, b. 1957)

This story is reminiscent of the cases discussed in the previous chapter in which lawyers used the 'girlfriend' defence to lighten the sentences of accused female ETA members. But the presence of the mother, the 'lady of the house', inside prison also underscores the explicitly political nature of women's traditional support roles in Basque nationalism. As the narrator puts it, even if she had only made dinner and washed underwear, 'she was in prison with pretty heavy charges'. The seemingly incongruous presence of the middle-aged Basque housewife in a Spanish prison undermines the symbolic opposition between home and prison, between the ETA prisoner on the inside and his mother on the outside lobbying for his release. The narrator herself is aware of this contradiction. On one hand, the ideal of the strong, nationalist, Basque-speaking rural housewife and mother holds a strong appeal for the young, middle-class, urban, Spanish-speaking narrator. On the other, she acknowledges that this was a restrictive stereotype against which she and other women activists struggled to define themselves:

> *What's your reaction, how do you see, how people talk about the mothers of prisoners? . . . Was there a contradiction between talking about women as mothers and talking about women as political beings?*
>
> Yes. Well, contradiction in the sense that it clashed, I think when we entered prison that was precisely what clashed, those two conceptions . . . When we insisted that we were prisoners, or when we put the feminine in all the documents or when we demanded that different treatment, what we were trying to do was to be recognised as political agents. Against

what? Against the traditional model of the Basque woman as mother. Because we weren't mothers, and on top of it we weren't at all sure about the question of maternity. I'm a mother by fluke. I'm a mother because there was a certain circumstance in my life, and I said I want to try this, and because biologically I can be a mother. But in theory I wasn't out to be a mother. The majority of us weren't out to be mothers. Why? Because first of all we were political beings, and that was in direct contradiction with the traditional figure of the mother, looking after the children and all that. (#10, b. 1957)

Prison, like living in exile or in hiding, was by definition a restricted, closed space in which the personal and political overlapped on a daily basis. Many stories about life behind bars echo memories of exile and clandestine activist life, where difficult living conditions and the ever-present physical threat represented by the police combined with chances for intense interpersonal relations. But unlike those other places on the outside, prison was literally, and forcibly, a sex-segregated space. As such, it is associated in narrators' memories with a unique opportunity for considering the gender politics of the radical nationalist movement, and for reflection on the changes prisoners had – and had not – seen in women's roles inside their movement and their own lives. Women's prison narratives therefore disrupt the sense of timelessness that characterises the narrative of 'the Basque prisoner' in more official discourses of radical nationalism. Even though in the stories of some narrators 'the Basque prisoner' appears as an archetype, a mythical hero whose social profile remains unchanged over time, others' direct memories of imprisonment are grounded in specific social and historical contexts. In particular, a comparison between interviews from different generations of female ETA prisoners brings out the significant changes in women's lives between the late 1960s and late 1970s.

These narratives of incarceration disturb the dichotomy between prison and home as it has been constructed in much literature and practice of the radical nationalist movement. Although prison was to a certain extent cut off from the 'real world', in the sense of being removed from activists' family, friends, work, community and activism, the language of the interviews suggests that, for many, imprisonment, is associated with new experiences. To speak of it as an 'education' in life is to risk minimising the punitive dimension of the prison experience. The interviews certainly do not deny this fundamental element. Yet, on the whole, memories of prison life – even among those narrators who were there for several years – accentuate the formation of new networks and new understandings of activism. Of central significance in these stories is the retrospective influence of feminism on narrators' understandings of their own lives, and of gender relations generally. It was also the language of feminism that helped some narrators to develop a political critique of the gender politics of radical nationalism. That relationship between nationalism and feminism is the subject of the next chapter.

7

Nationalism and feminism

> I remember that period as very, very rich. You share, you debate . . . We were very young, very brazen . . . We talked about the issue of sexuality, and within sexuality, the issue of masturbation . . . And we made posters, and put them up in the neighbourhood. I'm amazed! The things we did! [*laughter*]. (#10, b. 1957)

> I think all the women in the nationalist left are feminists. And all the new generations what are joining are feminist women. But I think we still haven't found the main point. This is unfinished business. (#16, b. 1958)

One of the central concerns for scholars of gender and nationalism is the relationship between nationalism and feminism. Many have highlighted the fraught nature of that relationship, particularly in the Western context.[1] Gisela Kaplan has noted that in Europe '(f)eminism and nationalism are almost always incompatible ideological positions'.[2] Similarly, Mary Condren has written of the Irish case in the twentieth century, '(b)oth nationalist and feminist movements are engaged in the politics of identity, but the interests of the latter are usually submerged to those of the former'.[3] In fact, nationalism and feminism have taken radically different approaches to the politics of identity – whereas most nationalist movements are invested in consolidating a community through the emphasis on a unique and unitary national identity, much feminist theory and practice is engaged with the project of challenging the very idea of a stable of fixed identity.

Lois A. West has used the term 'feminist nationalism' to define 'social movements simultaneously seeking rights for women and rights for nationalists within a variety of social, economic, and political contexts'.[4] While this provides a useful startingpoint for an investigation into the connections between the respective 'rights' of women and of nationalists, I propose to reverse the terms of West's expression. Whereas 'feminist nationalism' implies a nationalist movement that adopts a feminist agenda, this chapter will focus on 'nationalist feminism', or feminism as a movement that incorporates other differences, including the national. In this chapter I argue that the vibrant nationalist feminism of the period 1977–82 was less successful in having its demands recognised by the wider radical nationalist movement than it was in campaigning around broader feminist issues – most notably abortion rights and violence against women.

But the interviews suggest that the legacy of feminism went beyond its failures or successes as a political movement to its broader influence on understanding of gender identities and relations. In her oral history of lesbian AIDS activists in New York City, Ann Cvetkovich suggests that political activism can be understood as traumatic 'because of its emotional intensities and disappointments'.[5] While I am wary of labelling activist memory 'traumatic', I follow Cvetkovich's lead in stressing the feelings associated with activism, and considering the ways in which these may be expressed in oral history interviews. It is in memories of feminism that the passions of political engagement are most keenly felt. The final section of the chapter analyses more closely narrators' mixed memories of feminism. These range from stories of joy and laughter associated with the playful character of feminist actions or forming solidarities with women across boundaries of class and generation, to bitter recollections of the disrespect with which feminists were treated by many men in their own movement.

Basque nationalist feminism

Historical factors – most immediately the social, cultural and political restrictions imposed by the Franco dictatorship – contributed to the relatively late development of Spanish second-wave feminism. There was some early feminist organising within the broader pro-democracy movement in the 1960s,[6] but it was not until after Franco's death that women's political activity came into the open. The mid- to late 1970s saw the unprecedented mobilisation of women in feminist groups all over Spain.[7] These boom years of Spanish feminism were characterised as well by intense debate, especially over 'dual activism' – the question of whether women should be active simultaneously in the women's movement and in political parties. This debate involved wider theoretical problems concerning the relationship between Marxism, feminism and the material oppression of women,[8] which generated similarly heated discussion among feminists in the rest of Western Europe. But in Spain the close relationship of many feminists to parties on the Left, and the urgency of wider political issues such as amnesty for political prisoners and the establishment of democratic institutions, made the issue of 'dual activism' all the more urgent.

During the transition many Spanish feminists became disillusioned with the lack of commitment shown by the main opposition parties to women's issues, and with the small numbers of women in positions of power.[9] From 1979 the Spanish women's movement showed signs of fragmentation, part of the wider phenomenon of *desencanto* in Spanish society – the disenchantment and decline in popular activism that replaced the overall enthusiasm of the early transition years.[10] But the Basque country was an important exception to this pattern. Whereas the general political mobilisation that had propelled the pro-democracy efforts in most of Spain was largely dismantled by the end of the 1970s, the struggle over the Basque Autonomy Statute and the escalation of popular mobilisation, political violence, and police repression, provided a markedly different environment for the development of the Basque women's movement.[11]

Following the first formal meetings of women's groups in Spain, in 1976 Basque feminists organised themselves in provincial Women's Assemblies, which incorporated independent feminists as well as women from left-wing political parties.[12] While in the rest of Spain most 'dual activist' feminists were active in the Socialist and Communist parties, the unique political situation in the Basque country meant that a large number of feminists considered these parties both too reformist and too 'Spanish'.[13] Some of the women involved in the Assemblies were independent activists; but a significant number were members of small, vibrant Maoist and Trotskyist parties. Still others participated in the radical nationalist movement.

In December 1977 the first Basque feminist conference brought together over 3,000 women at the new Basque university in Lejona, outside Bilbao. As in the rest of Spain, Basque feminists were concerned with broader questions of democratic change, as well as international women's issues such as sexuality, violence against women, abortion, and domestic and paid labour.[14] But the specific political and cultural context of the Basque transition informed their approach to these more general questions at the same time as it prompted feminists to add specifically Basque issues to their agenda. Thus, while the Women's Assemblies did not define themselves as nationalist, they did incorporate some demands relating to Basque language, culture and identity, and to the Basque conflict. For instance, the first manifesto of the Women's Assembly of Vizcaya promoted teaching in Basque in public schools, called for the end of French and Spanish control of the Basque country, and demanded the immediate release of all Basque political prisoners.[15] At the same time, some women directly active in the nationalist left began to create separate nationalist feminist organisations, in order to demonstrate more fully their dual commitment to both movements.

Prior to more formal attempts to establish a radical nationalist women's organisation in the late 1970s, there had been several initiatives by nationalist feminists. The earliest of these were in the French Basque country, influenced by the French Women's Liberation Movement (MLF) and bringing together French Basque women with Spanish Basque women in exile.[16] South of the border some groups were formed by women independent of the radical nationalist movement,[17] while others, like those formed by activists in political parties and coalitions – LAIA, HASI and, later, Herri Batasuna[18] – brought together women in groups close to ETA. Most of these projects were short-lived, and their difficulties in forcing their parties to adopt women's issues foreshadowed those of subsequent nationalist feminist groups.[19]

The first attempt to create a feminist organisation within the political structure of the radical nationalist movement came in 1978 with the creation of KAS Emakumeak (KAS Women), which in 1981 was re-formed as Aizan.[20] KAS Emakumeak was founded by nationalist women in the French and Spanish Basque countries, including a few female ETA activists,[21] and between 1978 and 1981 local groups were set up in all four Spanish Basque provinces.[22] Like many other Basque women's groups, KAS Emakumeak was composed largely of women in their twenties and thirties from the middle and lower middle class (such as teachers, health workers, office workers, liberal professionals).[23] In addition to forming small collectives throughout the Basque country, these women participated both in other radical nationalist organisations and in wider feminist campaigns.

KAS Emakumeak echoed attempts of second-wave feminists in other countries to explore the connections between gender, class and ethnic identities. Following from earlier nationalist feminist groups (e.g. EEBAA, see n.16), KAS Emakumeak focused on what its members considered their 'triple oppression' as women, workers and Basques. When KAS Emakumeak dissolved in 1981, amid wider schisms within the radical nationalist left, its successor organisation, Aizan, coined the term Mujeres Trabajadoras Vascas (Basque Working Women). This was a feminist modification of the term Pueblo Trabajador Vasco, devised a decade before by ETA members inspired by Third World national liberation movements (see chapter 4). The theory of 'triple oppression' combined critiques of patriarchy and 'Spanish imperialism' with a challenge to capitalism. One narrator who joined Aizan in the early 1980s remembers the excitement engendered by these new ideas:

We coined the term Basque Working Women. For us that was already a conquest. To recognise that we wanted to unify those three things, for me that was really interesting . . . the combination of triple oppression . . . We spoke about oppression as women, as workers, as Basques . . . I felt one . . . It reunited me as a person. (#10, b. 1957)

As members of both KAS Emakumeak and Aizan discovered, however, it proved much easier to garner support and enthusiasm for new theories of 'triple oppression' among small groups of young female activists than to have such insights adapted by the wider radical nationalist movement. This frustration was highlighted by both associations' ongoing failure to be recognised as legitimate and equal alongside other radical nationalist groups within the radical nationalist coordinating committee KAS.[24] This exclusion reflected a resistance on the part of other collectives, including ETA(m), to recognise a separate nationalist women's organisation. Although ETA(m) was only one of several groups inside KAS, since it was respected as the armed 'vanguard', its leadership on all issues was taken seriously by other members of the coalition.

Throughout the early 1980s, ETA(m)'s publications *Zutabe* and *Zuzen* – dedicated to claiming responsibility for armed actions, as well as outlining political principles – contained some discussion about the Basque 'women's liberation movement', and listed feminism along with other Basque social movements whose activities it supported. At the same time, however, women's issues tended to be excluded from ETA(m)'s wider political analysis, and in its rhetoric women were still represented more often as the mothers of dead or imprisoned male ETA members than as activists.[25] The leadership of ETA(m) voiced support for the equality of women and men in the nationalist movement, but like the radical nationalist left generally they opposed the establishment of separate women's groups within the structure of that movement.[26]

The position of KAS Emakumeak and Aizan within KAS was always tenuous. Several narrators involved in the two organisations recall that exchanges about their status and political aims resulted in a series of clashes with other groups in the coalition. What were intended to be discussions over the strategy for incorporating a feminist agenda into the radical nationalist movement often got bogged down in disagreements over language. One narrator who joined Aizan in the early 1980s had a humorous take on the debate about expanding KAS's official slogan (calling for an 'Independent, reunified, socialist Basque country') to include a feminist element:

We wanted the qualitative 'non-patriarchal' . . . 'Independent, reunified, socialist and non-patriarchal'. It was taken poorly in terms of a strategic adjective. We couldn't propose in negative terms, it had to be in positive terms. So [they suggested] 'egalitarian'. And 'egalitarian' didn't convince us at all . . . And 'feminist' was not considered an objective, feminist was talked of in the sense of the feminist struggle. And it was assumed that when this future society was achieved, the feminist struggle might not be necessary . . . Well of course, 'a feminist state' sounded a bit weird! [*laughter*]. (#10, b. 1957)

Other narrators note that many radical nationalists considered feminism to be both petit bourgeois (a common insult on the Left generally at the time, in Spain and elsewhere) and *españolista* (pro-Spanish). The label '*españolista*' (which Robert Clark calls 'one of the worst epithets in the ETA lexicon') had been used against dissenters since the 1960s.[27] But the idea that women's independent organising was 'foreign' had its roots in the early twentieth century, in the rhetoric of early Basque nationalists who wanted to distinguish the activities of Basque nationalist women from those of other middle-class women moving into the public sphere.[28]

The difficulties experienced by the women in KAS Emakumeak and Aizan in persuading nationalist colleagues – both male and female – to incorporate feminism into the radical nationalist agenda were similar to those experienced by feminist 'dual activists' in other political movements, in Spain and elsewhere. But these wider problems have to be weighed against significant, if smaller-scale, actions and changes achieved in specific areas. In 1979, two campaigns brought nationalist women together with other feminist organisations: the fight for the decriminalisation of abortion, and the movement to end violence against women. Although neither of these was an exclusively nationalist issue, in both cases Basque nationalist feminists used the language of nationalism and feminism to challenge more traditional female identities and to map out new arenas for women's political engagement.

Abortion and violence against women

If suffrage was the issue that united Western feminists of the first wave, by the second wave the focus on women's relationship to the State had expanded beyond public rights to the more intimate issues of sexual and reproductive freedom. In Spain this development was aptly summed up in the words of a placard carried at one feminist demonstration: 'Right to vote 1931, right to abortion 1981'.[29] In Spain, as in Italy, the history of Fascist legislation defining women's bodies as the property of the State, and the influence of the Catholic Church, made abortion a particularly contested issue. Divorce was legalised in Spain in 1981 (still in the face of opposition from the Right and the Church), but the abortion rights movement would last well beyond the election of the Socialist Party in 1982.[30]

In the context of the cultural, social and political upheaval of the transition years, the abortion rights campaign was waged amid persisting traditional representations of motherhood as women's 'natural' and most valued role. At the same time, there was a more modern symbolic association of the new democracy with sexual freedom – most publicly seen in the proliferation of images of scantily clad young women in the newly democratic press of the late 1970s. In calling for the decriminalisation of abortion, Basque and Spanish feminists came up against both the traditional Catholic Right and the democratic Centre, whose reforms had left intact much of the legal framework of the Franco state.[31] The strength of the anti-abortion lobby is shown by the fact that a majority of Spanish women, especially those of the older generation, opposed legalisation.[32]

Abortion was also a markedly personal issue for the new generation of feminists, many of whom had come of age during the 'sexual revolution' – albeit in its belated Spanish form – but at a time when the availability of contraception was still restricted in Spain. The abortion rights campaign was part of a much wider feminist grassroots movement aimed at increasing women's control over their own reproductive capacities in order to improve, among other things, the quality of child-rearing. One of the most important feminist initiatives of the 1970s was the establishment of family planning clinics, such as the 'Planning' in the working-class Bilbao neighbourhood of Recalde, a centre mentioned by several of the narrators. Some of these women were involved in helping women to cross into France to obtain abortions, while some made the trip for themselves. One narrator active in one of the early Recalde women's groups, and later Aizan, recalls the personal and political impact of going to France to have a termination:

> My partner at the time was obviously involved in this whole story, he was with me in the movement . . . And even though this guy was supposedly progressive and everything, I felt totally abandoned. I had to do it on my own . . . I remember it perfectly. I had just had the abortion, I was coming from there, exhausted, and there was a demonstration against university taxes . . . So I found him at the demo . . . and I told him I'd had the abortion and [*shaking her hand*] he says, 'Well done, mate' . . . It's imprinted on my memory . . . And from then on I found women's issues much more interesting. (#10, b. 1957)

The abortion rights campaign reached its high point in Spain between 1979 and 1981, with the trial against eleven women (one accused abortionist and ten patients) from the working-class Bilbao suburb of Basauri. The trial represented as well the zenith of Basque feminist mobilisation, bringing together a wide range of women's groups, including

KAS Emakumeak and other nationalist feminists.[33] Hundreds of women from the Basque country and the rest of Spain participated in demonstrations and sit-ins against the trial, as did members of Basque popular organisations, unions and parties, among them radical nationalists. Feminists in other countries also sent messages of solidarity.[34]

The Basauri trial was interpreted by feminists and other activists not only as a women's issue, but also a class issue, and more generally – given the heavy-handed police actions against the demonstrators – as part of the wider Basque solidarity movement against state repression.[35] Even ETA(m) got involved in the campaign, expressing its support for the women's movement by attacking the property of a prominent anti-abortion doctor.[36] The trial had a positive outcome in 1982 for the women involved, with the acquittal of nine of the defendants, and a request for the pardon for the woman accused of performing the terminations.[37] Although this legal victory did not translate into wider legal reform, the trial itself, and in particular the popular response to it, are remembered by many narrators and recorded in written documents as a significant landmark for Basque feminism.

The year following the Basauri trial, another significant campaign was waged in the Basque country, this time focusing on violence against women. Like abortion, this was a staple issue of second-wave Western European feminism. Although an ongoing concern, it came to particular prominence in the Basque country in 1980 because of a series of sexual assaults – in some cases culminating in murder – against young Basque women.[38] What brought these particular attacks to the attention of the public, and to organisations on the Left and the radical nationalist movement, was the fact that some of the victims were said to have had connections to nationalist politics. In addition, ultra-right-wing groups claimed responsibility for some of the attacks.

Protest against the rapes and rape-murders brought together a wide spectrum of Basque social movements, far-left organisations and radical nationalist groups.[39] ETA(pm), for instance, responded with an action against cinemas screening pornographic films in Bilbao.[40] There was widespread interest in the assaults and the protests against them in the media, including the radical nationalist press. For its part, KAS Emakumeak responded to the series of violent crimes against women by orchestrating a propaganda campaign designed to draw links between anti-nationalist and sexist violence.[41] But, as in other situations in which 'war rape' has captured the particular attention of nationalists,[42] for the mainstream radical nationalist movement it was the ethnic and/or political identity of the victims, and not the type of attack, that made these crimes 'political'. Thus one article in the radical nationalist newspaper *Egin* distinguished between the '*machista* and sexist' implications of all rape, and the 'political intention' behind these particular attacks, implying that rape in itself was not a political problem.[43] The radical nationalist reaction to the 'war rapes' thus offers an example of what the editors of the volume *Nationalisms and Sexualities* have called the 'deeply ingrained . . . depiction of the homeland as a female body whose violation by foreigners requires its citizens and allies to rush to her defense'.[44]

In recent years feminist studies of societies with prolonged political conflicts have investigated the relationship between political and other forms of violence, including domestic violence and sexual assault, which have traditionally been labelled 'private' or 'social' crimes. In Northern Ireland and Israel/Palestine, for instance, feminist scholars have looked at the effects of high levels of military and paramilitary activity on violence against women and children in homes, making connections between the ethics of male-dominated military organisations and the targeting of certain female victims. An important part of this project has been to condemn the media's role in sensationalising political violence – often labelled 'terrorism' – while treating as much less newsworthy more common forms of force affecting the civilian population.[45] The general conclusion in such studies is that high levels of political violence in a society can often lead to increased levels of force against civilians, both directly, because of the increased numbers of weapons in circulation, and indirectly, through the social and psychological impact of high levels of militarisation. However, the seriousness of these kinds of attacks is typically eclipsed in the public eye by types of violence more obviously related to the conflict itself.

In Basque society during 1979–80, levels of political violence – by all three wings of ETA, by ultra-right-wing paramilitary groups and by the state security forces – had reached staggering levels. Bombs, rifle attacks, police assaults on unarmed demonstrators, mass arrests and torture were all almost daily occurrences. It was in this context of widespread political conflict that feminist activists – including those from nationalist organisations such as KAS Emakumeak – attempted to bring public attention to the devastating effects of the criminalisation of abortion, and of sexual assault and murder. Although both campaigns received significant attention in the mainstream and left-wing media, and although feminists enjoyed the support of other popular movements and parties on the Left during both campaigns, this solidarity did not necessarily translate into long-term support for women's issues generally. In this regard, the experience of nationalist feminists was not so different from that of women in other left-wing groups in these years.

It would be a mistake, however, to assess these campaigns based only on their limited immediate achievements. In subsequent years the women's movement in the Basque country and throughout Spain has continued to campaign on both issues, with important results, especially in the area of violence against women. Domestic violence in particular has gone from being an issue virtually ignored by the Spanish press in the period under study to one of national public concern that attracts regular media attention and government initiative. By taking up the key 1970s feminist concerns of abortion and violence against women, and campaigning for change in a specific cultural, social and political context, Basque feminists – nationalists and others – were attempting to build new identities incorporating gender, ethnicity and class in a way that anticipated much contemporary feminist theory and practice. Even if they did not always successfully confront the gendered power relations in the Basque nationalist movement itself, by campaigning for free choice on abortion and against violence against women, nationalist feminists joined other women in offering alternatives to the traditional roles offered to women within dominant Spanish and Basque visions of nationhood, including within radical nationalism. Like some of the women in ETA discussed in chapter 5, they constructed new female nationalist identities that were not premised on maternity. Like feminists in Northern Ireland, radical Basque nationalist feminists broke the silence around issues often considered within their own community to be personal, private or taboo.[46] Through protests and demonstrations they introduced into public a new language of women's pain, one that broke down the opposition discussed in chapter 6 between men's direct suffering and the indirect, mute suffering associated with motherhood.

This symbolic challenge to the gender politics of the political status quo and the radical nationalist movement was exemplified by the slogan 'Amnesty for Women', which was employed to direct public attention to the political nature of both the abortion and sexual violence issues. By taking up the cry of amnesty, one of the central demands of both the radical nationalist and wider pro-democracy movements, feminist activists called into question the democratic credentials of a state that continued to imprison women accused of performing or having abortions.[47] At the same time, the language of these campaigns undermined the dichotomy between political and other forms of violence. In this regard, radical nationalist feminism anticipated more recent feminist contributors to debates about human rights, who argue that sexual and domestic violence should be as much the focus of human rights campaigns as torture and other forms of political violence.[48]

Feminist memories, feminist legacies

The awkward relationship between nationalism and feminism is reflected in narrators' memories, both in direct assessments of the strengths and weaknesses of the two movements, and more broadly in the ways the discourses of nationalism and feminism figure in their life narratives. National identity and the nation are imagined as timeless entities. National conflict – in the form of both Spanish 'repression' and Basque 'resistance' – stretch back in time before narrators' own lives, as that which is always 'the same'.[49] In contrast to this narrative of continuity, feminism – and personal and political relationships among women in particular – often signal change in a life story, especially positive change. Even when narrators do not identify as feminists, their recollections demonstrate a consciousness in the changes in women's lives and in gender relations. This sense of change comes out most strongly in narrators' memories of their relationships with their own mothers, or in discussions about their daughters. One narrator, who remembered having a particularly difficult relationship with her mother, recalls:

> As a teenager I fought with my mother about everything . . . I had the impression that she only quarrelled with me. Maybe she, in the situation she was in. I don't know. I imagine at the command of my father, although my father never seemed very authoritarian to me. But maybe he wasn't with me and he was with her. But he didn't seem that way with her, either. But none of that occurred to me. The only thing that occurred to me was that my mother was only bossy towards me. (#1, b. 1947)

This reflection on her parents' relationship – which the narrator was able to make because, in her words, 'now I've lived' – recalls a similar story she tells of her partner's failure to help her with housework and childcare in the early 1970s, even though they were both politically active and raising a young child together. At that point, she said, she 'hadn't even considered women's tasks or men's tasks' (#1, b. 1947). Life experience and feminist consciousness do not supply answers to the past, but they do provide a new language with which to reframe and reconsider the meanings of experience.

In a different interview a narrator reflects upon the influence of the women's movement on her life by looking both backwards to her mother and forwards to her daughter. Children are often used as a gauge to measure change and continuity during a narrator's life. In the previous chapter we saw that the same narrator's memories of different generations of prisoners, culminating with the friends of her own children, led her to conclude that the profile of the prisoner had remained the same since the days her own father was imprisoned during the war a half-century before. A very different perception of time emerges when she talks about women's issues:

> The contact with women younger than me, those women who're 40, 40 something, for those of us who are 50, has taught us a great deal. Because, there was this change, that now women started thinking about contraception, about continuing working, about not having children at once. Maybe I'm one of the last ones who've lived in my mother's style . . . I wasn't convinced that I had to work to earn money, because I was outside doing other kinds of work. Well maybe that generation has ended with me. My daughter doesn't want that at all. (#3, b. 1944)

This excerpt reminds us that political inheritances are far from straightforward, and that they do not always take place within the confines of the family. The model of women's intergenerational community as set out by this last narrator goes against the grain of an historical nationalism that idealises tradition and sees change and modernity as a threat to national community and identity. Additionally, by noting that the style of her mother's generation ends with her, the narrator recognises the alternatives available to her own daughter. There is no hint here that the 'style' she and her mother followed was wrong; indeed, on one level the interview can be read as a tribute to the narrator's strong and fiercely nationalist mother, who had died a few years previously. But if there is a trace of mourning as well for the traditional model of maternity that her mother represented, and that the narrator sees as dying out with her own generation, there is no sense of regret that her daughter will have other models to follow.

If in the interviews in nationalism and feminism have a different relationship to notions of time and change, so too do they evoke quite different emotions. Whereas stories of nationalist politics are often recounted in a sombre tone, memories of feminist activism are frequently expressed with a sense of joy. For example, narrator #3, whose experience of having an abortion in France has already been reproduced above, describes the early years of the feminist organisation she joined in the Bilbao neighbourhood of Recalde:

> I remember that period as very, very rich. You share, you debate . . . We were very young, very brazen . . . We talked about the issue of sexuality, and within sexuality, the issue of masturbation . . . And we made posters, and put them up in the neighbourhood. I'm amazed! The things we did! [*laughter*] . . . And we made posters, huge ones. You can't imagine. Huge, and we put on them the conclusions we'd arrived at, the debates of the young women's group, and we put them up in the street. Well! 'Masturbation' this

that and the other. And I guess the people in Recaldeberri were amazed because we talked about masturbation as if it were the greatest thing in the world! (#10, b. 1957)

There is a trace of nostalgia here for the naiveté and cheekiness associated with youthful activism. But what makes this a happy memory is also the recollection of solidarity associated with an intense period of activism. As Kristin Ross notes in her study of the afterlives of 1968, the Paris May events are often remembered by participants as a time when all aspects of an activist's life collapsed together: politics, work, love, friendships.[50] In the excerpt above there is a sense as well of a dissolving of boundaries between private and public, through the act of hanging posters about the wonders of female masturbation in the public squares and streets of a working-class neighbourhood in Bilbao. (Of course, there was more than a little boldness in these actions in a country where, a few years previously, strict censorship laws had restricted representations of women's sexuality.) In this regard, feminist activist memories share something in common with memories of other forms of activism, including membership in ETA: a sense of time collapsing, life being lived at a dizzying pace that gives little time to stop and think, and requires one to live 'to the full' and 'in the moment' – what I called in the introduction 'activist time and space'. But, in addition to this, women's organisations are associated with a creativity and imagination that arise specifically out of working together with other women:

> I remember we did a campaign so that on March 8th women didn't work at home. So that day they have a holiday, or a strike. We made proposals, I remember they were novel, and there were some women who had a lot of imagination, who were really expressive when it came to making proposals. We had a really good time. I remember that in the feminist struggle I enjoyed myself, as well as being active, and in the political struggle I rarely enjoyed myself . . . I think women united struggle and celebration, more than the men. We have other potentials that men don't have. I think it's that way right up to today. It's another way of relating. It's a different kind of enthusiasm. (#14, b. 1956)

This narrator had been in ETA in the 1970s, and had spent some time in prison before becoming active in feminist politics in the later 1970s. Like several narrators, she had experienced at close quarters the loss of a family member in the conflict, and like many had become significantly distanced from radical nationalism by the time I met her. While the interview as a whole was more analytical than expressive of emotion, I was struck by her frequent association of feminist activism with pleasure. In this her memories echo the words of a Sandinista activist interviewed by

Margaret Randall in 1992 who recalled that solidarity with other women had taught her to learn to laugh even at life's tragedies; feminism had enabled her and other women to turn anger into laughter, adding a 'new dimension' to their lives.[51]

But a celebration of the creativity and pleasure associated with being a part of a new women's movement may also, on some level, be a response to a more sinister humorous portrayal of the women's movement; one that sees feminism as a bit of a joke. At moments the narrators betray frustration and even anger as they recall that feminism was rarely taken seriously. One woman lamented that over the years, in spite of the personal respect she commanded as a longtime activist, her attempts to raise women's issues in meetings were typically met with disrespect from male comrades.

> There were always problems with Aizan because we were feminists. And we explained it and proposed it very clearly. So [they said], 'Here come those twits from Aizan with the same old story.' . . . The cheap joke, 'Ah! Here she is again! Hey! Don't get mad! Give us a kiss.' Look. I got so. They took everything really seriously. And when the issue of women arose, the cheap joke. (#15, b. 1946)

Another woman remembers conversations about feminism with male comrades in and around ETA in similar ways:

> Well, yes, we spoke to them, with our male comrades, and we debated, but there was some confusion. Talking about feminism was also talking about women as liberated. For them. I mean women who it was easier to go to bed with. It was the round table, or rather the round beds, as it was called back then. The round bed. Imagine! And so when you were a feminist you were a woman who was easy to pull. I don't think we were ever able to get much further than that. (#14, b. 1956)

If there is a sense of exasperation in these excerpts, there is also an underlying suggestion that the men in question were a bit hopeless, that ultimately the joke was on them.

This last narrator ultimately took quite a 'philosophical' view – in the popular sense of the term – in her assessment of the outcomes of feminist activism. She emphasised the elements of comedy and enjoyment, and insisted on the value of qualitative successes over and above quantitative failures. When asked whether she thought the roles played by women had been taken into account in the history of radical nationalism, she replied:

> For me taking it into account means that there would be women in political positions. Let's say we're in a democratic society, and that they'd

occupy 50% of the positions, and the leadership, and they'd speak up. And there aren't. I don't even see any effort to make it reality. I think what has happened is that many of us women can live better . . . And then I guess the women's struggle here, like in the Spanish state, was useful in obtaining abortion and other women's rights. Otherwise I don't know where we'd be. (#14, b. 1956)[52]

I want to close this chapter with an excerpt from another narrator, #16, whose history is in many ways similar to that of #10, cited in the previous chapter. Both had grown up in the same working-class Bilbao neighbourhood in the 1960s, and had been part of the same activist circles in the 1970s and 1980s, including radical nationalist and later feminist organisations. Both had been accused of collaboration with ETA in the early 1980s and imprisoned. In fact, narrator #10 had mentioned narrator #16 several times in her interview as someone who could tell me much more about the history of radical nationalist feminism. Yet the interviews with the two narrators could not have been more different. Whereas the first was characterised from the outset by a friendly, even jovial, exchange between the narrator and me as interviewer, and evoked a series of funny memories, even in relation to prison, that with #16 was largely a serious encounter, and focused much more on the difficulties and sacrifices of nationalist activism. This contrast was probably due to a number of factors, including a different dynamic between the two narrators and myself, as well as the distinct experiences the two women had had of radical nationalist violence. Like several other narrators, narrator #16 had lost a close relative to 'anti-terrorist' violence. In contrast to interview #17 (see chapter 4), in which the narrator's story focused on her dead partner, in this case there was an unbroken silence about the death, a silence which no doubt contributed to my own unease. But precisely because of its sombre tone, the interview is particularly expressive of the intense emotions associated for many with commitment to ETA. It also contains valuable reflections on the fraught relationship between nationalism and feminism.

Towards the end of the interview, I asked the narrator, as I had with others, to reflect upon the past fifteen years. The excerpt is worth quoting at length because it encapsulates, both in its language and in the exasperation with which it was spoken, sentiments expressed by many of the narrators, and by many supporters of ETA in general at the time of the interviews:

And today [1997], how do you see the situation of women in the nationalist left? The issue of feminism, the roles women have?

How do I see it? Well I think the fundamental problem is we still don't believe that we women have to organise ourselves. In the end we don't believe it. And today it's not because there aren't feminist women. To the contrary, I think all the women in the nationalist left are feminists. And all the new generations that are joining are feminist women. But I think we still haven't found the main point. This is unfinished business. How do you organise women? There are different attempts around, but in the end they don't come off. And then you have to add to that . . . that there's a lot at stake. A lot. So we can't allow ourselves the luxury of losing time, or of becoming distracted.

When you say there's a lot at stake, are you talking about women or the nationalist left in general?

The nationalist left in general. When I say the MLNV[53] has a specific job to do . . . I mean we can't allow ourselves the luxury of stopping the machine . . . No. Because all the reorganising we've done throughout our history, we've had to do without letting down our guard. Because the moment you let down your guard. Because we've got tons of prisoners. Because we've got tons of people who are staking themselves out there and because, in short, the enemy is still advancing. It's advancing more and more. I think that's something that puts people back too. There are *loads* of women, there are more and more women who are activists, activists in Jarrai,[54] activists in HB. And you don't hook them into this story. And I don't think that's a coincidence. It's not a coincidence. I think it's a question of priorities . . . That people see it as essential to set up a Gestoras in their town. But they don't see it as so essential to set up a women's organisation. So I'm trying to tell you that we've got our work set out for us. It's not so easy as in other organisations. Why? Because what we've got at stake is a lot. It's a lot because, above all, it's not just theory. It's lives. It's the future of the whole process. (#16, b. 1958)

This passage combines a sense of disappointment that feminism has been a frustrated project for radical nationalists with the feeling of urgency associated with the Basque conflict itself, an urgency personified, as I suggested in the Introduction and chapter 6, by the hundreds of ETA members in Spanish and French prisons. The difficulty of imagining a political project that would combine feminism and nationalism is underlined by the fact that the narrator, herself a feminist activist, uses language reminiscent of that of the non-feminist radical nationalist mainstream to explain why feminism cannot be a priority at a time of crisis; the implication that feminism is a kind of luxury recalls the narrator's memory of others calling it 'petty bourgeois'.

This narrator's claim that feminism is 'unfinished business' for radical nationalists is echoed in other interviews in which narrators seemed reluctant to dwell on painful memories of conflicts with fellow nationalists over women's issues. Speaking of the moment in which the radical nationalist women's organisation was disbanded under pressure from other groups in the early 1980s, one narrator describes the move as 'lamentable'. 'It upsets me', she says (# 15, b. 1946). Still another claims, 'The period surrounding the whole mess with the split has been erased [from my mind]' (#9, b. 1958). I prefer to leave the words of these narrators to stand as they are, rather than interpreting them as 'traumatic' or 'repressed'. Moreover, I do not wish to emphasise the element of mourning over other emotions evoked by memories of feminism as we saw above, including joy. It is worth considering here Cvetkovich's claim that '[o]ne value of oral history projects is that they can provide a public space for the emotional work of mourning at a time when the collectivity of activism may have faded and people are more isolated'.[55]

The potent combination of nostalgia and regret in these memories reflects in part the fact that, while the radical nationalist movement continued at the time of the interviews, the radical nationalist feminist organisations in which several narrators had been active had largely disintegrated. So had the energy and mobilisation of Basque and Spanish second-wave feminism, which was at its peak between the mid-1970s and 1980s. Ultimately, feminism in the interviews is itself a kind of conflict – not only between the pleasures and pain associated with feminist activism in the past, but also between a recognition that much remained to be done to improve women's lives at the time of the interviews, and the conviction that in the context of an ongoing 'war' against the Spanish state the nationalist cause must be given highest priority.

8

Women and the Basque conflict in the new millennium

In January 1986, almost eighteen years after the death of Txabi Etxebarrieta at the hands of the Civil Guard, the first female activist in the history of ETA – Bakartxu Arzelus – was killed by police during the course of an armed action. Although in radical nationalist circles there was a certain celebration of this first female 'martyr', the aftermath of Arzelus's death underlined the extent to which the female activist remained an anomaly. During her funeral there were clashes between Arzelus's father, Iñaki, a lifelong supporter of the Basque Nationalist Party (PNV), and radical nationalist activists who tried to claim Arzelus and her dead body as their own. According to the Basque mainstream and moderate nationalist press, one group of radical nationalist women insulted Iñaki Arzelus as a 'bad father', while various leaders of Herri Batasuna (HB), the party close to ETA, accused him of trying to take Arzelus away from her true family.[1]

These incidents exposed significant tensions within the radical nationalist idea of family. On one level there was a struggle between the activist's natural father and what could be called – following the argument in chapter 4 – her adopted father, ETA. On another there was a clash between two divergent visions of Basque nationalism (those of the PNV and HB respectively), both claiming to represent 'the Basque people'. Whereas an idealised family is celebrated in both traditions as the basis of community, and ETA members are typically claimed as 'children of the people', in this case there was an apparently irreconcilable conflict between the family of origin and the greater nationalist family.

Moreover, this funeral for a dead female ETA activist underscored the importance of gender relations in the construction of the ETA martyr. In most funerals for ETA militants, the mother of the dead activist plays a central and visible role.[2] But Arzelus's mother was confined to the background of these events (she was hardly mentioned in press accounts), suggesting that the figure of the mother at the public funeral functions above all to draw attention to the fallen son. The impression that Arzelus was being welcomed in death into a new family was made, moreover, by the central presence of a childless older female figure, HB leader Itziar Aizpurua. At the funeral, Aizpurua, who had made the conscious choice not to have her own children,[3] welcomed Arzelus into the collective of 'Basque youth' who had shown their love of their people through their own deaths. She paid tribute to Arzelus as the 'first woman to fall at the front from bullets of the Civil Guard, even if her father doesn't want to acknowledge it'.[4]

While Arzelus's family had attempted to bury her in a private ceremony, radical nationalist activists attempted, in the words of her father, to 'kidnap' her body. Here, and in the events that followed (including debates in the moderate and radical nationalist press), the struggle for the meaning of the Basque nation and nationalist family were quite literally waged over Arzelus's dead body.[5] Through the events and commentary surrounding her funeral, Arzelus's life and death became a metaphor for the contested terrain of the Basque nation/people/family. Although she was hailed as ETA's first female martyr, the contest over Arzelus's corpse suggested that, unlike her male comrades, who in death were celebrated as Christ-like figures transcending earthly existence, the female activist would remain defined by her body.[6] Arzelus's body became the disputed property of rival families, a struggle that briefly made material the symbolic nationalist connection between the homeland and the female body. These events provide further examples of the multiple ways – some of which were discussed in chapters 5 and 6 – that bodies of female activists were constructed and defined as different from men through the competing discourses of the Basque conflict.

In the midst of these events a letter from Arzelus's local feminist collective to the radical nationalist daily *Egin* attempted to address the complex personal and political realities of her life, including her choices and commitment as a nationalist, as an ETA activist and as a woman.[7] The letter acknowledges the difficulties she had experienced, including tensions with her family and her partner, as well as the dangers she faced as an ETA activist. While it shares with the wider radical nationalist press the tone of homage to a martyr, the letter stood alone amid the commotion surrounding Arzelus's death in its attempts to place her activism within a wider context of social relations, including gender and ethnicity. It also stressed her political agency, not just her status as a victim or heroine.

Eight months after the death of Bakartxu Arzelus, the killing of another former ETA activist, Dolores González Catarain – widely known by her nickname 'Yoyes' – captured the attention of the Basque and Spanish public.[8] Although the tale of Yoyes is much better known than that of Arzelus, both stories hint at the same basic tensions within the radical nationalist community with regards to gender and women's activist roles. In 1979, having become the first female member of ETA-militar (ETA[m])'s executive committee, Yoyes left the organisation over disagreements of policy and strategy. After spending six years in exile in Mexico, during which time she reconsidered her position on nationalism and the armed struggle, became more committed to feminism and gave birth to a son, Yoyes sought permission from the ETA(m) executive committee to return to the Basque country without returning to ETA. While her former comrades refused her request, Yoyes received authorisation from the Spanish government to go back to Spain in 1985. Almost immediately upon her arrival there was heated national debate about the meaning of the pardon apparently granted to this former female 'terrorist'. In the mainstream Basque and Spanish press, Yoyes's return was hailed as a major blow to ETA and a boost to the so-called 'peace process' (more imaginary than real, since ETA continued its violence and the years of Yoyes's return coincided with those of the GAL).[9] Anxious to prove these predictions false, radical nationalist supporters accused Yoyes of being a traitor, and graffiti calling her an informer appeared on shop windows in her hometown of Ordizia in the Goierri region of Guipízcoa. A year later, in September 1986, while walking with her young son in the square during the local autumn festival in Ordizia, Yoyes was shot and killed by two male members of ETA(m).

ETA's official defence of Yoyes's death was that as a former member of the executive committee her presence in Spain posed a grave security risk to the organisation.[10] Implicit in this argument was the belief that she had collaborated with the Spanish government in exchange for a personal pardon. This is a view still shared by many radical nationalist activists, including some narrators for this study.[11] Following the killing of Yoyes, the general consensus expressed in the mainstream Basque nationalist and Spanish press was that the ETA(m) executive had ordered Yoyes's death as a warning against those ETA prisoners and exiles who were tempted to choose a path similar to hers – that is, government-sanctioned individual pardon as opposed to a collective amnesty.[12] Her death was therefore interpreted as a strike against the 'social reinsertion' programme, through which the Spanish government had granted pardons to ETA prisoners and exiles willing to renounce the use of arms. The process had begun in 1982 with the dissolution of ETA(pm) and had led dozens of former activists publicly to abandon their weapons.[13] ETA(m)'s leadership was vehemently opposed to 'social reinsertion' and accused of treason all who took up the government's offer. Though most *reinsertados* adamantly denied they were 'repentant', many supporters of ETA(m) viewed them as Italian-style *arrepentidos*.[14] As Begoña Aretxaga stresses, therefore, prior to Yoyes's death dozens of other *reinsertados* had also been accused of collaboration and treason; moreover, by the time of her murder the original furore surrounding 'social reinsertion' had waned substantially, raising the question of why Yoyes's 'treason' was considered worse than that of other *reinsertados*.[15]

While the fact that Yoyes was a woman, and in particular a mother, was widely remarked upon, accounts of her death did not focus on gender as a relation of power. Yet on both a symbolic and material level gender was an important element in the events surrounding Yoyes's activism, her abandonment of ETA, and ultimately her death. Her feminist activism during her days in the French Basque country and many of the entries in her diary (published by friends and family members the year after her death) attest to the fact that Yoyes had been conscious of her difference as a woman in ETA.[16] She was equally aware that her relationship to the organisation continued to be informed by this fact after she left. While it would be altogether too simplistic to say that Yoyes was killed *because* she was a woman, she herself had written, just two years before her death, that her life was in the hands of ETA, 'as if it were a husband whom the wife had left, but as long as not everyone knows, holds on to the hope that she will return'.[17] Some who knew her drew the same conclusion. In the words of one narrator close to Yoyes, her murder was 'like the revenge of a spited man'.[18]

Yoyes was killed by two male ETA activists precisely at a moment when her life was furthest removed, both physically and symbolically, from her time as an activist. She had returned to her hometown in the Goierri, that idealised region in the heart of rural Guipízcoa that ETA members held up as the essence of Euskadi,[19] but which most had had to leave behind – along with their families – in order to enter the military organisation. Most importantly, Yoyes was a mother, walking through town with her child, an action unimaginable in her days as an activist. Through all the political justifications of her death there remains an additional, and equally political, significance: Yoyes's life story, that of a woman who had chosen first to be an armed activist and later to be a mother, constituted a transgression of the separation between the masculine military organisation and the supposedly feminine world of the home, epitomised by the mother. As with the case of Irish Republicanism, similarly grounded in a strong tradition of Catholicism and Marian worship, mother and warrior were incompatible identities.[20] As the late Begoña Aretxaga wrote in her analysis of the cultural meanings of Yoyes's murder,

A mother by definition cannot be a hero or traitor in the cultural context of radical nationalism; she is beyond these categories. Yoyes collapsed gender differentiations at a moment when ETA(m) needed them more rigidly than ever.[21]

As had been the case with the ETA community in exile in the 1970s (see chapter 4), during the debates around 'social reinsertion' the maintenance of strictly defined gender roles and spaces within the radical nationalist community, and in particular in and around ETA, served to create an illusion of strength and stability in the face of outside threats.

The controversy and discomfort that still surrounded the figure of Yoyes at the time of my interviews, a decade after her death, is suggested through recurring silence. Although her name was mentioned in several interviews as the primary example of a woman who had made it to the top of ETA, few narrators – including those who had known her personally – offered memories of Yoyes as a person, or opinions on the circumstances of her death. I was given an eerie reminder of the seeming desire to erase Yoyes from radical nationalist memories when, in the course of an archival search at the library of the Benedictine monastery in Lazkao (Guipízcoa), I came across a photograph of her with a male ETA activist and his female partner. I had previously seen the photograph reproduced in radical nationalist publications from the 1990s. It was taken in the French Basque country in the late 1970s, and in it the three young people are smiling broadly in front of a French road sign, dressed in jeans and baggy jumpers. But in the reproductions I had seen previously the couple stood alone – Yoyes had literally been cut out of the picture.

In recent years there has been a tendency on the part of some commentators to claim Yoyes as a kind of hero, even a victim – albeit not an entirely innocent one – of a violence she herself had rejected. Yet, while there is no evidence that Yoyes collaborated with the Spanish authorities upon her return to Spain, nor is it clear that she abandoned her previous commitment to political violence. Notwithstanding ETA's accusation of treason, Yoyes never made a public statement explaining why she had left the organisation. By guarding her silence Yoyes was complying with the conditions of her former colleagues, but, as Aretxaga points out, she may also have had personal and political reasons for remaining mute about her break with ETA, and about the organisation's continuing use of arms.[22] In other words, Yoyes's silence itself is open to different interpretations.

The lives and deaths of Bakartxu Arzelus and Yoyes illuminate the dilemmas of trying to define women's armed activism without recourse to the categories 'terrorist' and 'victim'. The label 'terrorist' denies the activist's political commitment as well as the historical context in which she acts – including the violence of the Spanish state. The idea of the woman activist as a 'victim', on the other hand, eliminates the concept of personal choice and agency, at the same time that it obscures the brutal effects of ETA's political violence and the pain of its victims. Against the terrorist/victim dichotomy I prefer to allow these stories to stand as testimony to the complexity of the categories 'victim' and 'perpetrator', especially in relation to the gender politics of conflict.

Women and ETA at the turn of the millennium

A notable feature of the social changes in Basque society at the turn of the millennium has been the increasing participation of women in all areas of public activity, including politics. Over the past decade a woman has led one of the smaller, non-violent Basque nationalist parties, and in the Basque regional elections of April 2005, women were elected to a record majority of parliamentary seats (40 out of 75).[23] Within the radical nationalist movement itself, since the 1990s women have increasingly been visible as spokespeople. In ETA as well there has been a gradual rise in the numbers of women. Although the organisation remains overwhelmingly male, the qualitative nature of women's participation appears to have changed somewhat.[24] Female ETA members became more publicly visible from the 1980s onwards as they were directly implicated in some of the group's worst atrocities, including the high-fatality car bombings of the Madrid commando and the 1987 Hipercor massacre, which killed twenty-one people at a Barcelona shopping centre. Moreover, over the last twenty years police sources have identified several women as ETA leaders.[25] During ETA's short-lived ceasefire of 1998-99, which raised hopes of a peace process, one 'historical' female activist (Belén González) was cited as a possible negotiator with the Spanish government, while another (Soledad Iparagirre) was accused of being instrumental in ending the truce.[26]

In the 1960s, women were recruited to ETA through very different routes from men. However, with the steady increase over the last twenty years of women's participation in all levels of education, work and politics, as well as the creation of a co-ed youth culture within the radical nationalist community (about which, more below), young women have been more likely to enter the organisation through similar routes to their male counterparts. An analysis of the profiles of fourteen women accused of armed activity or leadership positions in ETA from the early 1980s until 2003 demonstrates that, like early women recruits, later female activists have come from similar social backgrounds to their male comrades.[27]

While the majority are from ethnic Basque or mixed families, a significant minority are from 'immigrant' families (i.e. with parents or ancestors born in other parts of Spain), reflecting a general change in the profile of ETA activists over the past two decades.[28] Almost all were involved in radical nationalist or left-wing activism before joining ETA. In addition, their entry into the organisation followed a similar pattern to that of male comrades: they were typically 'legal' activists before police identification forced them to go underground and become full-time 'illegal' militants.

The most immediate factor differentiating these female ETA members from their male comrades is that the significant majority of them (nine of fourteen) reportedly had male partners inside the organisation. Although this statistic seems to confirm the 'couple terrorism' thesis outlined in chapter 5, further analysis shows that that theory does not account for the specific social and cultural circumstances in which these women joined ETA. First, press reports do not specify when they formed their relationships with male comrades; as chapter 5 demonstrated, there are cases of couples forming after both members join the organisation. Moreover, while reports of female activists almost invariably include their romantic liaisons, press accounts of the arrest or death of a male activist are less likely to report details of his personal relationships, making comparisons difficult.

But even if heterosexual couples have been a common phenomenon inside ETA, they are only one of a wide range of personal relationships among ETA members. In a discernible pattern dating back to ETA's early days, and noted by several other scholars, male and female activists are commonly recruited to the organisation through friends, relatives or members of their *cuadrilla* (see chapter 2).[29] Thus, for example, of the fourteen female activists sampled above only one had no reported partner or relative previously or currently inside ETA, and several had more than one – including cousins, siblings, uncles, and even parents – as well as partners. If we consider that many women probably also had activist friends, the network of social relations expands even further beyond the heterosexual couple. A cursory look at the profiles of prominent ETA activists indicates the importance of familial ties in the political formation and recruitment of many ETA members, male as well as female.[30]

In spite of the substantial changes in Basque women's social and political roles, the Basque conflict remains dominated by men, whether as politicians, members of the security forces or armed activists.[31] This tends to confirm the argument made in chapter 4 and above, that in the context of an armed conflict the policing of gender roles takes on particular importance. Contemporary radical nationalist feminists also note that feminism has not been fully incorporated into their movement's political agenda or culture.[32] These observations echo those made by narrator #16 a decade ago that feminism was 'unfinished business' (see chapter 7). This narrator noted in particular the contradiction between the rising number of young women active in the radical nationalist youth movement (then Jarrai), and the persisting lack of impact of feminism on the movement as a whole. Recent anthropological and linguistic studies of youth and Basque culture help to shed some light on this issue. Sharryn Kasmir's study of the Basque punk movement in the 1980s and 1990s, for example, argues that, although the youth culture in Basque industrial towns in this period was mixed, punk itself 'presents a masculinist version of Basqueness that attributes agency and cultural innovation to men, affirms the manliness of key political and social spaces, and writes a masculinist narrative of the nation'.[33] Furthermore, Kasmir's analysis of the Basque-language lyrics of songs by the popular 1980s group Hertzainak reveals a narrative of intergenerational conflict between sons and fathers reminiscent of the break between ETA and the PNV forty years before (see chapter 1), 'reinscribing the knowledge that political agency is masculine'.[34]

Sociolinguistic research likewise points to what one author calls the privileging of masculinity in the constructions of contemporary Basque identity among youth. In her study of the teaching of Basque in *ikastolas* in San Sebastián during the 1990s, Begoña Echeverria demonstrates that both language texts and the teaching of certain grammatical structures (in particular, the familiar form of 'you', *hika*) reinforce the association between 'authentic' – and, by implication, nationalist – Basque culture, and masculinity. At the same time, visual representations of women in the classroom continue to promote the traditionalist nationalist association of women with the private sphere.[35] Furthermore, Echeverria suggests that the unequal usage of *hika* among women and men in Basque society may be grounded in the historical gender division of the Basque workforce during industrialisation. Whereas rural Basque-speaking men formed the new proletariat in local factories, where the vernacular was most likely to be used, women more typically went into the service industry, where more formal language was required.[36] Thus in practice men were more likely than women to retain the peculiarities of the 'peasant language' which has been associated in nationalist rhetoric with 'real' Basque tradition. This link between vernacular, cultural authenticity, nationalism and masculinity is found in practice in the contemporary radical nationalist movement. 'Indeed *hika* usage', Echeverria writes, 'is associated with nationalist militancy more generally, and most of the protagonists here, too, are male.'[37] Echeverria's conclusions point to an important historical connection between the different patterns of women's and men's social, economic and cultural roles in the 1960s, explored in chapter 2, and the contemporary gender politics of radical nationalism.

Representations of women in ETA[38]

Another area that highlights the continuities of the last twenty-five years is the realm of representation. As the number of women in ETA has increased over this period, and more women have made the news, there has been a kind of normalisation in representations of these women, moving away from some of the more sensationalised portrayals of 'dangerous elements' described in chapter 5. In recent years most reports of women accused of ETA-related offences have not dwelt obsessively on the women's femininity or speculated widely on their sexuality. Instead, anxieties and fantasies about women in ETA seem to have been projected on to a small number of female activists. The most conspicuous example is that of accused member of the Madrid commando Idoia López Riaño, whose reported exploits during the 1980s, and subsequent arrest and extradition from France to Spain in 1994 and 2001 respectively, prompted ongoing speculation and commentary in the Spanish press, incorporating almost every imaginable misogynist stereotype. Few reports about López Riaño (nicknamed, among other things, 'the Tigress' – a name which, tellingly, was also reportedly used inside ETA) spared descriptions of her appearance ('tall', 'green eyes', 'magnificent beauty', 'spectacular physique', 'slave to her body and her hair') and her lifestyle (in particular, her supposed enthusiasm for nightlife), as well as references to her apparently 'cold' and calculated approach to armed actions.[39] Representations of López Riaño as a 'dangerous *etarra*' (ETA member) played with the tension between women's 'nature', a hyper-sexualised femininity, female rebellion and violence.[40] In the words of one male journalist – whose confessed feelings of simultaneous fascination and repulsion for female 'terrorists' led him to write an entire book on women in ETA based largely on speculation and fantasy – 'Seduction and the pistol were her weapons.'[41]

If images of López Riaño suggest male fantasies of exaggerated femininity and hyper-heterosexuality, a counter-example points to the anxieties provoked by the phantom of the female activist who does not hide her purported masculinity. Another sensationalist book about the Basque conflict provides the following description of Iñaxi Zeberio, who was killed by Basque police (*ertzainas*) during a raid on the flat where she was hiding in 1998:

> The *etarra* [member of ETA] looks like a brute, [with] wide shoulders, and the *ertzainas* who take part in the entry of the house where the *etarra* is hiding are sure, after suitably frisking her, that they're standing beside a man . . . [they] verify that an abundant mop of black hair is coming out of the ETA member's chest.[42]

Just as women's armed activism is directly linked to sexual deviance – whether promiscuity or implied lesbianism – it is also regarded as a perversion of their destiny as mothers. Several of the more lurid descriptions of female ETA members make direct reference to their reproductive functions. In 1996, for example, *El Mundo* columnist Martín Prieto wrote of Belén González that '[she] has menstruated more blood from her gun than from her vagina!' Five years later he repeated the same cliché almost word for word in reference to López Riaño: '*La Tigresa* is more worried about her menstruation than about the blood she lets spill from others.'[43] By linking their menstrual blood with their fatal actions, these statements imply that, by killing, female activists transgress their natural duty to give life.

As seen in chapter 4, the belief in the incompatibility of armed activism with maternity is common to many cultures, and can be traced as well in radical nationalist discourse. The case of Yoyes, described above, underscores the power of the cultural prohibition on activist motherhood. Yet one of the notable features of stories of women arrested for ETA participation since the 1990s is the presence of small numbers of mothers among them, including some accused of armed actions.[44] This development suggests that there has been on some level a shift in the gendered boundaries inside the radical nationalist community, one as yet difficult to measure or assess. Like one narrator who dreamed of having a daughter with her *nom de guerre* (#21, b. 1945), these activists add a new dimension to the nationalist narrative of generation and political inheritance. And if the archetypal figure of the mother of the male activist continues to hold sway, the addition of female activists to the ranks of ETA prisoners and martyrs, makes the mother–daughter relationship a part of this narrative in a way it was not in ETA's early years.[45] Nonetheless, in my conversations with young and not-so-young nationalist women over the past decade I have heard many laments about the conventional attitudes of their male comrades and the clichéd representations of women as the mothers of the nation. In a society which, like other Western European regions, has seen an important drop in birth rates since the late twentieth century, the gap between the gendered discourse of nationalism and changing social patterns is especially glaring.

Representations of female ETA members have shifted over the past four decades, from images of innocent victims to 'dangerous elements'. Yet these depictions have remained within the same ideological framework, assuming women's political activism is an extension of their personal relationships, and specifically their sexuality. Moreover, there is significant evidence in the case of ETA that male and female perpetrators are subject to different treatment, not only in the press but also by the security forces. One is struck in reading accounts of arrests of female ETA members in the Spanish and Basque press over the past two decades by the frequent speculation about some of these women's sexual activities. This is in contrast to the almost total lack of reporting of the accusations of sexual and gender-specific torture made by some female detainees.[46] Yet throughout this period the radical nationalist press reported testimonies that included harassment, threats of rape and actual sexual assault, and in 2000 Amnesty International raised concerns about the claim of sexual torture made by one accused female ETA member.[47] Media silence surrounding these cases is all the more notable given the significant reporting in the Spanish media in recent years – following decades of silence – of cases of domestic violence against women.

The point, as I stressed above, is not to argue that women who commit political violence are first and foremost victims, be it as unwitting girlfriends or as targets of police violence. But nor is it valid to make the opposite claim: that female terrorists are more dangerous than their male counterparts.[48] While several women are currently serving lengthy sentences in Spanish and French prisons accused of armed actions causing multiple deaths, there is no empirical evidence that women in ETA on average commit more – or more fatal – violent actions than men. On the contrary, sentencing patterns indicate that a substantial majority of ETA members imprisoned for 'blood crimes' are men.[49]

The implications of this evidence go beyond the case of ETA. As the media frenzy surrounding the female US soldier accused of torturing Iraqi prisoners indicates, the fact that violence by women is presumed to be extraordinary can make torture itself appear exceptional.[50] This forecloses serious discussion about the systemic use of torture and state violence, as well as about the wider gender politics of conflict. In the context of the international 'war on terror', in which political leaders have declared that all 'terrorism' is the same, case studies of female armed activists are an important intellectual and political resource for understanding not only why some women participate in political violence, but also how representations of women armed activists and combatants serve a variety of interests in wars and political conflicts.

Conclusion

With this book I have contributed to the 'gendering' of the history of ETA and radical Basque nationalism through a study of the roles of women in the movement since the 1960s. The book has shown how women's recruitment into and participation in ETA differed from those of men in the organisation's first few decades, how these differences were shaped by the historical conditions of late Franco and transitional Spain, and how the gender politics of radical nationalism have shifted since the 1960s. The changing political, economic and social conditions of Spain and the Basque country, and the development of a strong Basque feminist movement from the 1970s onwards, contributed to women's increased participation in all areas of nationalist politics, including as ETA activists. However, the emphasis on the military organisation, with its attendant masculinist ethic, over and above other nationalist initiatives and organisations, deepened gender divisions and restricted women's roles.

Yet if these conclusions tend to confirm the view of other scholars of gender and nationalism over the past two decades that nationalism is largely negative for women, this book serves as a warning against overgeneralisation in this regard. In chapter 2, I demonstrated that in the specific context of 1960s Spain, under a military dictatorship with an entrenched gender hierarchy, the new radical nationalist movement actually opened new spaces for women's public activities and political activism. This expansion was facilitated by the fact that nationalist rhetoric associated women with the realm of culture and language. Although this link was part of the gendered division of labour within radical nationalism, under conditions of historical change and crisis the movement's grounding in local communities and families allowed for the incorporation of women in a manner not possible in a more conventional political movement or party. Furthermore, several factors (the predominantly male character of the Spanish and Basque security forces, examples of police stereotyping of female ETA members as 'dangerous elements' and cases of sexual torture) show that the militarisation of ETA in the 1970s, with its attendant strengthening of gender divisions, cannot be explained solely by the legacy of traditional nationalism. Instead, it must be understood in the context of ETA's escalating conflict with the Spanish state.

If I have stressed, therefore, the need for careful historical contextualisation in the assessment of the advantages and disadvantages of nationalism for women, I also hope this book will contribute to the wider literature on gender and nationalism by highlighting the variety of women's nationalist roles, including those that go beyond the realm of motherhood and reproduction. Nationalist rhetoric has emphasised – and to a large extent continues to privilege – the figure of the mother of the male activist as the ideal nationalist woman. However, my analysis has demonstrated that 'patriotic motherhood' is itself a political construct (chapter 4), one that privileges some forms of maternity and maternal relations while ignoring or castigating others. What is at stake is the reproduction of (mostly male) nationalist activists and nationalism itself.

My oral history interviews shed light on the ambivalence felt by many former activists, whether mothers or not, towards the conventional role of motherhood as described in nationalist rhetoric, including the idea of a 'Basque matriarchy'. This mixture of feelings is shown most clearly in interviews with former ETA activists, for whom the development of new activist identities involved two things: a rejection of the association of militarism with masculinity and a denial of the automatic link between femininity and peace. In contrast to the findings of some comparative studies and representations of women in armed organisations, my interviews with women in ETA show that their feelings about political violence were determined neither by a commitment to maternity nor by a process of 'masculinisation'. With these conclusions I hope to contribute as well to the growing literature on women and political violence.[1]

I have also suggested that the idea of nationalist reproduction must be expanded to include the roles of fathers and of masculinity. This has been shown clearly in the discussion of fathers as role models (chapter 1), the importance of paternity among male ETA activists (chapter 4) and the examples of the ongoing construction of a 'masculinised' narrative of the nation through contemporary Basque linguistic and cultural practices (chapter 8). By looking at some of the ways radical nationalist masculinities have been constructed through the memories of female narrators (chapters 3 and 4), I have emphasised the need for more detailed investigation into, and theorisation of, the relationship between individual and national memories, and between memory and gender.

In addition to the work to be done on radical nationalist masculinities, more research is needed into the roles of women in other radical nationalist organisations outside ETA, especially over the past twenty-five years, including the youth movement and the street violence or *kale borroka* of the 1990s (see Introduction). Over the past decade anthropologists in particular have turned their attention to radical Basque youth culture and politics;[2] but to my knowledge no detailed study of the gender politics of the *kale borroka* has been undertaken.[3] On the other end of the spectrum is women's participation in the human rights and peace movements in the Basque country, from associations such as the ETA victims' support group Gesto por la Paz to the pro-negotiation initiative Elkarri.[4] Anecdotally it appears that, as with the case of radical nationalist prisoners' rights groups such as Gestoras pro amnistía (see chapter 6), women have had a relatively high profile in these organisations. But further research could help to illuminate how gender relations have shaped the impact of the Basque conflict on people's lives and their reactions to it. Although I have argued against assuming that women are innately more peaceful than men, comparative studies of conflict show that the gendered nature of political violence and nationalism means that women bring particular perspectives to peace talks.[5]

If nationalism was one of the academic key words of the 1990s, in the new millennium scholars have increasingly turned their attention to other concepts. In the field of Basque studies a recurring theme in recent publications is the challenges faced by Basque nationalism in the age of globalisation and postnationalism, as well as the potentials such phenomena may bring to a resolution of the Basque conflict.[6] In the remainder of this concluding chapter I will explore briefly the position of gender in these debates, and in particular whether the gender politics associated with postnationalism differ from those of radical Basque nationalism as outlined in this book.

In Spain, the idea of postnationalism is associated in the public mind primarily with a loose collective of male Basque-Spanish intellectuals, most now resident outside the Basque country, who have dedicated much of their writing over the past twenty years to a vociferous critique of ETA violence specifically, and of Basque nationalism more generally. Among these the most prolific and prominent have been the philosopher Fernando Savater and the literary critic Jon Juaristi.[7] I have argued elsewhere that Juaristi's highly personalised history of Basque nationalism, as developed in his best-selling book *El bucle melancólico*,[8] betrays a privileging of patriarchal political lineages and a denigration of the feminine – including the association of femininity with the worst excesses of radical nationalist violence – that mirror in significant ways the gender politics of Basque nationalism.[9] Similarly, when other Spanish postnationalist writers refer to women at all it is either in the form of stereotypical portrayals of women[10] or dismissals of feminism.[11] For this reason, as well as for their tendency to conflate all forms of Basque nationalism with 'terrorism',[12] I have always been sceptical of the postnationalist critique of ETA as produced in Spain. I am much less convinced by this intellectual project, for instance, than Paul Julian Smith, who, in his book *The Moderns*, admires both Savater's 'critically denaturalized vision of violence and nationalism'[13] and the postnationalist vision presented by Juaristi, along with Juan Aranzadi and Patxo Unzueta in their collection of essays *Auto de terminación*.[14]

Smith finds a parallel to the postnationalist project of Savater, Juaristi and company in the films of Basque-Spanish director Julio Medem. It is worth considering this connection in some detail because Medem's 2003 documentary on the Basque conflict, *La pelota vasca: la piel contra la piedra* (Basque Ball: Skin Against Stone) clearly reveals the overlap between the gender politics of nationalism and those of postnationalism. In his analysis of Medem's 1995 fictional film *Tierra* (Land), Smith writes:

> [T]he postnationalists share with Medem not only their impatience with national boundaries and antagonisms but also their engagement with fantasy and irrationality. Juxtaposing film and text we might read *Tierra* as an allegory of a Basque nationalism brought down to earth.[15]

Other British critics of Spanish culture have found in Medem's fictional cinema a subversion of the identity politics associated with Basque nationalism.[16] But *La pelota vasca* shows a decided shift in its relationship to nationalism, one that fits better with Cameron Watson's definition of postnationalism than that of the group of intellectuals cited by Smith. According to Watson:

> Postnationalism does not, as many observers seem to think, imply the end of nationalism, but rather, I suspect, a kind of accommodation (much like that of postmodernity with the modern condition) between nationalism and changing social, economic, political, and cultural realities.[17]

The director of several previous feature-length fictional films, Medem is one of Spain's most celebrated contemporary directors, so his documentary on the Basque conflict was bound to receive national and international attention. *La pelota vasca* consists of a dizzying series of talking heads (politicians, journalists and others), set against mostly rural Basque landscapes, commentating on the Basque conflict. The rapid shifting between the figures interviewed in the film is meant to evoke the fast rhythm of a *pelota* match (*pelota* is a popular Basque sport played by two people – usually men – in which a ball is struck against the wall with the hand, a bat or a scoop). Medem himself has said that *pelota* represents a kind of dialogue between the two players.[18] On one hand *La pelota vasca* can be read within Medem's overall oeuvre, much of which concerns itself with themes present in *La pelota vasca*. For example, Medem's first film, *Vacas* (Cows; 1992), a story of two rival Basque families, is replete with references to history, violence and war, as well as national identity and its relationship to the land and Basque tradition, in particular sports. (In *La pelota vasca*, scenes from *Vacas*, in which the protagonist engages in another traditional Basque sport, woodchopping, are interspersed among the talking heads along with a series of archival footage, including television images of ETA violence and black-and-white images of men engaged in other 'typical' Basque sports).

But, while aesthetically and thematically *La pelota vasca* owes much to Medem's earlier work, in terms of wider representations of political violence in the Basque country it is perhaps best located within a tradition of documentary films on ETA and the Basque conflict, including Imanol Uribe's *El proceso de Burgos* (The Burgos Trial; 1979). That film is also made up of a series of interviews, in this case of the former ETA members tried at Burgos in 1970. There are other similarities between Uribe's film and Medem's. Rob Stone has described the earlier documentary as 'a record of the remembrances and testimony of those involved, interspersed with footage of Basque landscape and overlaid with folk songs, thereby establishing an historical, near-mythic context for the remembered events'.[19] With the difference that *La pelota vasca* concerns itself less with memory than with reflection on contemporary events, Stone's description could largely be applied to Medem's film.

For, in spite of its explicit plea for democracy, dialogue and plurality – all values associated, in the Spanish context, with the championing of 'modernity' and transnational identity, in particular Europeanness[20] – *La pelota vasca* offers up a fantasy of a very different kind: a vision of a mythic, Basque Golden Age. In it Medem portrays a rural sense of national identity (notwithstanding the overwhelmingly urban character of the contemporary Basque country, most of the talking heads are filmed against a backdrop of fields, mountains or sea), one that resembles the images of the countryside in Basque nationalist writings dating back to Sabino Arana and the early PNV. The film's background music, which features haunting melodies sung in *euskera* by popular folk singer Mikel Laboa, adds to its generally folkloric feel. Moreover, the documentary offers an almost exclusively masculine image of Basqueness, whether nationalist, anti-nationalist or 'neutral'. In the book version of *La pelota vasca* there are several interviews with women – a historian, a writer and a journalist, among them.[21] But in the film released in cinemas, most of the women have been edited out. In the most public and visible form of *La pelota vasca*, therefore, men occupy the sphere of politics and leisure, in particular politics and sports, while women are assigned archetypal roles associated with the private sphere, namely wives and mothers, and are represented above all as victims of the conflict.

One of the most moving and disturbing interviews in the film is with a young woman who describes in detail her experience of being arrested and held for several days in the police station in Pamplona before being released without charges. This testimony of a woman detained in 2002 includes some of the forms of torture reported by women arrested in the 1970s and 1980s and listed in chapter 6. In this regard *La pelota vasca* breaks a silence around a largely taboo topic, and does so with specific reference to women. But almost all the other women in the film are present as widows and mothers of male victims. Through the move back and forth between these women's stories the impression is created that their common suffering 'as women' links them in spite of their political differences.

This is a familiar strategy, one hardly unique to *La pelota vasca*, and has indeed been used by women on both sides of the Basque and other conflicts as the basis for dialogue and peace. But, as I have noted in earlier chapters, the strategy of privileging women – and mothers in particular – as representatives of peace carries with it the risk of excluding them from other political subject positions, a move all too apparent in *La pelota vasca*. Indeed, it could be argued that the dialogue between the men in the film depends to a certain extent on the exclusion of women from the political sphere. By making gender divisions and hierarchies appear natural, and pushing women to the margins of dialogue about conflict and political violence in the Basque country, *La pelota vasca* reflects the conservative gender politics typical of both nationalism and its postnationalist critics, as outlined above. These different examples of postnationalism offer important critiques of the ethnic exclusivity associated with Basque and other nationalisms. But until their authors engage critically with all forms of social power relations, including class and gender, they cannot offer fully democratic alternatives to nationalism.

In his review of *La pelota vasca*, Paul Julian Smith argues that the film implies a false moral equivalence between the violence suffered by people on both sides of the Basque conflict.[22] While I do not concur with Smith that the film suggests Medem is an apologist for ETA's armed actions, I agree that the strategy of moving between victims in a way that implies their commonality is dubious. Several years ago a woman who worked with victims of ETA commented to me that, although it was important to recognise the violence suffered by ETA members and supporters, those who had been targeted by radical nationalist violence had the right to have their pain represented without comparison to that of ETA prisoners. In other words, she was advocating the representation of the specific nature of the suffering of ETA victims. It is precisely this representation that Medem's film fails to offer. Its attempt to occupy the 'middle ground' therefore presents ethical as well as political problems. In its dogged defence of 'dialogue', *La pelota vasca* positions people on both sides of the Basque conflict first and foremost as victims, and assumes that their common victimhood can bring them together across the political divide. This assumption places the supposedly universal feelings of pain and suffering above political difference and agency.

As examples from South Africa, Latin America and elsewhere have shown, processes of 'truth and reconciliation' can be important elements in transitions from racist or authoritarian to democratic regimes. Indeed, the fact that in Spain no such process was undertaken after the death of Franco may help explain the national preoccupation with 'historical memory', and in particular with the 'recuperation' of the memory of the victims of Francoism, from the late 1990s onwards. Although the memory boom in Spain has been led by grassroots movements, academics, film-makers and journalists have made an important contribution to the debates, and to uncovering evidence of victims and their histories. This is just one example of the positive role outside professionals can play in promoting dialogue, understanding and democracy in areas with histories of conflict.

But, while the memories and needs of victims must be central to any process of peace or democratisation, it is important that outsiders – including researchers – resist the temptation to identify too closely with victimhood. In his important work on history and trauma, Dominick LaCapra warns that historians (and, by implication, other academics) can at best be 'secondary witnesses' to acts of violence.[23] In other words, we can empathise with those who tell their stories of suffering, but our representations of those stories must always be done at a distance that acknowledges our removal from the immediate impact of the violence itself. Crucially, LaCapra also stresses that academics must demonstrate some degree of understanding in relation to the memories of perpetrators of violence:

With respect to perpetrators, one may justifiably resist empathy in the sense of feeling or understanding that may serve to validate or excuse certain acts. In fact, one may feel antipathy or hatred. But one may nonetheless argue that one should recognize and imaginatively apprehend that certain forms of behaviour . . . may be possible for oneself in certain circumstances, however much the events in question beggar the imagination.[24]

If, as LaCapra suggests, listening to perpetrators involves an ethical commitment on the part of the academic, on a political level perpetrators cannot be ignored. As the example of the Northern Irish peace process, which has served as a fundamental inspiration to Basque nationalists, attests, perpetrators on all sides must be involved in negotiations, even though their participation often causes distress and anger for survivors. Finally, I would add that even in relation to victims, researchers should resist the temptation to focus on those victims whose stories lend themselves most readily to reconciliation (as I believe is the case with *La pelota vasca*). A more balanced and complete study of conflict must also accommodate as well responses to violence that include anger, hatred or silence.

The challenges of a politics of memory that avoids a distinction between worthy and unworthy victims are all the more apparent following ETA's declaration of a permanent cease fire in March 2006. In contemporary debates about memory in Spain, which tend to contrast memories of the losers of the Civil War (republicans) with those of the winners (Francoists), members of ETA and supporters of radical Basque nationalism occupy a problematic position. Although they (or, more accurately, their ancestors) were victims of Francoism, for the past forty years they have been both victims of state and paramilitary persecution (including torture and murder) and perpetrators of violence against others.[25] This paradox points to a complexity in memory not often represented in current discussions about the 'recuperation' of republican memories in Spain. Recent 'memory work' in Spain and elsewhere often emphasises, or at least assumes, the healing or even redemptive potential of collective remembering of past violence. But, just as radical nationalists have used memories of state repression to justify violence against others, today many Basques and Spaniards oppose negotiations with ETA because of recent memories of nationalist violence. Although there is no question of forgetting the violence, peace in the Basque country may depend, at least in part, on a willingness to act against memory.

Glossary

* indicates term also included in glossary

Aberri Eguna Basque Patriot Day celebrated on Easter Sunday
abertzale Basque nationalist or patriot; since 1970s usually refers to supporters of ETA* and the radical nationalist movement
Aizan radical nationalist feminist organisation founded in 1981
andereño female teacher in *ikastola**
baserri(ak) traditional Basque family farmstead(s)
CC.AA. (Comandos Autónomos) armed organisation loosely connected to ETA*, formed in 1977
CC.OO. (Comisiones Obreras – Workers' Commissions) clandestine trade unions formed by Catholic and communist activists in the 1950s
cuadrilla friendship group
EAB (Emakume Abertzale Batza – Women's Patriotic League) women's nationalist organisation, founded in 1922
EGI (Eusko Gaztedi del Interior – Basque Youth of the Interior) youth section of the PNV* during Franco period
Egizan radical nationalist feminist organisation, founded in 1980s; successor to Aizan*
EHAS (Eusko Herriko Alderdi Sozialista – Basque Popular Worker's Party) formed in 1974 from a break with ETA*'s Cultural Front
Ekin clandestine study group founded by young middle-class male students from nationalist families in 1952; predecessor to ETA*
emakume(ak) woman/women
EMK (Euskadiko Mugimendu Komunista) See ETA-Berri*
ertzaina literally 'soldier'; member of Basque autonomous police force
españolista pro-Spanish
ETA (Euskadi ta Askatasuna – Basque Homeland and Freedom) Basque independence movement founded in 1959
ETA-V 'mili' faction which emerged from schism at ETA*'s Sixth Assembly in 1970

ETA-VI left-wing faction which emerged from schism at ETA*'s Sixth Assembly in 1970

ETA-Berri left-wing organisation which emerged out of the expulsion of the Political Office at ETA*'s Fifth Assembly in 1966; later became Maoist Movimiento Comunista de España (MCE*, EMK* in Basque) in 1970

ETA(m) (ETA-militar) militarist wing of ETA*, formed in 1974; since 1982 the only active wing of ETA

ETA(p-m) (ETA-político-militar) wing of ETA*, formed from a split within ETA in 1974; disbanded in 1982

etarra member of ETA*

etxe house

etxekoandre housewife (literally 'lady of the house')

Euskadi/Euskal Herria the Basque country

euskaldun Basque-speaker/ing

euskera the Basque language

GAL (Grupo Anti-terrorista de Liberación – Anti-Terrorist Liberation Group) illegal paramilitary squad with connections to the PSOE* government which targeted ETA members and supporters in the 1980s

GRAPO (Grupo Revolucionario Anti-fascista Primero de Octubre – First of October Anti-Fascist Group) Spanish far-left armed organisation founded in 1975

Gestoras pro-amnistía radical nationalist prisoners' rights organisation founded in 1976; close to ETA(m)*

gudari Basque soldier

HASI (Herriko Alderdi Sozialista Iraultzalea – Popular Revolutionary Socialist Party) grew out of EHAS*

HB (Herri Batasuna – Popular Unity) radical nationalist party close to ETA(m)* founded in 1978; dissolved in late 1990s

herri people/country/nation

Herri Gaztedi (People's Youth) young people's Catholic organisation founded in *euskaldun** zones during the 1960s

HOAC (Hermandad Obrera de Acción Católica – Catholic Action Workers' Brotherhood) Catholic workers' association

ikastola school where children taught in *euskera**

ikurriña the Basque flag

Iparralde the French Basque country

JOC (Juventud Obrera Católica – Catholic Workers Youth) Catholic youth workers' association

KAS (Koordinadora Abertzale Sozialista – Socialist Nationalist Coordinating Committee) radical nationalist political coalition founded in 1975; close to HB* and ETA(m)*

KAS Emakumeak (KAS Women) radical nationalist feminist organisation founded in 1978

LAB (Langile Abertzaleen Batzordeak – Nationalist Workers' Commissions) radical nationalist trade Union, founded 1975

LAIA (Langile Abertzale Iraultzalean Alderdia – Nationalist Revolutionary Workers' Party) founded in 1974 following a split in ETA's Workers' Front

LCR/LKI (Liga Comunista Revolucionario – Revolutionary Communist League) Spanish wing of the Trotskyist LCR (IV International), merged with ETA-VI* in 1973; LKI in Basque (Liga Komunista Iraultzailea)

liberado/a paid full-time member of ETA*

LKI See LCR

MCE See ETA-Berri*

MLNV (Movimiento de Liberación Nacional Vasco – Basque National Liberation Movement) popular name for radical nationalism from 1980s onwards

PCE (Partido Comunista de España) Spanish Communist Party

PNV (Partido Nacionalista Vasco – Basque Nationalist Party) founded by Sabino Arana in 1895

poteo going drinking from bar to bar; typically done in *cuadrilla**

PSOE (Partido Socialista Obrero Español) Spanish Socialist Party

PTV (Pueblo Trabajador Vasco – Basque Working People) expression adopted at the second half of ETA*'s Fifth Assembly in 1966 in an attempt to combine the notions of class and national struggle

Sección Feminina de Falange (SF) women's section of the Spanish Falange, founded in 1934; went on to become a state agency under Franco

Appendix 1: interviews

Interviews cited in the book, including informants' dates of birth and the month and year of each interview:

#1: b. 1947; February 1996
#2: b. 1959; February 1996
#3: b. 1944; March 1996
#4: b. 1936; March and July 1996
#5: b. 1949; March 1996
#6: b. 1946; April 1996
#7: b. 1943; May 1996
#8a: b. 1948; May 1996
#8b: b. 1947; May 1996
#9: b. 1958; May 1996
#10: b. 1957; June 1996
#11a: b. 1946; July 1996
#11b: b. 1944; July 1996
#11c: b. 1945; July 1996
#12: b. 1947; August 1996
#13: b. 1941; August 1996
#14: b. 1956; August 1996, and untaped conversation, June 1996
#15: b. 1946; January 1997
#16: b. 1958; January 1997
#17: b. 1958; February 1997
#18: b. 1961; March 1997
#19: b. 1944; March 1997
#20: b. 1945; March 1997
#21: b. 1945; April 1997
#22: b. 1943; August 1996 (untaped)

Appendix 2: women in ETA

ETA women prisoners 1975–83

A note on sources

The data below are based on lists of ETA prisoners, published by prisoners' rights groups and other radical nationalist organisations. Only those lists on which individual prisoners' political affiliation are given are included. Consequently, there are no lists for the period before 1975, when lists of 'Basque political prisoners' habitually included members of all illegal political organisations, often without distinction.[1] The lists used below are neither complete nor entirely accurate. There are several inconsistencies among them, including missing or misspelled names, inaccurate birth dates and places of origin. There are also biases in the collecting process. Those lists compiled by Gestoras pro-amnistía in the late 1970s and early 1980s, by which time the prisoners' rights group was clearly closely aligned to ETA(m), are likely more complete and accurate about the details of ETA(m) prisoners than about those in ETA(pm) and CC.AA. The lack of a coherent group representing the prisoners of those organisations, as well as the fact that both ceased to exist during the 1980s, makes it especially difficult to obtain accurate information about their activists. Since there are only lists available for specific dates, they omit people who served short sentences between these dates. Finally, the lists do not include ETA members who were

Date	Prisoners	Women	%
November 1975[2]	356	34	10
January 1976[3]	373	38	10
July 1980[4]	138	4	3
1981[5]	351	36	10
February 1983[6]	349	22	6
July/August 1983[7]	403	33	8

never imprisoned. Notwithstanding these shortcomings, and because for security reasons, the organisation does not release membership lists, lists of prisoners are the closest thing we have to an ETA membership list.

Patterns of women's participation in ETA

Sources

This section is based on information about individual female ETA members gathered from written sources (and in a few cases supplemented with oral sources) for the period 1966 to 1982. Included here are 329 women arrested and charged with ETA-related offences and/or imprisoned or exiled for the same reasons. In the cases of those women never charged or imprisoned, I have relied on published confirmation of their participation in the organisation.[8] In a few cases I have gathered additional information about individual activists from the interviews. The written sources consist primarily of newspaper and magazine reports of arrests and trials, and lists of arrests and prisoners published by Gestoras pro-amnistía and other radical nationalist organisations. In some cases, information was gathered from published interviews with or articles about individual members or groups of activists.[9] I have also relied on the Editorial Txalaparta series, which includes lists of prisoners and people arrested for ETA-related activities.[10] Finally, I have drawn on Robert Clark's biographical material about 'historical' ETA activists.[11]

Patterns of participation

In this category, women from the three ETA organisations (ETA(m), ETA(pm) and CC.AA.) have been grouped together, since there is not enough information to make a satisfactory comparison among them. However, the subjects are divided into three time periods: 1996–1970 (including the Burgos trial), 1971–75 and 1976–82. Where possible, information has been gathered on the following: place of origin, age, occupation and activities in ETA.

Age at time of arrest, trial or exile
Total sample: 142 of 329

Group A: 1966–70
Total sample   15
Mean age   27 years
Modal age   24 years
Range   33 (from 18 to 51 years)

Group B: 1971–75
Total sample   56
Mean age   26 years
Modal ages   18, 20 and 22 years
Range   41 (from 16 to 57 years)

Group C: 1976–82
Total sample   71
Mean age   27 years
Modal ages   20 and 24 years
Range   44 (from 17 to 61 years)

Notes
The average ages of women activists did not vary greatly between the late 1960s and early 1980s, although the middle period (1971–75) indicates a drop in modal age to as low as 18. This probably reflects a greater number of student activists in these years. The large range in ages, and the inflated mean age, indicates two different kinds of activism: the direct participation of activists in their late teens and early twenties; and the collaboration of middle-aged women who lodged ETA members in their homes.

Occupation
Total sample: 131 of 329

Group A: 1966–70

Occupation	Number	%
Office worker	7	39
Teacher	4	22
Student	3	17
Other*	4	22
Total	18	100

* Hairdresser, farm worker, dressmaker, social worker

Group B: 1971–75

Occupation	Number	%
Student	15	46
Office worker	4	12
Saleswoman	4	12
Homemaker	4	12
Health worker/nurse	3	9
Worker (general)	2	6
Teacher	1	3
Total	33	100

Group C: 1976–82

Occupation	Number	%
Student	14	18
Office worker	14	18
Teacher	12	15
Health worker/nurse	8	10
Unemployed	6	7.5
Worker (general)	6	7.5
Bartender/waiter	5	6
Homemaker	3	3.5
Journalist	3	3.5
Social worker	2	3
Other*	7	8
Total	80	100

* University professor, psychologist, saleswoman, civil servant, market worker, school director, security guard

Family connections
Group A: 1966–70 (34 total)
Family members: 10 (all men) = 29 per cent of cases

Group B: 1971–75 (84 total)
Family members: 32 (24 men, 8 women) = 38 per cent of cases

Group C: 1976–82 (211 total)
Family members: 58 (50 men, 8 women) = 27 per cent of cases

Activities in ETA

This section is based on information about the charges brought against individual activists. Where no charge has been noted, level of participation has been estimated based on length of prison sentence (i.e. short sentences of one to four years indicate collaborative or infrastructure-type activity). Collaboration includes cultural activities, printing and distributing propaganda, collecting information about potential targets, making links with *liberados* (full-time members of ETA), carrying information or weapons between *liberados*, hiding weapons and lodging ETA members.

Total sample: 242 OF 329

Group A: 1966–70

Activity	Number	%
Collaboration	23	72
Present at Assemblies	5	16
Full-time armed activists	3	9
Armed robbery	1	3
Total	32	100

Group B: 1971–75

Activity	Number	%
Collaboration	52	93
Armed actions	4	7
Total	56	100

Group C: 1976–82

Activity	Number	%
Collaboration	132	86
Armed activities*	19	12
Leaders**	3	2
Total	154	100

* Robbery, kidnapping, bombings
** Member of ETA Executive Committee

Female Basque political prisoners 1983–2002

February 1983
Total: 349; women: 22 (6 per cent)[12]

July/August 1983
Total: 403; women: 33 (8 per cent)[13]

January 1987
Total: 308; women: 23 (7 per cent)[14]

October 1989
Total: 541; women: 53 (10 per cent)[15]

June 1991
Total: 513; women: 63 (12 per cent)[16]

January 1992
Total: 553; women: 61 (11 per cent)[17]

May 1993
Total: 561; women: 71 (13 per cent)[18]

August 1994
Total: 495; women: 57 (12 per cent)[19]

September 1994
Total: 550; women: 62 (11 per cent)[20]

January 1996
Total: 544; women: 68 (13 per cent)[21]

December 1997
Total: 537; women: 65 (12 per cent)[22]

June 1999 (ceasefire September 1998–December 1999)
Total: 464; women: 50 (11 per cent)[23]

February 2002
Total: 540; women: 63 (12 per cent)[24]

Notes

Introduction

1 I use the phrase 'Basque country' in reference to the four Basque provinces (Vizcaya, Guipúzcoa, Alava and Navarre) which are part of Spain. Although Navarre is not part of the Basque Autonomous Community (established in 1980), it has had a vibrant radical nationalist movement since the 1960s and some of the narrators quoted in this book were born in Navarre. I use 'French Basque country' to refer to the three Basque provinces in France.
2 Over the years many different terms have been used to denote the political movement around ETA (see Glossary). For the sake of consistency I have chosen to use the term 'radical nationalism' throughout the book, although it probably did not come into widespread use until the 1970s.
3 Major works in Spanish include Antonio Elorza et al., *Historia de ETA* (Madrid: Temas de Hoy, 2000); José María Garmendia, *Historia de ETA*, 2 vols (San Sebastián: Haranburu, 1980); Florencio Domínguez Iribarren, *ETA: estrategia organizativa y actuaciones 1978–1992* (Bilbao: Universidad del País Vasco, 1998); Gurutz Jáuregui Bereciartu, *Ideología y estrategia política de ETA 1959–1968* (Madrid: Siglo XXI, 1981); Francisco Letamendia Belzunce, *Historia del nacionalismo vasco y de ETA*, 3 vols (San Sebastián: R&B Ediciones, 1994); José Manuel Mata López, *El nacionalismo vasco radical* (Bilbao: Universidad del País Vasco, 1993). In English the main works are Robert P. Clark, *The Basque Insurgents: ETA, 1952–1980* (Madison: University of Wisconsin Press, 1984), and John Sullivan, *ETA and Basque Nationalism: The Fight for Euskadi 1890–1986* (London: Routledge, 1988).
4 See Begoña Aretxaga, *Los funerales en el nacionalismo radical vasco* (San Sebastián: Baroja, 1988).
5 Some studies include small sections on women's participation in ETA. See Miren Alcedo, *Militar en ETA: historias de vida y muerte* (San Sebastián: Haranburu, 1996); Domínguez Iribarren, *ETA*; and Fernando Reinares, *Patriotas de la muerte: quienes han militado en ETA y por qué* (Madrid: Taurus, 2001).
6 See chapter 2 for more detailed discussion of this argument.
7 Nira Yuval-Davis and Floya Anthias (eds), *Woman–Nation–State* (London: Methuen, 1989), p. 7. Studies of women and nationalism in a wide variety

of contexts stress the importance of the role accorded women as mothers and as bearers of national 'tradition'. See various articles in special journal issues on gender and nationalism: *Feminist Review*, 44 (summer 1993); *Gender and History*, 5:2 (summer 1993); and *Nations and Nationalism*, 6:4 (October 2000), as well as Andrew Parker *et al.* (eds), *Nationalisms and Sexualities* (New York: Routledge, 1992), and Nira Yuval-Davis, *Gender and Nation* (London: Sage, 1997).

8 See Catherine Hall *et al.*, 'Introduction', *Gender and History*, 5:2 (summer 1993), 159–64, and Annie Whitehead *et al.*, 'Editorial', *Feminist Review*, 44 (summer 1993), 1–2.

9 Valentine M. Moghadam, 'Introduction and overview: gender dynamics of nationalism, revolution and Islamization', in Moghadam (ed.), *Gender and National Identity: Women and Politics in Muslim Societies* (London: Zed Books, 1994), pp. 3–4.

10 Mary Nash makes a similar argument in relation to Republican propaganda during the Civil War. See Nash, ' "Milicianas" and homefront heroines: images of women in revolutionary Spain (1936–1939)', *History of European Ideas*, 11 (1989), 235–44.

11 For a summary of these, see Appendix 2.

12 Selma Leydesdorff *et al.*, 'Introduction', *International Yearbook of Oral History and Life Stories*, vol. 4 'Gender and Memory' (Oxford: Oxford University Press, 1996), p. 4.

13 For a useful summary of these issues and their implications for feminist oral history, see Penny Summerfield, *Reconstructing Women's Wartime Lives* (Manchester: Manchester University Press, 1998), pp. 9–16. See also various chapters in Sherna Berger Gluck and Daphne Patai (eds), *Women's Words: The Feminist Practice of Oral History* (New York and London: Routledge, 1991).

14 James Fentress and Chris Wickham, *Social Memory* (Oxford: Blackwell, 1992).

15 See, for example, Iwona Irwin-Zarecka, *Frames of Remembrance: Social and Cultural Dynamics of Collective Memory* (London: Transaction, 1993); David Middleton and Derek Edwards (eds), *Collective Remembering* (London: Sage, 1990); and Eviatar Zerubavel, *Time Maps: Collective Memory and the Social Shape of the Past* (Chicago and London: University of Chicago Press, 2003). For examples in the Spanish context, see Paloma Aguilar Fernández, *Memoria y olvido de la guerra civil española* (Madrid: Alianza Editorial, 1996); Paloma Aguilar and Corsten Humlebaek, 'Collective memory and national identity in the Spanish democracy: the legacy of Francoism and the civil war', *Memory and History*, 14:12 (autumn 2002), 121–64; and Michael Richards, 'Collective memory, the nation-state and post-Franco society', in Barry Jordan and Rikki Morgan-Tamosunas (eds), *Contemporary Spanish Cultural Studies* (London: Arnold, 2000), pp. 38–47.

16 Carrie Hamilton, 'Memories of violence in interviews with Basque nationalist women', in Katharine Hodgkin and Susannah Radstone (eds), *Contested*

Pasts: The Politics of Memory (New York and London: Routledge, 2003), pp. 120–35.
17 For a discussion of some of the methodological problems associated with defining collective memory, see Elizabeth Jelin, *State Repression and the Struggles for Memory* (London: Latin American Bureau, 2003), pp. 10–12.
18 Hamilton, 'Memories of violence', pp. 130–1.
19 See Kerwin Lee Klein, 'On the emergence of memory in historical discourse', *Representations*, 69 (winter 2000), 127–50.
20 Hamilton, 'Memories of violence'.
21 Summerfield, *Reconstructing Women's Wartime Lives*, pp. 115–60.
22 Some anthropological studies make references to masculine identities in relation to ETA. See Alcedo, *Militar en ETA*, and Joseba Zulaika, *Basque Violence: Metaphor and Sacrament* (Reno: University of Nevada Press, 1988). Some work has been done on masculinity and Basque nationalism in the area of literary theory. See Joseba Gabilondo, 'Terrorism as memory: the historical novel and masculine masochism in contemporary Basque literature', *Arizona Journal of Hispanic Cultural Studies*, 2 (1998), 113–46.
23 A more detailed history of radical nationalist masculinity would contribute to the growing historical literature on masculinity and conflict. See Stefan Dudink, Karen Hagemanna and John Tosh (eds), *Masculinities in Politics and War: Gendering Modern History* (Manchester: Manchester University Press, 2004).
24 Wendy Bracewell, 'Rape in Kosovo: masculinity and Serbian nationalism', *Nations and Nationalism*, 6:4 (October 2000), 566.
25 Hodgkin and Radstone (eds.), 'Introduction', *Contested Pasts*, p. 5.
26 Leydesdorff *et al.*, 'Introduction', p. 6.
27 Hodgkin and Radstone (eds), 'Introduction', *Contested Pasts*, p. 5.
28 Joan Sangster, 'Telling our stories: feminist debates and the use of oral history', in Robert Perks and Alistair Thomson (eds), *The Oral History Reader* (London: Routledge, 1997), p. 96.
29 All the narrators were members or supporters of ETA-militar (ETA[m]), the wing of the organisation that remains active today. I was not able to locate women formerly active in other wings – ETA-político-militar (ETA[pm]) and the Comandos Autónomos (CC.AA.) – who were willing to be interviewed. Some written sources, including published interviews with female ETA(pm) activists cited in later chapters of this book, do indicate that these women shared a number of common experiences with women in ETA(m). Both Alcedo, *Militar en ETA*, and Reinares, *Patriotas de la muerte*, contain interviews with ETA(pm) as well as ETA(m) activists; however, neither author makes explicit comparisons between the experiences of activists from the different wings of ETA. There may have been differences between the two organisations with regard to women's roles, and it is hoped that future studies of radical nationalism can provide the basis for comparison in this area.
30 Paul Thompson, *The Voice of the Past: Oral History* (Oxford: Oxford University Press, 2nd edition, 1988).

31 Alessandro Portelli, 'The peculiarities of oral history', *History Workshop*, 12 (autumn 1981), 97.
32 There is disagreement among scholars over the merits of literal transcription. Some historians have noted that literal transcriptions may be an embarrassment to narrators if they make them appear inarticulate, and that therefore grammatical errors and long sentences should be corrected. See Brana Gurewitsch (ed.), *Mothers, Sisters, Resisters: Oral Histories of Women Who Survived the Holocaust* (Tuscaloosa and London: University of Alabama Press, 1998), pp. xx–xxi.
33 My limited fluency in the Basque language euskera eliminated the option of interviews in that language. However, only a minority of the narrators were what could be regarded 'native speakers' of Basque. This concept is complicated in the Basque country. Decades of declining use of euskera, followed by direct repression under Franco, and more recently a rise in use among young people (as well as widespread adult literacy programmes), have combined to produce a wide variety of degrees of fluency.
34 All interviews will be indicated in the text by number and date of birth, as here. For a full list of interviews, see Appendix 1.
35 Hamilton, 'Memories of violence'.
36 Ronald J. Grele, 'Private memories and public presentation: the art of oral history', in Grele *et al.*, *Envelopes of Sound: The Art of Oral History* (New York: Praeger, 2nd edition, 1991), p. 247.
37 The GAL (Grupo Anti-terrorista de Liberación – Anti-terrorist Liberation Group) was a paramilitary squad formed largely by off-duty police officers and having connections to the governing Spanish party (PSOE) which killed several suspected ETA members in the French Basque country during the 1980s. For a history of the GAL and the dirty war against ETA, see Paddy Woodworth, *Dirty War, Clean Hands: ETA, the GAL and Spanish Democracy* (New Haven, CN, and London: Yale University Press, 2001).
38 Luisa Passerini, 'Introduction' in Passerini (ed.), *International Yearbook of Oral History and Life Stories*, vol. 1 'Totalitarianism' (Oxford: Oxford University Press, 1992), p. 12.
39 Luisa Passerini, 'Lacerations in the memory: women in the Italian underground organizations', *International Social Movement Research*, 4 (1992), 161–212.
40 Eilish Rooney, 'Political division, practical alliance: problems for women in conflict', *Journal of Women's History*, 6:4/7:1 (winter/spring 1995), 42.
41 For a description of the political and economic consequences of the *kale borroka*, see Ludger Mees, *Nationalism, Violence and Democracy: The Basque Clash of Identities* (Basingstoke: Palgrave Macmillan, 2003), pp. 77–9. See also Hanspeter van der Broek, 'Borroka – the legitimation of street violence in the political discourse of radical Basque nationalists', *Terrorism and Political Violence*, 16:4 (winter 2004), 714–36; and Pedro J. Oiarzabal, 'Reconstructing Basque youth political violence from mass media discourses', *Journal of the Society of Basque Studies in America*, 23 (2003–4), 29–44.

42 For a discussion of the interrelationship between the personal and the political in people's decisions to leave radical nationalism, see Mikel Arriaga Landeta, *Y nosotros que éramos de HB . . . sociología de una heterodoxia abertzale* (Alegia: Aramburu, 1997).
43 Amando de Miguel, 'Estructura social y juventud española', *Revista del Instituto de la Juventud*, 0 (1965), 35.
44 Statistics on the economic crisis of the 1980s and 1990s are provided by Sharryn Kasmir, ' "More Basque than you": class, youth and identity in an industrial Basque town', *Identities*, 9:1 (January–March 2002), 49–51.
45 Saul Benison *et al.*, 'It's not the song, it's the singing. Panel discussion on oral history', in Grele *et al.*, *Envelopes of Sound*, p. 73.
46 Sangster, 'Telling our stories', pp. 92–4.
47 Daniel James, *Doña María's Story: Life History, Memory and Political Identity* (Durham, NC, and London: Duke University Press, 2000), p. 139.
48 *Ibid.*
49 *Ibid.*, p. 140.
50 *Ibid.*
51 *Ibid.*, p. 141. See Doris Sommer, 'Resistant texts and incompetent readers', *Latin American Literary Review*, 4 (1992), 104–8.
52 Major works include Cathy Caruth (ed.), *Trauma: Explorations in Memory* (Baltimore: Johns Hopkins University Press, 1995); Cathy Caruth, *Unclaimed Experience: Trauma, Narrative and Experience* (Baltimore: Johns Hopkins University Press, 1996); Shoshana Felman and Dori Laub, *Testimony: Crises of Witnessing in Literature, Psychoanalaysis and History* (New York: Routledge, 1992); and Dominick LaCapra, *Representing the Holocaust: History, Theory, Trauma* (Ithaca: Cornell University Press, 1994).
53 Susannah Radstone, 'Social bonds and psychical order: testimonies', *Cultural Values*, 5:1 (January 2001), 59.
54 I discuss at greater length the problem of identifying with victimhood, and of equating different form of violence, in the Conclusion.
55 Passerini, 'Lacerations', p. 197.
56 *Ibid.*
57 Hamilton, 'Memories of violence'. Some of these silences are now being addressed by the popular movement for the 'recuperation of historical memory' in Spain.
58 Passerini, 'Lacerations', p. 191.
59 *Ibid.*, p. 205.
60 Ronaldo Munck, 'Deconstructing terror: insurgency, repression and peace', in Ronaldo Munck and Purnaka da Silva (eds), *Postmodern Insurgencies: Political Violence, Identity Formation and Peacemaking in Comparative Perspective* (Basingstoke: Macmillan, 2000), p. 9.
61 Kristin Ross, *May '68 and its Afterlives* (Chicago: University of Chicago Press, 2002), pp. 1–2.
62 *Ibid.*, pp. 102–4.

63 *Ibid.*, p. 102.
64 See Reinares, *Patriotas de la muerte*, pp. 126–45.
65 Jesus Casquete, *El poder en la calle: ensayos sobre acción colectiva* (Madrid: Centro de Estudios Políticos y Constitucionales, 2006).
66 Benedict Anderson, *Imagined Communities: Reflections on the Origins and Spread of Nationalism* (London: Verso, 1991 [1983]), pp. 141–2.

Chapter 1

1 Mercedes Ugalde, *Mujeres y nacionalismo vasco: Emakume Abertzale Batza 1906–1936* (Bilbao: Universidad del País Vasco, 1993), p. 46.
2 *Ibid.*
3 *Ibid.*, p. 37. For a more detailed analysis of gender and women in Arana's writing, see pp. 32–50. Several scholars of gender and nationalism have noted the 'femininization' of the enemy in nationalist discourse. See Diana Taylor, *Disappearing Acts: Spectacles of Gender and Nationalism in Argentina's Dirty War* (Durham, NC: Duke University Press, 1997), pp. 35–6.
4 Arana labelled 'immigrant' Spanish workers to the Basque country *maketos* and denounced them as dangerous socialists, in contrast to 'pure' Basques, who valued tradition and Catholicism; Antonio Elorza, *Ideologías del nacionalismo vasco 1876–1937 (de los 'euskeros' a Jagi Jagi)* (San Sebastián: Haranburu, 1978), p. 177, and John Sullivan, *ETA and Basque Nationalism: The Fight for Euskadi 1890–1986* (London: Routledge, 1988), chapter 1.
5 Ugalde, *Mujeres y nacionalismo vasco*, p. 383.
6 *Ibid.*, pp. 137, 249.
7 *Ibid.*, pp. 372–3.
8 I use 'ethnic Basque' to designate individuals, families and communities whose history in the Basque country predates the large waves of migration to the region in the late nineteenth century and the mid-twentieth century.
9 Ugalde, *Mujeres y nacionalismo vasco*, pp. 561–74.
10 *Ibid.*, p. 571.
11 *Ibid.*, p. 367.
12 *Ibid.*, p. 244. For the relationship between Basque nationalists and Spanish Republicans, see Juan Pablo Fusi, 'The Basque question 1931–37', in Paul Preston (ed.), *Revolution and War in Spain 1931–1939* (London: Methuen, 1984), pp. 182–201.
13 Basque nationalists, like other Basque and Navarrese traditionalists, voted in favour of women's suffrage, in line with the popular perception that women were more likely to vote for conservative Catholic parties; Ugalde, *Mujeres y nacionalismo vasco*, p. 215.
14 For a study of women's organisations during the Civil War see Mary Nash, *Defying Male Civilization: Women in the Spanish Civil War* (Denver, CO: Arden Press, 1995).

15 For the negotiation of Basque autonomy under the Second Republic, see Fusi, 'The Basque question'.
16 The expression *gran hogar* was used by the Spanish fascist party, the Falange. Geraldine M. Scanlon, *La polémica feminista en la España contemporánea 1868–1974* (Madrid: Akal, 1976), p. 317.
17 In Alava and Navarre, Carlists and other traditionalist forces (including the majority in the PNV) sided with the rebels in July 1936.
18 Shlomo Ben-Ami, 'Basque nationalism between archaism and modernity', *Journal of Contemporary History*, 26 (1991), 499.
19 Robert P. Clark, *The Basques: The Franco Years and Beyond* (Reno: University of Nevada Press, 1979), p. 81; José María Garmendia, *Historia de ETA*, 2 vols. (San Sebastián: Haranburu, 1980), vol. 1, p. 86; Francisco Letamendia Belzunce, *Historia del nacionalismo vasco y de ETA*, 3 vols (San Sebastián: R&B Ediciones, 1994), vol. 1, p. 317; and Sullivan, *ETA and Basque Nationalism*, pp. 27–8, 34.
20 Elorza, *Ideologías del nacionalismo vasco*, p. 175.
21 *Ibid.*, p. 176.
22 The *fueros* or foral laws were a series of local laws, privileges and exemptions (particularly in the areas of customs, taxation and military service) common to much of medieval Western Europe. Though the Basque provinces and Navarre had been incorporated into the Castilian Kingdom between the thirteenth and sixteenth centuries, the *fueros* in these regions remained largely intact until the nineteenth century. See Stanley Payne, *Basque Nationalism* (Reno: University of Nevada Press, 1975), p. 17.
23 For a discussion of the historical roots of 'universal nobility and the myth of egalitarianism' and their exploitation by early Basque nationalists, see Letamendia Belzunce, *Historia del nacionalismo vasco*, vol. 1, pp. 47–52, 144–6.
24 ' "Invented traditions" is taken to mean a set of practices, normally governed by overtly or tacitly accepted rules and of a ritual or symbolic nature, which seek to inculcate certain values and norms of behavior by repetition, which automatically implies continuity with the past.' Eric Hobsbawm, 'Introduction: inventing traditions' in Eric Hobsbawm and Terence Ranger (eds), *The Invention of Tradition* (Cambridge: Cambridge University Press 1997 [1983]), p. 1.
25 Joseba Zulaika, *Basque Violence: Metaphor and Sacrament* (Reno: University of Nevada Press, 1988), pp. 103–24, and Begoña Aretxaga, *Los funerales en el nacionalismo radical vasco* (San Sebastián: Baroja, 1988), p. 27.
26 According to Ugalde, the notion of gender equality under the foral laws was derived largely from the prerogatives granted to women with regards to inheritance laws, under which, in the case of the absence of a male heir, women were able to take on certain political responsibilities. She argues that the assertion of gender equality worked together with the celebration of the mother in nationalist discourse to mask the gender hierarchy that existed

both under the foral laws and in the PNV of the 1930s; Ugalde, *Mujeres y nacionalism vasco*, p. 377.
27 For an example of the contemporary durability of the matriarchy theory among some Basque women, see Margaret Bullen, 'Gender and identity in the *Alardes* of two Basque towns, in William A. Douglass *et al.* (eds), *Basque Cultural Studies* (Reno: University of Nevada Basque Studies Program, 1999), p. 166.
28 A. Ortiz Osés and F. K. Mayr, *El matriarcalismo vasco: reinterpretación de la cultura vasca* (Bilbao: Universidad de Deusto, 1980). See also Txema Hornilla, *La ginococracia vasca* (Bilbao: Editorial Geu Argitaldaria, 1981). For a critique of the Basque matriarchy theory, see Juan Aranzadi, *Milenarismo vasco: edad de oro, etnia y nativismo* (Madrid: Taurus, 2nd edition, 2000), pp. 499–553. On a popular level, there were frequent debates about the matriarchy theory in the left-wing and radical nationalist press in the late 1970s. See various letters in *Punto y Hora de Euskal Herria*, 47 (4–10 August 1977), 48 (11–17 August 1977) and 51 (1–7 September 1977).
29 Teresa del Valle *et al.*, *Mujer vasca: imagen y realidad* (Barcelona: Anthropos, 1985).
30 *Ibid.*, p. 141.
31 *Ibid.*, pp. 78, 135, 141. Sharryn Kasmir's study of the cooperatives of Mondragón highlights the same gender division of leisure time and space among Basque and migrant workers in industrial areas; Sharryn Kasmir, *The Myth of Mondragón: Cooperatives, Politics and Working-Class Life in a Basque Town* (Albany: State University of New York Press, 1996), p. 81.
32 Antonio Elorza, 'Some perspectives on the nation-state and Autonomies in Spain' in Helen Graham and Jo Labanyi (eds), *Spanish Cultural Studies: An Introduction* (Oxford: Oxford University Press, 1995), p. 332. See also Clark, *The Basques*, pp. 121–4; Ander Gurruchaga, *El código nacionalista vasco durante el franquismo* (Barcelona: Anthropos, 1985), p. 311; Letamendia Belzunce, *Historia del nacionalismo vasco*, vol. 1, p. 249; Alfonso Pérez-Agote, *La reproducción del nacionalismo: el caso vasco* (Madrid: Centro de Investigaciones Sociológicas, 1984), pp. 88–98; and Sullivan, *ETA and Basque Nationalism*, pp. 33–4.
33 Aurora G. Morcillo, *True Catholic Womanhood: Gender Ideology in Franco's Spain* (DeKalb: Northern Illinois University Press, 2000), p. 162. See also Kathleen Richmond, *Women and Spanish Fascism: The Women's Section of the Falange 1934–1959* (London: Routledge, 2003). For comparative studies of motherhood and authoritarianism, see Renate Bridenthal, Atina Grossmann and Marion Kaplan, *When Biology Became Destiny: Women in Weimar and Nazi Germany* (New York: Monthly Review Press, 1984); Victoria de Grazia, *How Fascism Ruled Women: Italy 1922–1945* (Berkeley: University of California Press, 1992); Claudia Koonz, *Mothers in the Fatherland: Women, the Family, and Nazi Politics* (New York: St Martin's Press, 1987); and Kevin Passmore (ed.), *Women, Gender and Fascism in Europe 1919–1945* (Manchester: Manchester University Press, 2003).

34 Del Valle *et al.*, *Mujer vasca*, pp. 124–5.
35 Judith Stacey, 'Are feminists afraid to leave home?', in Juliet Mitchell and Ann Oakley (eds), *Who's Afraid of Feminism? Seeing Through the Backlash* (New York: Pantheon Books, 1986), p. 226.
36 When EAB women demonstrated in the streets of Bilbao in support of male nationalist prisoners, during the Second Republic, Socialist trade unionists accused male PNV members of lacking virility for allowing women to take on men's roles in the streets. Basque nationalist men retorted that the women were acting as mothers, wives and daughters of prisoners; Ugalde, *Mujeres y nacionalismo vasco*, p. 400.
37 Thousands of women were also imprisoned and/or executed, the majority for their support of workers' parties and movements.
38 Jeremy MacClancy, 'At play with identity in the Basque arena', in Sharon Macdonald (ed.), *Inside European Identities: Ethnography in Western Europe* (Oxford: Berg, 1993), p. 87.
39 Sullivan, *ETA and Basque Nationalism*, p. 28.
40 Robert P. Clark, *The Basque Insurgents: ETA, 1952–1980* (Madison: University of Wisconsin Press, 1984), p. 25.
41 For the generation difference between Francoist supporters and their sons, see Barry Jordan, 'The emergence of a dissident intelligentsia', in Graham and Labanyi (eds), *Spanish Cultural Studies*, pp. 245–7.
42 Juan Díez Medrano, *Divided Nations: Class, Politics, and Nationalism in the Basque Country and Catalonia* (Ithaca, NY, and London: Cornell University Press, 1995), p. 130.
43 For the Ekin years, see Clark, *Basque Insurgents*, pp. 24–7; Letamendia Belzunce, *Historia de nacionalismo vasco*, vol. 1, pp. 252–9; and Sullivan, *ETA and Basque Nationalism*, pp. 27–33.
44 Clark, *Basque Insurgents*, p. 26. For a similar argument from a member of the PNV, see Sullivan, *ETA and Basque Nationalism*, p. 33. Zulaika also notes that the schism is often portrayed as the younger men's rejection of the 'cowardly' paternal party, PNV. Zulaika, *Basque Violence*, p. 274.
45 Carrie Hamilton, 'Re-membering the Basque nationalist family: daughters, fathers and the reproduction of the radical nationalist community', *Journal of Spanish Cultural Studies*, 1:2 (autumn 2000), 158–9.
46 Clark, *Basque Insurgents*, p. 162, and Zulaika, *Basque Violence*, pp. 274–75.
47 Kristin Ross, *May '68 and its Afterlives* (Chicago: University of Chicago Press, 2002), p. 204.
48 The *requeté* was the Carlist militia during the Spanish Civil War. Carlism was a traditionalist Catholic movement with its popular base in the rural regions of northern Spain, especially parts of the Basque country and Navarre. The movement emerged in the 1830s in defence of the pretender to the throne, Don Carlos, against liberal reformers in Madrid. During the 1930s Carlism re-emerged as a reactionary political force against the liberalising reforms of the Second Republic. Its base was strongest in Navarre and the rural Basque

regions, explaining the widespread support for the military uprising of July 1936 in Navarre and Alava. For a study of Carlism in Navarre in the twentieth century, see Jeremy MacClancy, *The Decline of Carlism* (Reno: University of Nevada Press, 2000).
49 Leader of the PNV and head of the Basque government from its establishment in October 1936 until his death in 1960. During the Franco regime the PNV-led Basque government was in exile in Paris.
50 The girl later died of her injuries.
51 Sally Alexander, 'Memory, generation and history', in *Becoming a Woman and Other Essays in Nineteenth- and Twentieth-Century Feminist History* (London: Virago, 1994), p. 234.
52 *Ibid.*
53 This slip of the tongue ('reli') suggests that the narrator was thinking of nuns (*religiosas*). But, while some individual nuns may have been nationalists, nuns generally did not play the same pivotal role in the resurgence of Basque nationalism in the 1950s and 1960s as Basque priests. See chapter 2.
54 Andrew Parker *et al.*, 'Introduction' in Parker *et al.* (eds), *Nationalisms and Sexualities* (New York: Routledge, 1992), p. 6.
55 *Ibid.*, pp. 6–7.
56 Ugalde, *Mujeres y nacionalismo vasco*, p. 43.
57 Hamilton, 'Re-membering the Basque nationalism family'.
58 Gilles Deleuze and Félix Guattari, *Anti-Oedipus: Capitalism and Schizophrenia* (London: The Athlone Press, 1984 [1972]).
59 *Ibid.*, p. 97.
60 *Ibid.*
61 Ronald J. Grele, 'Private memories and public presentation: the art of oral history', in Grele *et al.*, *Envelopes of Sound: The Art of Oral History* (New York: Praeger, 2nd edition, 1991), pp. 255–6.
62 *Ibid.*, p. 256.

Chapter 2

1 Miren Alcedo, *Militar en ETA: historias de vida y muerte* (San Sebastián: Haranburu, 1996), p. 108; Robert P. Clark, *The Basque Insurgents: ETA, 1952–1980* (Madison: University of Wisconsin Press, 1984), p. 162, and *The Basques: The Franco Years and Beyond* (Reno: University of Nevada Press, 1979), pp. 120–4; Ander Gurruchaga, *El código nacionalista vasco durante el franquismo* (Barcelona: Anthropos, 1985), p. 311; Francisco Letamendia Belzunce, *Historia del nacionalismo vasco y de ETA*, 3 vols (San Sebastián: R&B Ediciones, 1994), vol.1, pp. 249–50; John Sullivan, *ETA and Basque Nationalism: The Fight for Euskadi 1890–1986* (London: Routledge, 1988), p. 33; and Joseba Zulaika, *Basque Violence: Metaphor and Sacrament* (Reno: University of Nevada Press, 1988), p. 106.

2 Frances Lannon, 'Catholicism and social change' in Helen Graham and Jo Labanyi (eds), *Spanish Cultural Studies: An Introduction* (Oxford: Oxford University Press), pp. 276–82.
3 Amando de Miguel, 'Religiosidad y clericalismo en los jovenes españoles', *Revista del Instituto de la Juventud*, 8 (1966), 67–70.
4 William A. Christian Jr, *Visionaries: The Spanish Republic and the Reign of Christ* (Berkeley and Los Angeles: University of California Press, 1996), pp. 38, 245, and William A. Douglass, *Death in Murélaga: Funeral Ritual in a Spanish Basque Village* (Seattle: University of Washington Press, 1969), pp. 193–5.
5 Zulaika, *Basque Violence*, p. 50.
6 For an outline of Herri Gaztedi's activities, see Paulo Iztueta, *Sociología del fenómeno contestario del clero vasco, 1940–1975* (San Sebastián: Elkar, 1981), pp. 283–93.
7 Zulaika, *Basque Violence*, p. 40.
8 The use of cultural societies as covers for ETA activity was specified in ETA's *Libro blanco*, which outlined the organisation's principles and security policies in the early 1960s. *Documentos Y*, 18 vols (San Sebastián: Hordago, 1979–81), vol. 1, p. 151.
9 *Yoyes: desde su ventana* (Pamplona, 1987), pp. 25–7. For more on Yoyes, see chapter 8.
10 Several narrators claimed that few of the nuns in Basque girls' schools were Basque. According to Father Agirre at the Benedictine monastery in Lazkao, each religious order had its own regulations about transferring members to convents in different regions of Spain. Personal correspondence, June 1998.
11 Frances Lannon, *Privilege, Persecution and Prophecy: The Catholic Church in Spain 1875–1975* (Oxford: Oxford University Press, 1987), p. 58.
12 Christian, *Visionaries*, pp. 33–8.
13 Regular state television broadcasts began in 1956. Aurora G. Morcillo, *True Catholic Womanhood: Gender Ideology in Franco's Spain* (DeKalb: Northern Illinois University Press, 2000), p. 56. Already in the 1930s Basque priests had expressed alarm about the corrupting influences of cinema and new dancing fashions on local youth; Christian, *Visionaries*, p. 38.
14 Morcillo, *True Catholic Womanhood*, pp. 56–63.
15 Jean Franco, 'Going Public', in George Yudice, Jean Franco and Juan Flores (eds), *On Edge: The Crisis of Contemporary Latin American Culture* (Minneapolis and London: University of Minnesota Press, 1992), p. 68.
16 *Ibid.*
17 Clark, *Basque Insurgents*, p. 162; Gurruchaga, *El código nacionalista vasco*, pp. 360–74, 377–8; Letamendia Belzunce, *Historia del nacionalismo vasco*, vol. 1, p. 249; Alfonso Pérez-Agote, *La reproducción del nacionalismo: el caso vasco* (Madrid: Centro de Investigaciones Sociológicas, 1984), pp. 105–10; Sullivan, *ETA and Basque Nationalism*, pp. 33–4; and Cyrus Ernesto Zirakzadeh, *A Rebellious People: Basques, Protests and Politics* (Reno: University of Nevada Press, 1991), p. 149.

18 Jesus Arpal, 'Solidaridades elementales y organizaciones colectivas en el País Vasco (cuadrillas, txokos, asociaciones)', *Euskal Herriko Soziologiazko Ikastaroa*, Cuaderno de Formación 3 (Bilbao: IPES, n.d.), 54–5, and Eugenia Ramírez Goicoechea, 'Cuadrillas en el País Vasco: identidad local y revitalización étnica', *Revista Española de Investigaciones Sociológicas*, 25 (January–March, 1984), 213–20. For a general description of the *cuadrilla*, see Gurruchaga, *El código nacionalista vasco*, pp. 360–74.
19 Arpal, 'Solidaridades', p. 55, and Ramírez Goicoechea, 'Cuadrillas,' p. 214.
20 Arpal, 'Solidaridades', p. 52, and Zulaika, *Basque Violence*, pp. 110–11.
21 Sullivan, *ETA and Basque Nationalism*, pp. 33, 194.
22 See Gregorio Morán, *Los españoles que dejaron de serlo: Euskadi 1937–1982* (Barcelona: Planeta, 1982), pp. 78–9.
23 Alcedo, *Militar en ETA*, p. 108.
24 Ramírez Goicoechea, 'Cuadrillas', pp. 218–19.
25 Clark, *Basque Insurgents*, pp. 156–7.
26 Sharryn Kasmir notes that, during the 1960s in the industrial town of Mondragón, Guipúzcoa, an important centre of both labour and radical nationalist activism, bars were dominated by ethnic Basque men. Kasmir, ' "More Basque than you": class, youth and identity in an industrial Basque town', *Identities*, 9:1 (January–March 2002), 42.
27 Lynda Edgerton, 'Public protest, domestic acquiescence: women in Northern Ireland', in Rosemary Ridd and Helen Callaway (eds), *Caught up in the Conflict: Women's Responses to Political Strife* (London: Macmillan, 1986), p. 74.
28 Kathy Peiss, 'Gender relations and working-class leisure: New York City, 1880–1920', in Carol Gronemon and Mary Beth Norton (eds), *'To Toil the Livelong Day': America's Women at Work, 1780–1980* (Ithaca: Cornell University Press, 1987), p. 102. For other leisure activities among Basque men – including hunting and traditional rural sports – and their implications for the 'us vs them' nationalist model, see Zulaika, *Basque Violence*.
29 For a description of one such all-male ritual, the pre-wedding bachelor party, see Arpal, 'Solidaridades', p. 56.
30 See, for example, the comments of Basque socialist Ramón Jáuregui about his negative experience of the *cuadrilla* in Jon Juaristi, 'Un cadáver en el jardín', in Juan Aranzadi et al., *Auto de terminación* (Madrid: El País/Aguilar, 1994), p. 195.
31 Juan Aranzadi, *Milenarismo vasco: edad de oro, etnia y nativismo* (Madrid: Torres, 2nd edition, 2000), p. 536.
32 In her study of the controversy surrounding women's participation in the annual Alardes (patron festivals) of Hondarribia and Irun in the late 1990s, Margaret Bullen argues that the association of the mock military parade with masculinity must be understood in relation to wider social constructions of masculinity, including through sporting events. She cites the work of Carmen Díez on Basque football, pointing in particular to the following characteristics of initiation and socialisation: 'the marking of the passage from the

domestic world of the home and family to an exclusively male sport domain; the acceptance of masculine authority and insertion in a hierarchical order; the desire for success and approval in the public sphere; the control of the body and mind and resistance to pain as specifically male attributes.' Margaret Bullen, 'Gender and identity in the *Alardes* of two Basque towns' in William A. Douglass *et al.* (eds), *Basque Cultural Studies* (Reno: University of Nevada Basque Studies Program, 1999), p. 177, n. 36. See also Díez, 'Deporte y la construcción de las relaciones de género', *Gazeta de Antropología*, 12 (1996), 93–100. On the Alarde, see also J. P. Linstroth, 'History, tradition, and memory among the Basques', *History and Anthropology*, 13:3 (2002), 159–89. Another area of study in relation to initiation rites and male bonding is the military service most young men would have performed before entering ETA. I am indebted to an earlier reader of the book manuscript for suggesting this point. For a discussion of military service as initiation rite, including its role in reinforcing sexual difference, see Joseba Zulaika, *Chivos y soldados: la mili como ritual de iniciación* (San Sebastián: Baroja, 1989).

33 Helen Graham, 'Gender and the state: women in the 1940s' in Graham and Labanyi (eds), *Spanish Cultural Studies*, p. 182.
34 Anny Brooksbank Jones, *Women in Contemporary Spain* (Manchester: Manchester University Press, 1997), p. 75.
35 Graham, 'Gender and the state,' p. 189.
36 Jones, *Women in Contemporary Spain*, p. 78.
37 Gobierno Vasco, *Situación de la mujer en Euskadi* (1982), pp. 299–318. For Spain generally, see Morcillo, *True Catholic Womanhood*, p. 65.
38 During the 1971–72 academic course year, 3% of the Spanish population were registered at university, 28% of them women; Catherine Matsell, 'Spain' in Joni Lovenduski and Jill Hills (eds), *The Politics of the Second Electorate: Women and Public Participation* (London: Routledge & Kegan Paul, 1981), p. 141. For a discussion of the principle of gender segregation that governed educational legislation under Franco, at primary, secondary and tertiary levels, see Morcillo, *True Catholic Womanhood*.
39 Florencio Domínguez Iribarren, *ETA: estrategia organizativa y actuaciones 1978–1992* (Bilbao: Universidad del País Vasco, 1998), pp. 44–5, and Patxo Unzueta, *Los nietos de la ira* (Madrid: El País/Aguilar, 1988), pp. 63–5.
40 Linda K. Kerber, 'Separate spheres, female worlds, woman's place: the rhetoric of women's history', *Journal of American History*, 75:1 (June 1988), 28. For a discussion of the concept of 'separate spheres' in Spanish women's history, see Victoria Lorée Enders and Pamela Beth Radcliff, 'General introduction: contesting identities/contesting categories' in Enders and Radcliff (eds), *Constructing Spanish Womanhood: Female Identity in Modern Spain* (Albany: State University of New York Press, 1999), pp. 3–4.
41 The importance of paid work outside the home in expanding women's social activities is suggested as well by Sharryn Kasmir's study of the cooperatives of Mondragón, where working-class bars became more mixed in the 1970s

after women began to work in factories and to socialise with male *cuadrillas* in bars after work; Kasmir, 'From the margins: punk rock and the repositioning of ethnicity and gender in Basque identity', in Douglass *et al.* (eds), *Basque Cultural Studies*, p.194, and *The Myth of Mondragón: Cooperatives, Politics and Working-Class Life in a Basque Town* (Albany: State University of New York Press, 1996), p. 81.

42 Letamendia Belzunce, *Historia del nacionalismo vasco*, vol. 1, p. 317, and Sullivan, *ETA and Basque Nationalism*, pp. 27, 38.
43 Clark, *Basque Insurgents*, p. 203; José María Garmendia, *Historia de ETA*, 2 vols (San Sebastián: Haranburu, 1980) vol. 2, pp. 142–3; and Letamendia Belzunce, *Historia del nacionalismo vasco*, vol. 1, p. 374.
44 See the testimonies of the Burgos defendants in Morán, *Los españoles que dejaron de serlo*, pp. 73–95.
45 Letamendia Belzunce, *Historia del nacionalismo vasco*, vol. 1, p. 317.
46 Zulaika, *Basque Violence*, p. 136.
47 Miren Etxezarreta, *El caserío vasco* (Bilbao: Elexpuru Hnos., 1977), p. 168. See also Douglass, *Death in Murélaga*, pp. 109–10, 147–8.
48 See, for example, *Anaitasuna* 128 (1965) and 131 (1966).
49 Clark, *Basque Insurgents*, pp. 32–3.
50 Clark, *The Basques*, pp. 256–63.
51 *Ibid.*, pp. 41–2.
52 Zirakzadeh, *A Rebellious People*, pp. 153–6.
53 *Zutik*, 15 (1961).
54 *Zutik*, 'Especial prensa' (1965).
55 Quoted in Teresa del Valle *et al.*, *Mujer vasca: imagen y realidad* (Barcelona: Anthropos, 1985), p. 235. Full document in Editorial Txalaparta, *Euskadi eta Askatasuna/Euskal Herria y la libertad*, 8 vols (Tafalla: Editorial Txalaparta, 1993), vol. 1, pp. 290–6.
56 *Zutik*, 25 (1964).
57 'Carta a los intelectuales' (2nd edition), Editorial Txalaparta, *Euskadi eta Askatasuna*, vol. 1, p. 295.
58 *Zutik*, 29 (May 1965).
59 Letamendia Belzunce, *Historia del nacionalismo vasco*, vol. 1, p. 300.
60 It is noteworthy that in none of the interviews is the Sección Femenina (SF) mentioned directly, although all of the narrators would have had to perform the compulsory SF social service for women during the Franco period. This silence may indicate that this was simply considered a duty to be performed, and was not accorded importance as a part of narrators' political or social development in contrast to radical nationalist activities. Nonetheless, by not asking directly about SF I may have missed an opportunity to investigate its role in the social and political development of young Basque nationalist women under Franco. For a history of SF's activities during the first two decades of the Franco regime, see Kathleen Richmond, *Women and Spanish Fascism: The Women's Section of the Falange 1934–1959* (London: Routledge, 2003).

61 *Zutik*, 29 (May 1965).
62 *Zutik*, 29 (May 1965). Gurutz Jáuregui Bereciartu, *Ideología y estrategia política de ETA 1959–1968* (Madrid: Siglo XXI, 1981), p. 488.
63 For a discussion of the impact of Third World liberation movements on ETA's development and ideology, see chapter 4.
64 Editorial Txalaparta, *Euskadi eta Askatasuna*, vol. 3, p. 167. The most serious incident occurred at the Aberri Eguna in Irun in 1966, when the Civil Guard opened fire on a group of young people arriving at the event on foot, seriously wounding two teenagers.
65 Cultural work included organising mountain outings where young people could raise the *ikurriña*, folk dance, singing and speaking in *euskera*, preparing cultural newsletters in *euskera*, and sewing *ikurriñas*. Support tasks included making and distributing propaganda, collecting money, making lists of local people who attended certain cultural events and who were sympathetic to the nationalist cause, and hiding people in their homes. Later, those activists who became more directly involved could end up having direct contacts with ETA *liberados* (full-time activists) and were involved in more direct actions, such as painting graffiti on town walls and destroying Francoist monuments, and even looking for and delivering arms.
66 The *ikastola* movement dated from the years of the Second Republic and continued clandestinely in people's homes and churches during the 1940s and 1950s. With the loosening of Francoist legislation against the Basque and Catalan languages by the early 1960s, *ikastolas* gradually became legal; Daniele Conversi, *The Basques, the Catalans and Spain: Alternative Routes to Nationalist Mobilization* (London: Hurst & Company, 1997), p. 104.
67 Del Valle *et al.*, *Mujer vasca*, p. 250. See also Begoña Echeverria, 'Privileging masculinity in the social construction of Basque identity', *Nations and Nationalism*, 7:3 (2001), 339–63, and Teresa del Valle, *Korrika: rituals de la lengua en el espacio* (Barcelona: Anthropos, 1988), pp. 49–64.
68 *Enbata*, 338 (13 Februrary 1975).

Chapter 3

1 See Jean Grugel and Tim Rees, *Franco's Spain* (London: Arnold, 1997), pp. 140–2 and various articles in Helen Graham and Jo Labanyi (eds), *Spanish Cultural Studies: An Introduction* (Oxford: Oxford University Press, 1995), pp. 196–228.
2 Raymond Carr and Juan Pablo Fusi, *Spain: Dictatorship to Democracy* (London: George Allen and Unwin, 1979), pp. 109–10.
3 Juan Pablo Fusi, *Franco: A Biography* (London: Unwin Hyman, 1987), p. 77.
4 Michael Richards, 'Collective memory, the nation-state and post-Franco society', in Barry Jordan and Rikki Morgan-Tamosunas (eds), *Contemporary Spanish Cultural Studies* (London: Arnold, 2000), p. 42.

5 Paul Preston, *The Politics of Revenge: Fascism and the Military in 20th Century Spain* (London: Routledge, 2nd edition, 1995), p. 42.
6 Daniele Conversi, *The Basques, the Catalans and Spain: Alternative Routes to Nationalist Mobilization* (London: Hurst & Company, 1997), p. 104.
7 Anne McClintock, *Imperial Leather: Race, Gender and Sexuality in the Colonial Contest* (New York: Routledge, 1995), pp. 374–5.
8 *Ibid.*, p. 375.
9 *Ibid.*, p. 371.
10 *Documentos Y*, 18 vols (San Sebastián: Hordago), vol. 2, p. 5.
11 For more on radical nationalist rituals see José Manuel Mata López, *El nacionalismo vasco radical* (Bilbao: Universidad del País Vasco, 1993), p. 75.
12 Diana Taylor, *Disappearing Acts: Spectacles of Gender and Nationalism in Argentina's Dirty War* (Durham, NC: Duke University Press, 1997), p. 29.
13 *Ibid.*, p. 9.
14 Joseba Zulaika, *Basque Violence: Metaphor and Sacrament* (Reno: University of Nevada Press, 1988), p. 286.
15 Paul Preston, *The Triumph of Democracy in Spain* (London: Routledge, 1993 [1986]), p. 18.
16 John Sullivan, *ETA and Basque Nationalism: The Fight for Euskadi 1890–1986* (London: Routledge, 1988), pp. 69–70.
17 'El primer mártir de la revolución', *Documentos Y*, vol. 7, p. 484.
18 Richard Dyer, *Stars* (London: British Film Institute, revised edition, 1998), pp. 30–2.
19 *Ibid.*, p. 31.
20 *Ibid.*, p. 32.
21 *Punto y Hora de Euskal Herria*, 518 (June 1988).
22 Miren Alcedo, *Militar en ETA: historias de vida y muerte* (San Sebastián: Haranburu, 1996), p. 133.
23 Luisa Passerini, *Autobiography of a Generation: Italy 1968* (Hanover and London: Wesleyan University Press, 1996), p. 84.
24 *Ibid.*
25 *Ibid.*, p. 81.
26 *Ibid.*, p. 83.
27 *Ibid.*, pp. 99–100.
28 S. N. Eisenstadt, 'Introduction', in Max Weber, *On Charisma and Institution Building* (Chicago and London: University of Chicago Press, 1968), p. xviii.
29 John Horne, 'Masculinity in politics and war in the age of nation-states and world wars, 1850–1950', in Stefan Dudink *et al.* (eds), *Masculinities in Politics and War: Gendering Modern History* (Manchester: Manchester University Press, 2004), p. 30.
30 *Ibid.*
31 *Ibid.*
32 Zulaika, *Basque Violence*, p. 62.
33 Alfonso Pérez-Agote, *La reproducción del nacionalismo: el caso vasco* (Madrid: Centro de Investigaciones Sociológicas, 1984), pp. 116–17.

34 Taylor, *Disappearing Acts*, p. 119.
35 *Ibid.*, p. 121.
36 *El Correo Español* (3 August 1968).
37 Imanol Uribe's 1979 documentary of the trial, *El juicio de Burgos*, is more balanced, including interviews with the female defendants and lawyers.
38 *ABC* (8 December 1970).
39 The reference is to the fact that under Franco demonstrators used Spanish words, including *libertad* (freedom). By the time of the interview in 1996 it was common to use Basque terms (in this case, *askatu*) at political protests. Izco de la Iglesias was the ETA member accused of being the actual killer of Manzanas.
40 *Grises* (greys) was a popular name for the National Police. The security forces have often been identified by radical nationalist activists by the colour of their uniforms – the Civil Guard are called *verdes* (greens) and the riot squads of the Basque police are known as *beltzak* (blacks).
41 *Documentos Y*, vol. 1, p. 5.
42 See Gregorio Morán, *Los españoles que dejaron de serlo: Euskadi 1937–1982* (Barcelona: Planeta, 1982), pp. 73–95.
43 Robert P. Clark, *The Basque Insurgents: ETA, 1952–1980* (Madison: University of Wisconsin Press, 1984), p. 283.

Chapter 4

1 I borrow the term 'homefront heroine' from Mary Nash, ' "Milicianas" and homefront heroines: images of women in revolutionary Spain (1936–1939)', *History of European Ideas*, 11 (1989), 235–44.
2 See epigraph for chapter 2.
3 Federico Krutwig, *Vasconia* (Buenos Aires: Ediciones Norbait, 2nd edition, 1973[1963]).
4 Julen Madariaga *et al.*, 'Insurección en Euskadi', in Editorial Txalaparta, *Euskadi eta Askatasuna/Euskal Herria y la libertad*, 8 vols (Tafalla: Editiorial Txalaparta, 1993), vol. 1, pp. 272–89.
5 Robert P. Clark, *The Basque Insurgents: ETA, 1952–1980* (Madison: University of Wisconsin Press, 1984), p. 34
6 *Ibid.*, p. 45.
7 *Zutik*, 44 (January 1967).
8 Antonio Elorza, 'Some perspectives on the nation-state and Autonomies in Spain', in Helen Graham and Jo Labanyi (eds), *Spanish Cultural Studies: An Introduction* (Oxford: Oxford University Press, 1995), pp. 332–3.
9 According to one early ETA member and Burgos defendant, this was true even in the 1960s. See interview with Teo Uriarte, *Muga*, 17 (1980).
10 Clark, *Basque Insurgents*, p. 133.
11 Cynthia Enloe, *Does Khaki Become You? The Militarization of Women's Lives* (London: Pandora, 1988), and Jean Bethke Elshtain, *Women and War* (Brighton: Harvester Press, 1987).

12 Ilene Rose Feinman, *Citizenship Rites: Feminist Soldiers and Feminist Antimilitarists* (New York and London: New York University Press, 2000).
13 Genevieve Lloyd, 'Selfhood, war and masculinity', in Carole Pateman and Elizabeth Grosz (eds), *Feminist Challenges: Social and Political Theory* (Boston: Northeastern University Press, 1987), p. 75.
14 Klaus Theweleit, *Male Fantasies*, 2 vols (Cambridge: Polity Press, 1987, 1989).
15 Mary Condren, 'Sacrifice and political legitimation: the production of a gendered social order', *Journal of Women's History*, 6:4/7:1 (winter/spring 1995), 166.
16 Nancy Huston, 'The matrix of war: mothers and heroes', in Susan Ruben Suleiman (ed.), *The Female Body in Western Culture: Contemporary Perspectives* (Cambridge, MA and London: Harvard University Press, 1985), p. 127.
17 'Libro blanco' in *Documentos Y*, 18 vols (San Sebastián: Hordago, 1979–81), vol. 1, pp. 151–60.
18 Robert P. Clark, *Basque Insurgents*, p. 161, and Joseba Zulaika, *Basque Violence: Metaphor and Sacrament* (Reno: University of Nevada Press, 1988), p. 90
19 Sarah Benton, 'Women disarmed: the militarization of politics in Ireland 1913–23', *Feminist Review*, 50 (summer 1995), 162.
20 Conversation with narrator #14, b. 1956; June 1996.
21 Benton, 'Women disarmed', pp. 150–1.
22 *Ibid.*, p. 162.
23 *Ibid.*
24 Penny Summerfield, *Reconstructing Women's Wartime Lives* (Manchester: Manchester University Press, 1998), p. 116.
25 My evidence that several male ETA members in the 1970s and 1980s were fathers, and that fatherhood was a source of personal and political support for some, contradicts Zulaika's findings that 'the father figure is totally absent within the ranks of ETA operatives'; Zulaika, *Basque Violence*, p. 274. Zulaika bases his findings on observations of ETA members in his home town of Itziar, Guipúzcoa, and does not consider ETA members in exile in France. My conclusions suggest a need to reconsider Zulaika's claim, as well as his argument that '(f)atherhood seems to clash directly with the charismatic image of the revolutionary who has given up everything for the country' (*ibid.*).
26 See Introduction, n.37.
27 Miren Alcedo, *Militar en ETA: historias de vida y muerte* (San Sebastián: Haranburu, 1996), p. 211.
28 Juan Aranzadi, 'Etnicidad y violencia en el país vasco', in Aranzadi *et al.*, *Auto de terminación* (Madrid: El País/Aguilar, 1994), p. 233.
29 Statistics on the number of ETA members in exile in France vary greatly, and are almost impossible to verify, since many self-designated 'refugees' were illegal. Two lists from 1974 put the numbers at 105 and 150 respectively;

Editorial Txalaparta, *Euskadi eta Askatasuna*, vol. 4, pp. 247–51. By 1979, according to the same publication, there were 450 exiles (vol. 5, p. 80). An article in *Policía Española*, cited in *Egin* (4 January 1981), estimated there were about 200 full-time ETA activists in France. There were also exiles who were members of other illegal radical nationalist organisations and political parties. The number of exiles varied depending on the political situation in Spain. Thus it rose during states of emergency, and dropped with the amnesty of 1976. See the Spanish government's lengthy list of people permitted to return to Spain; Editorial Txalaparta, *Euskadi eta Askatasuna*, vol. 4, pp. 275–89. These numbers do not take into account partners and families, which swelled the exile community considerably. Although Robert Clark suggests that few ETA members carried on a 'normal' married and family life (Clark, *Basque Insurgents*, p. 163), evidence from my narrators indicates that several male ETA members in France in the 1970s had female partners, only a minority of whom were also members of the organisation.

30 See the description of an 'exemplary' exile couple dedicated to the Basque cause – Juan José Etxabe and his wife Agurtzane Arregi, who 'was always ready to help and collaborate'; *Enbata*, 516 (13 July 1978). Arregi was later killed in an attack by far-right gunmen while living in exile.

31 *Enbata*, 591 (20 December 1979).

32 Alfonso Pérez-Agote, *La reproducción del nacionalismo: el caso vasco* (Madrid: Centro de Investigaciones Sociológicas, 1984), p. 195.

33 Benedict Anderson, 'Exodus', *Critical Inquiry*, 20 (winter 1994), 319.

34 Nira Yuval-Davis, *Gender and Nation* (London: Sage, 1997), p. 46. Yuval-Davis insists that there is an important difference between diasporic and exile communities: 'The latter are usually individuals or families who have been part of political struggles in the homeland; their identity and collectivity membership continue to be directed singularly or at least primarily towards there, and they aim to "go back" the moment the political situation changes' (p. 18).

35 The narrator compared this 'man's world' to the Alarde in Irun, a local festival celebrating an historic Basque battle. During the summer of the interview (1996), much media attention focused on debates between local women who tried to take part in the festival's mock military parade and upholders of 'tradition', who defended the exclusion of women. For an analysis of these controversies, see Margaret Bullen, 'Gender and identity in the *Alardes* of two Basque towns' in William A. Douglass *et al.*, *Basque Cultural Studies* (Reno: University of Nevada Basque Studies Program, 1999), pp. 149–77.

36 Another narrator, who spent some time with the ETA exile community in Venezuela in the early 1980s, similarly recalls that 'they were not adapted at all because they were always thinking about Euskadi, thinking about Euskadi, thinking about Euskadi' (#19, b. 1944).

37 Julia Kristeva, *Strangers to Ourselves* (New York and London: Harvester Wheatsheaf, 1991), p. 9.

38 Paul Preston, *The Politics of Revenge: Fascism and the Military in 20th Century Spain* (London: Routledge, 2nd edition, 1995), p. 42.
39 *Hautsi*, 7 (October 1975). For a study women's roles in the funerals of ETA militants, see Begoña Aretxaga, *Los funerales en el nacionalismo radical vasco* (San Sebastián: Baroja, 1988).
40 *Enbata*, 624 (August 1980). According to Robert Clark, Otaegi's mother, like the families of many ETA activists of his generation, did not support his joining the organization; Clark, *Basque Insurgents*, p. 156.
41 For example, the first anniversary of the assassination of José Miguel Beñorán Ordenaña, 'Argala', a prominent ETA(m) leader killed by far-right paramilitaries in France in 1978, was marked in the radical nationalist newspaper *Egin* with a feature interview with his mother. Sitting in her kitchen surrounded by photos of her dead son, preparing lunch for her other children, Argala's mother reportedly declared: 'He wouldn't even be able to order the killing of his own killers'; *Egin* (21 December 1979). A similar interview following the death of another activist in 1981, announced: ' "Gogor" is not a thug.' Accompanied by photos of smiling mother and son in embrace, and the mother's description of him as loving, caring and good with children, the article proclaimed, 'His mother's commentaries are incontestable'; *Punto y Hora de Euskal Herria*, 240 (23–30 October 1981).
42 'Arrasateko Herriak Euskadi Osoari', November 1978.
43 Lloyd, 'Selfhood, war and masculinity,' p. 76.
44 *Deia* (2 September 1977 and 20–24 January 1978). Soon afterwards, Apala himself escaped and disappeared. For further details of the Apala/Pertur affair, see Clark, *Basque Insurgents*, pp. 92–3.
45 *ABC* (3 December 1970), *La Gaceta del Norte* (9 April 1976) and *Cambio 16*, 338 (28 May 1978).
46 For a description of the fear experienced by families of Spanish police stationed in the Basque country, see *Interviu*, 217 (10–16 July 1980). There were cases of wives of the national police protesting the transfer of their husbands to the Basque country; Gestoras pro-amnistía, 'Relato diario de acontecimientos' (n.d.), p. 11.
47 During most of the 1970s, ETA's primary targets were the Spanish police and military, and consequently female victims were exceptional. There were at least two cases in which the organisation killed the female companions of members of the security forces who were the main targets (*Egin* [7 and10 October 1979 and 23 March 1982]), and one female police officer was killed in a shootout (*Zuzen*, 10 [July 1981]). During the 1970s there was only one case of ETA deliberately targeting a woman – the attempted assassination of the former Francoist mayor of Bilbao, Pilar Careaga (*Egin* [28 March 1979]). The proportion of female victims rose in the 1980s and 1990s as ETA targeted more politicians and civilians, in particular in bomb attacks. According to data from the Association of the Victims of Terrorism between June 1968 and June 1998, ETA killed 809 people – 746 males, 60 females and 3 'unborns'. Among these were 338 civilians, 199 Civil Guards, 175

police officers and 97 soldiers (*ABC* [7 June 1998]). For a full list of ETA's female victims to 1986, see *El País* (11 September 1986).

48 The limited data available on popular support for radical nationalism in the 1970s suggest that gender was not as important as class and ethnicity in determining votes for radical nationalist parties; Juan Linz, *Conflicto en Euskadi* (Madrid: Espasa Calpe, 1986), pp. 573–5. For a discussion of the difficulties in measuring voter support for ETA, see William A. Douglass and Joseba Zulaika, 'On the interpretation of terrorist violence: ETA and the Basque political process', *Comparative Studies in History and Society*, 32:2 (1990), 238–57.
49 *Cambio 16*, 576 (13 December 1982).
50 Condren, 'Sacrifice and political legitimation', p. 177.

Chapter 5

1 Editorial Txalaparta, *Euskadi eta Askatasuna/Euskal Herria y la libertad*, 8 vols (Tafalla: Editional Txalaparta, 1993), vol. 1, p. 297.
2 Two of these women, Arantza Arruti and Jone Dorronsoro, were eventually arrested and tried at Burgos in 1970. The third, María Asunción Goenaga, left ETA soon after going into exile in 1969. A fourth woman in ETA, Itziar Aizpurua, was also tried and sentenced at Burgos.
3 The case of Yoyes, who left ETA in 1979 and was killed by her former comrades in 1986, will be discussed in chapter 8.
4 Joseba Zulaika, *Basque Violence: Metaphor and Sacrament* (Reno: University of Nevada Press, 1988), p. 182.
5 Fernando Reinares, *Patriotas de la muerte: quienes han militado en ETA y por qué* (Madrid: Taurus, 2001), p. 21.
6 Alcedo dedicates a short chapter to interviews with former female activists; Miren Alcedo, *Militar en ETA: historias de vida y muerte* (San Sebastián: Haranburu, 1996), pp. 353–66.
7 Reinares, *Patriotas de la muerte*, pp. 21, 150. See also Florencio Domínguez Iribarren, *ETA: Estrategia organizativa y actuaciones 1978–1992* (Bilbao: Universidad del País Vasco, 1998), p. 23.
8 Robin Morgan, *The Demon Lover: The Roots of Terrorism* (London: Piatkus, 2001 [1989]), p. xviii.
9 *Ibid.*, p. 204.
10 Reinares, *Patriotas de la muerte*, pp. 20–1.
11 Morgan, *Demon Lover*, p. 214.
12 *El Correo Español* (1 August 1970).
13 *La Gaceta del Norte* (29 October 1975).
14 *El Correo Español* (6 March 1973).
15 See interviews with Burgos defendant Itziar Aizpurua, Editorial Txalaparta, *Euskadi eta Askatasuna*, vol. 3, p. 172, and *Egin* (6 August and 22 November 1980, 7 February 1981).
16 *Egin* (26 September 1981).

17 Frantz Fanon, *Studies in a Dying Colonialism* (London: Earthscan Publications, 1989 [1965]).
18 *Hitz*, 4 (August 1975). See also the example of Mikel Lejarza (Lobo), who infiltrated ETA in the 1970s and claimed that being paired with a female activist aided their mission because they could pass as a couple; Manuel Cerdán and Antonio Rubio, *Lobo: un topo en las entrañas de ETA* (Barcelona: Plaza & Janés, 2003), pp. 41–2.
19 *Egin* (26 April 1983).
20 *Deia* (25 April 1983). The contrast between González and the supposedly stupid police officer relies on an ethnocentric depiction of southern Spanish masculinity as personified by members of the security forces. An important area of future research is the relationship between gender and constructions of Basque and Spanish ethnicity.
21 Cameron Watson, 'Imagining ETA', in William A. Douglass *et al.* (eds), *Basque Politics and Nationalism on the Eve of the Millennium* (Reno: University of Nevada Basque Studies Program, 1999), pp. 102.
22 *Ibid.*, p. 101.
23 *Ibid.*
24 Paula Schwartz argues in her study of partisans in the French Resistance that 'it was commonly recognized that of all resisters, they had the best disguises: they were women!': '*Partisanes* and gender politics in Vichy France', *French Historical Studies*, 16:1 (spring 1989), 131.
25 *ABC* (7 January 1969). Arruti was married to the male ETA member mentioned in the article, but other evidence indicates they entered the organisation separately and met inside (personal communications, 1996).
26 These images, with their focus on women's supposedly deviant sexuality, are strikingly similar to media representations of female armed activists elsewhere in the 1970s and 1980s. See, for example, Ulrike Hanna Meinhof, 'Revolting women: subversion and its media representations in West Germany and Britain', in Sîan Reynolds (ed.), *Women, State and Revolution: Essays on Power and Gender in Europe since 1789* (Brighton: Wheatshaft Books, 1986), pp. 141–60.
27 *Interviu*, 156 (10–16 May 1979).
28 *Cambio 16*, 576 (13 December 1982).
29 This press coverage of women in ETA was part of a wider media fascination with armed women in these years. In the late 1970s, the same period in which ETA's violent actions attracted constant attention from the newly democratic Spanish press, magazines such as the self-consciously risqué current affairs weekly *Interviu* ran stories on women guerrillas in the Middle East, female soldiers in the American army, and even an Italian 'terrorist' grandmother, as well as pin-up spreads with semi-nude models posing as combat women; *Interviu*, 222 (14–20 August 1980), 224 (28 August – 3 September, 1980), 232 (23–29 October 1980) and 220 (31 July–6 August 1980), 71–3.
30 Alcedo, *Militar en ETA*, p. 360.

31 See, for example, H. H. A. Cooper, 'Woman as terrorist', in Freda Adler and Rita James Simon (eds), *The Criminology of Deviant Women* (Boston: Houghton Mifflin Company, 1979), pp. 150–7, and Mike Benson, Mariah Evans and Rita Simon, 'Women as political terrorists', *Law, Deviance and Social Control*, 4 (1982), 121–30.

32 Ineke Haen Marshall, Vincent Webb and Dennis Hoffman, 'A review of explicit and implicit propositions about women as terrorists', *Resources for Feminist Research*, 14:4 (1986), 22. For further critique of this literature, see Rhiannon Talbot, 'Myths in the representation of women terrorists', *Eire-Ireland*, 35 (autumn/winter 2000/01), 165–86, and Gilda Zwerman, 'Conservative and feminist images of women associated with armed, clandestine organizations in the United States', *International Social Movement Research*, 4 (1992), 133–59.

33 Miren Alcedo, 'Mujeres de ETA: la cuestión del género en la clandestinidad', *La Factoria*, 4 (October 1997); Eileen MacDonald, *Shoot the Women First* (London: Arrow, 1991), pp. 35–6; and Gilda Zwerman, 'Mothering on the lam: politics, gender fantasies and maternal thinking in women associated with armed, clandestine organizations in the United States', *Feminist Review*, 47 (summer 1994), 41.

34 Ronald J. Grele, 'Private memories and public presentation: the art of oral history', in Grele et al., *Envelopes of Sound: The Art of Oral History* (New York: Praeger, 2nd edition, 1991), p. 255.

35 Luisa Passerini, 'Lacerations in the memory: women in the Italian underground organizations,' *International Social Movement Research*, 4 (1992), 176.

36 *Ibid.*, 175.

37 Luisa Passerini, *Fascism in Popular Memory* (Cambridge: Cambridge University Press, 1987), pp. 27–8.

38 Morgan, *Demon Lover*, p. 214.

39 Cameron Watson makes the interesting suggestion that, because the Franco regime excluded both Basques and women from the status of full subjects, 'for many Basque women [including ETA members] . . . a rebellion against the condition of passive womanhood was, in fact, a rebellion against the condition of being Spanish itself'; Cameron Watson, 'The tragedy of Yoyes' in Cameron Watson and Linda White (eds), *Amatxu, Amuma, Amona: Writings in Honor of Basque Women* (Reno, NV: Centre for Basque Studies, 2003), p 138.

40 *Interviu*, 156 (10–16 May 1979). See also the comments of Burgos defendant Arantza Arruti in *Punto y Hora de Euskal Herria*, 518 (June 1988), and interviews with former female activists in Alcedo, *Militar en ETA*, pp. 353–66, and Teresa del Valle et al., *Mujer vasca: imagen y realidad* (Barcelona: Anthropos, 1985), p. 246.

41 *Pipa* means 'pipe', and is slang in Spanish for 'gun'.

42 *Cambio 16*, 576 (13 December 1982).

43 Zwerman, 'Mothering on the lam', p. 44.

44 Zwerman, 'Conservative and feminist images', p. 147.
45 Zwerman, 'Mothering on the lam', pp. 34–5.
46 *Ibid.*, p. 54.
47 *Ibid.*, p. 45; Zwerman, 'Conservative and feminist images', p. 151.
48 Zwerman, 'Mothering on the lam', pp. 51–2.
49 This situation has changed over the past two decades, during which time there have been cases of women activists with children being arrested. See chapter 8.
50 Passerini, *Fascism*, p. 27.
51 Zwerman, 'Mothering on the lam', p. 44.
52 For example, Alcedo claims that women who take up arms 'imitate the most external, and perhaps roughest, elements of manly behaviour';. *Militar en ETA*, p. 355. But she does not cite any specific examples of this behaviour, and the claim is unsubstantiated in the stories of her own female interviewees.
53 Anna Krylova, 'Stalinist identity from the viewpoint of gender: rearing a generation of professionally violent women-fighters in 1930s Stalinist Russia' in Shani D'Cruze and Anupama Rao (eds), *Violence, Vulnerability and Embodiment* (Oxford: Blackwell, 2005), pp. 151–2.
54 Zwerman, 'Mothering on the lam', p. 54.
55 *Ibid.*, p. 48.

Chapter 6

1 Miren Alcedo, *Militar en ETA: historias de vida y muerte* (San Sebastián: Haranburu, 1996), p. 285.
2 *Ibid.*, pp. 285–6, 296.
3 *Punto y Hora de Euskal Herria*, 257 (12–19 March 1982). See also the cover of *Berriak* 13 (8 December 1976).
4 Gestoras pro-amnistía, *Euskadi 1977–1987: 10 años de represión* (1987).
5 Gestoras pro-amnistía, 'Alemaniado egoera' (1979).
6 'Mujer joven y cuestión nacional', *Euskadiko Emakume Gazteen Topaketak* (Orio: October 1986).
7 Gestoras pro-amnistía, *Euskadi 1977–1987* and *Euskadi Torturaren Aurka* (1987).
8 See Appendix 2.
9 *Ibid.*
10 Comisión Gestora pro-amnistía de Nabarra, *Boletín*, 9 (20 December 1978).
11 Puerto de Santa María, a coastal town in Andalucía, southern Spain, has a prison where ETA prisoners are still held at the time of writing. Santoña was the city in Santander where Basque soldiers surrendered to Franco's Italian allies in the summer of 1937.
12 *Egin* (22 September 1978).
13 *Egin* (20 December 1980) and *Punto y Hora de Euskal Herria*, 255 (26 February–6 March 1982).

14 For a discussion of 'militant motherhood' in twentieth-century Latin America, see Nikki Craske, *Women and Politics in Latin America* (Cambridge: Polity Press, 1999).
15 Diana Taylor, *Disappearing Acts: Spectacles of Gender and Nationalism in Argentina's Dirty War* (Durham, NC: Duke University Press, 1997), pp. 184–5.
16 Suzann Buckley and Pamela Lonergan, 'Women and the Troubles, 1969–1980', in Yonah Alexander and Alexander O'Day (eds), *Terrorism in Ireland* (Aldershot: Croom Helm, 1984), p. 84.
17 Mujeres KAS, 'Con respecto al hombre', *¿Es necesario una organización de mujeres?*, n.d., p. 3.
18 For a study of Spanish women prisoners in the early Franco period, see Fernando Hernández Holgado, *Mujeres encarceladas: en la prisión de Ventas: de la República al franquismo, 1931–1941* (Madrid: Marcial Pons, 2003).
19 For a brief discussion of these debates in the US context, see Ann Cvetkovich, *An Archive of Feelings: Trauma, Sexuality and Lesbian Public Cultures* (Durham, NC: Duke University Press, 2003), pp. 33–4 and especially p. 295, n. 35.
20 For the controversy surrounding the *testimonio* of Nobel prize-winner Rigoberta Menchú, see Arturo Arias (ed.), *The Rigoberta Menchú Controversy* (London: University of Minnesota Press, 2001), and David Stoll, *Rigoberta Menchú and the Story of All Poor Guatemalans* (Boulder, CO and Oxford: Westview Press, 1999).
21 *Euskadi: el último estado de excepción de Franco* (Chatillon-sous-Bagneux: Ruedo Ibérico, 1975); Justo de la Cueva *et al.*, *Tortura y sociedad* (Madrid: Editorial Revolución, 1982); and *La tortura en Euskadi* (Madrid: Editorial Revolución, 1986).
22 Elaine Scarry, *The Body in Pain: The Making and Unmaking of the World* (New York and Oxford: Oxford University Press, 1985), p. 35. The staged character of torture is suggested by Scarry's description of similarities in torture methods and language used by different authoritarian regimes during the twentieth century (p. 40). For another analysis of torture as a spectacle staged by the torturers, see Taylor, *Disappearing Acts*, p. 99.
23 See one woman's testimony in *Egin* (3 May 1980).
24 Gestoras pro-amnistía, *Euskadi 1977–1987*.
25 *Egin* (1 November 1979).
26 *Egin* (3 January 1981).
27 *Interviu* (22 (May 1980).
28 Various testimonies in Aizan agendas 1986 and 1988; Aizan, 'Tema: Tortura específica', n.d., and Egizan, 'Emakumea eta tortura', c. 1992.
29 Eva Forest (ed.), *Testimonios de lucha y resistencia: en la prisión de Yeserías* (Hendaye: Mugalde, 1977).
30 Eva Forest, 'Mujer y tortura', LAB, n.d.
31 *Ibid.*

32 Interview with Itziar Aizpurua, *Egin* (16 February 1997). See also the comments of one former ETA(m) male prisoner in Alcedo, *Militar en ETA*, pp. 292–3.
33 Thanks to Anna Davin for suggesting these points to me.
34 Begoña Aretxaga, *Shattering Silence: Women, Nationalism and Political Subjectivity in Northern Ireland* (Princeton, NJ: Princeton University Press, 1997), pp. 48–50, 105–21.
35 Nancy Caro Hollander, 'The gendering of human rights: women and the Latin American terrorist state', *Feminist Studies*, 22:1 (spring 1996), 70. See also Jean Franco, 'Gender, death, and resistance: facing the ethical vacuum', in Juan E. Corradi, Patricia Weiss Fagen and Manuel Antonio Garretón (eds), *Fear at the Edge: State Terror and Resistance in Latin America* (Berkeley: University of California Press, 1992), pp. 111–12. In using examples from Latin America I do not claim either that the forms of torture experienced there and by Basque women were the same, or that the political contexts were identical. However, given the similarities (including military regimes and some shared cultural heritage, such as Catholicism), the work on gender and torture in Latin America is helpful for an analysis of Basque prisoners in Spain.
36 There was no purging of the Francoist security forces during – or following – the transition to democracy, so many of the police officers involved in the arrest and torture of political prisoners from the mid-1970s to the early 1980s would have been trained under the military regime.
37 In François Maspero, *Batasuna: la répression au pays basque* (Paris: Cahiers Libres, 1970), pp. 76–7.
38 Other women arrested during the same period denounced the treatment they received at the hands of the police, who allegedly insulted them 'as women and even as mothers'; *Egin* (3 November 1981).
39 Forest, 'Mujer y tortura', and de la Cueva *et al.*, *Tortura y sociedad*, p. 207. An understanding of the sexual power relations involved in the torture of political prisoners in Spain at this time would require analysis of men's torture testimonies as well as those of women. For an example of such analysis in the case of the Argentine junta, see Taylor, *Disappearing Acts*, chapter 6. See also Franco, 'Gender, death and resistance', p. 109.
40 Taylor, *Disappearing Acts*, pp. 152–3. On the victim as a body to be penetrated, see also Franco, 'Gender, death and resistance', p. 108. Taylor refers to a Latin American model of male homosexuality, in which the partner defined as 'active' (i.e. the one who penetrates) retains his masculine identity and therefore socially sanctioned status as heterosexual male, whereas the 'passive', penetrated partner is stigmatised and marginalised as effeminate and gay. On a wider cultural level this model fits with studies of the 'Mediterranean' model of homosexuality. See Alberto Mira, 'Laws of silence: homosexual identity and visibility in contemporary Spanish culture', in Barry Jordan and Rikki Morgan-Tamosunas, *Contemporary Spanish Cultural Studies* (London: Arnold, 2000), pp. 241–50. I am not

making any sociological claims about male homosexual practice in Spain and Latin America; rather, I suggest that the active/passive model associated with Latin and Mediterranean cultures fits with wider national discourses in Franco (and to some extent post-Franco) Spain that allied masculinity with national strength and military victory, and femininity with passivity, vulnerability and military defeat (being conquered), which are helpful in turn for an analysis of the torture situation. For a discussion of gender constructions and metaphors of violation in Francoist historical discourse, see Maria Escudero, ' "Cortes and Marina": gender and the reconquest of America under the Franco regime', in Victoria Enders Lorée and Pamela Beth Radcliff (eds), *Constructing Spanish Womanhood: Female Identity in Modern Spain* (Albany: State University of New York Press, 1999), pp. 71–93.

41 Temma Kaplan, 'Reversing the shame and gendering the memory', *Signs*, 28:1 (2002), 179–99.
42 Franco, 'Gender, death and resistance', p. 104, and Scarry, *The Body in Pain*, p. 29.
43 Alcedo, *Militar en ETA*, p. 322.
44 Conversation with narrator #14, June 1996.
45 See, for example, Alcedo, *Militar en ETA*, p. 286.
46 Untaped post-interview conversation with narrator #10.
47 See also interview with Itziar Aizpurua, Editorial Txalaparta, *Euskadi eta Askatasuna/Euskal Herria y la libertad*, 8 vols (Tafalla: Editorial Txalaparta, 1993), vol. 3, p. 172.
48 *Hautsi*, 4 (September–October 1973).
49 Begoña Aretxaga, *Los funerales en el nacionalismo radical vasco* (San Sebastián: Baroja, 1988), p. 73.
50 See Appendix 2.
51 Comuna de ETA-m de Yeserías, 'Compañero/as de la Gestora pro-amnistía' (Madrid, 1 August 1982).
52 Conversation with narrator #14, June 1996. Itziar Aizpurua similarly recalls learning a great deal from communist prisoners; Editorial Txalaparta, *Euskadi eta Askatasuna*, vol. 3, p. 173.
53 Basauri is a prison in greater Bilbao where ETA prisoners were sometimes kept while awaiting trial.
54 The sale of contraceptives was legalised in Spain in 1978. In the previous year the Basque gay rights organisation EHGAM was founded. Various short-lived lesbian organisations were formed during the same period.
55 GRAPO (Grupo Revolucionario Anti-fascista Primero de Octubre), an armed organisation attached to a dissident Spanish communist party, the PCEr, was formed in 1975. For a history of GRAPO, including the roles of female activists, see Rafael Gómez Parra, *GRAPO: los hijos de Mao* (Madrid: Fundamentos, 1991).
56 Narrator #14 had similar memories of the GRAPO prisoners, untaped conversation, June 1996.

57 See chapter 5.
58 *Punto y Hora de Euskal Herria*, 257 (12–19 March 1982).

Chapter 7

1 As regards previously colonial regions, where many nationalist movements developed in direct opposition to European rule, feminist scholars have highlighted the potentially liberating nature of nationalist movements for women; Valentine M. Moghadam, 'Introduction and overview: gender dynamics of nationalism, revolution and Islamization', in Valentine Moghadam (ed.), *Gender and National Identity: Women and Politics in Muslim Societies* (London: Zed Books, 1994), p. 3.
2 Gisela Kaplan, 'Feminism and nationalism: the European case', in Lois A. West (ed.), *Feminist Nationalism* (New York and London: Routledge, 1997), p. 3.
3 Mary Condren, 'Sacrifice and political legitimation: the production of a gendered social order', *Journal of Women's History*, 6:4/7:1 (winter/spring 1995), 175.
4 Lois A. West, 'Introduction: feminism constructs nationalism', in West (ed.), *Feminist Nationalism*, p. xxx.
5 Ann Cvetkovich, *An Archive of Feelings: Trauma, Sexuality and Lesbian Public Cultures* (Durham, NC: Duke University Press, 2003), p. 230.
6 For women and feminism under Franco, see Mercedes Carbayo-Abengozar, 'Feminism in Spain: a history of love and hate', in Lesley Twomey (ed.), *Women in Contemporary Culture: Roles and Identities in France and Spain* (Bristol: Intellect, 2000), pp. 111–25, and Pilar folguera Crespo, 'El franquismo: el retorno a la esfera privada (1939–1975)', in Elisa Garrido (ed.), *Historia de las mujeres en España* (Madrid: Editorial Síntesis, 1997), pp. 527–48.
7 For the Spanish women's movement, see María Angeles Durán and María Teresa Gallego, 'The women's movement in Spain and the new Spanish democracy', in Drude Dahlerup (ed.), *The New Women's Movement: Feminism and Political Power in Europe and the USA* (London: Sage, 1986), pp. 200–16; Pilar Folguera (ed.), *El feminismo en España: dos siglos de su historia* (Madrid: Pablo Iglesias, 1988); Anny Brooksbank Jones, *Women in Contemporary Spain* (Manchester: Manchester University Press, 1997); Amparo Moreno, *Mujeres en la lucha: el movimiento feminista en España* (Barcelona: Anagrama, 1977); Neus Moreno and Montserrat Cervera, 'Algunas reflexiones sobre los 10 años de lucha feminista en el Estado Español (1975–1985)', in *Jornadas – 10 años de lucha del movimiento feminista* (Barcelona, 1–3 November 1985), pp. 65–71; Geraldine M. Scanlon, *La polémica feminista en la España contemporánea 1868–1974* (Madrid: Akal, 1976); Monica Threlfall, 'The women's movement in Spain', *New Left Review*, 151 (1985), 44–73, and 'Feminist politics and social change in Spain', in Monica Threlfall (ed.), *Mapping the Movement: Feminist Politics*

and Social Transformation in the North (London and New York: Verso, 1996), pp. 115–51.
8 Moreno, *Mujeres en la lucha*, pp. 71–3.
9 In the first democratic elections held in June 1977 women made up 13 per cent of candidates and were elected to 6 per cent of parliamentary seats. In 1979 the numbers were similar, and in 1982, with the election of the Socialist Party, the percentage of seats held by women rose to 11 per cent; Pilar Folguera, 'De la transición política a la democracia: la evolución del feminismo en España durante el periodo 1975–1988', in Folguera (ed.), *El feminismo*, p. 118.
10 Paul Preston, *The Triumph of Democracy in Spain* (London: Routledge, 1993 [1986]), p. 160, n. 17.
11 The PNV supported the autonomy statute, which gave a degree of administrative devolution to a new Basque regional government. The new 'Basque Autonomous Community' included the provinces of Vizcaya, Guipúzcoa and Alava. Radical nationalists opposed it on the grounds that it excluded the province of Navarre and fell far short of their ultimate aim of total independence.
12 For the history of the Basque women's movement, see Carmen Pérez Pérez, 'Historia y actualidad del movimiento feminista en Euskadi', *Inguruak* (December 1987), 53–9; *Berriak* (September 1976), 31–41; and *Egin* (8 October 1977).
13 There has never been a feminist organisation inside the PNV. In the past two decades the PNV-led Basque government has begun to address women's issues through its Women's Institute, Emakunde, founded in 1988. See Arantxa Elizondo and Eva Martínez, 'Presencia de mujeres y políticas para la Igualdad entre los sexos: el caso de las instituciones políticas vascas', *Revista de Estudios Políticos*, 89 (1995), 345–68, and Garbiñe Mendizabal and Esther Ortíz de Pinedo, 'El movimiento feminista y las políticas públicas de la igualdad', *Inguruak*, 13 (1995), 61–78.
14 *Euskadiko Emakumeen Lehenengo Topaketak/Jornadas de la mujer de Euskadi/Rencontre des femmes d'Euskadi* (Lejona, 1977).
15 'Manifiesto inicial de la Asamblea de Mujeres de Vizcaya', in Moreno, *Mujeres en la lucha*, pp. 173–9.
16 In 1974 the group Emazteak Iraultzan (Women in Revolution) was founded in Bayonne, followed by EEBAA (Euskal Emazteak Beren Askatasunaren Alde – Basque Women for Their Freedom). Aizan, 'Un análisis y una propuesta en la lucha feminista de Euskadi', Asambleas de Mujeres de Euskadi y Aizan, *Ponencias de las II Jornadas Feministas de Euskadi (1984)* (Bilbao, 1986), pp. 243–4; Aizan, 'Historia del Movimiento Feminista en Euskadi y su situación actual', n.d.; 'Emazteak mugimenduan,' *Ateka*, 5 (February 1984), 12–13; 'Feminismo e izquierda abertzale en Hego Euskal Herria', *Ezpala*, 0 (1996), 30; and Nekane Jurado, 'Mujer vasca: aportación oculta a la economía', in Miguel Angel Barencilla et al., *La mujer en Euskal Herria: hacía un feminismo propio* (San Sebastián: Basandere Argitaletxea, 2001), p. 163.

17 Conversation with former members of Euskal Emakumeak Borrokan (Basque Women in Struggle), June 1996. The Borrokan group never had official links to any radical nationalist organisation and was eventually absorbed into the Women's Assembly of Guipúzcoa. In Alava there was an Association of Abertzale Women, and in Vizcaya 'Oihuka' (Bizkaiko Emakume Abertzaleen Taldea – Vizcayan Abertzale Women's Group); Aizan, 'Un análisis y una propuesta', p. 244; *Berriak* (September 1976), and *Punto y Hora de Euskal Herria*, 147 (18–25 October 1979) and 165 (8–13 March 1980).

18 LAIAko emakumeak, 'Hacia un debate sobre la opresión de la mujer', n.d. LAIA (Langile Abertzale Iraultzalean Alderdia – Nationalist Revolutionary Workers' Party) was founded in 1974 following a split in ETA's Workers' Front. HASI (Herriko Alderdi Sozialista Iraultzalea – Popular Revolutionary Socialist Party) grew out of EHAS (Eusko Herriko Alderdi Sozialista – Basque Popular Worker's Party), which in turn came from a break with ETA's Cultural Front in 1974. In 1977 EHAS changed its name to HASI. Both LAIA and HASI were among the founding parties of Herri Batasuna, the radical nationalist electoral coalition close to ETA-militar, formed in 1978.

19 Conversation with three former members of the HASI women's group, March 1997. The group disbanded following the political crisis within HASI and KAS in 1980. For a description of the crisis see Francisco Letamendia Belzunce, *Historia del nacionalismo vasco y de ETA*, 3 vols (San Sebastián: R&B Ediciones, 1994), vol. 2, pp. 371–87. In addition, in 1979 a group of women in Herri Batasuna came together to discuss the lack of attention to women's issues and the low number of women candidates; cassette 'Mujeres HB 1979'. There were also feminist initiatives in the ETA(pm) camp; 'Aportaciones para la Asamblea de Mujeres del Partido' (San Sebastián, 1–2 September 1980), and *Hitz*, 15 (c. 1981) and 18 (c. 1982).

20 KAS (Koordinadora Abertzale Sozialista – Socialist Nationalist Coordinating Committee) was formed in 1975, and by the late 1970s was the umbrella organisation for various political groups in the ETA-militar faction, including ETA(m) itself.

21 Aizan, 'Un análisis y una propuesta', in Asambleas de Mujeres de Euskadi y Aizan, *Ponencias de las II Jornadas Feministas de Euskadi (1984)*, p. 244.

22 Untaped conversation with narrator #9 (b. 1958), March 1997.

23 #10, b. 1957; conversations with Mujeres Borrokan (June 1996) and former members of HASI women (March 1997), and MCE/EMK, 'Boletín especial: feminismo', *Kongresua* 2 (December 1982).

24 Notwithstanding its name, and the fact that there existed personal and political contacts at local and provincial levels between KAS Emakumeak and various other groups in KAS, the women's organisation was never officially integrated into the structure of KAS itself (#9, b. 1958).

25 *Zuzen*, 6 (March 1981).

26 *Zutabe*, 22 (1980).

27 Robert P. Clark, *The Basque Insurgents: ETA, 1952–1980* (Madison: University of Wisconsin Press, 1984), p. 33.
28 Mercedes Ugalde Solano, 'The discourse of gender and the Basque nationalist movement in the first third of the 20th century', *History of European Ideas*, 15:4–6 (1992), 697.
29 *Punto y Hora de Euskal Herria*, 245 (15–21 October 1981).
30 Abortion was not legalised until 1985, by the Socialist administration, and then only under limited circumstances (rape, damage to the foetus, or a serious threat to the mother's health). See Jones, *Women in Contemporary Spain*, p. 86.
31 One report estimated that as many as 3,000 Spanish women died annually as a result of illegal botched abortions in the years following Franco's death. *Cambio 16*, 413 (November 1979). The same article calculated that 300,000 Spanish women had abortions annually, including 13,000 who went to London in 1978 alone. See also *Punto y Hora de Euskal Herria*, 120 (12–19 April 1979), and *Sugarra*, 14 (1979). Spanish feminist Lidia Falcón estimated that up to 30% of women in Spanish prisons in this period were serving sentences related to abortion offences; Gisela Kaplan, *Contemporary Western European Feminism* (London: UCL Press Limited, 1992), p. 202.
32 Catherine Matsell, 'Spain', in Joni Lovenduski and Jill Hills (eds), *The Politics of the Second Electorate: Women and Public Participation* (London: Routledge & Kegan Paul, 1981), p. 147.
33 For KAS Emakumeak demands on abortion, see *Mujeres KAS* (16 June 1981).
34 The publicity accorded the trial prompted debates over abortion in municipal governments throughout the Basque country. The trial was followed all over Spain and Europe, solidarity committees were set up in France, Switzerland, Belgium, the Netherlands and Canada (*Sugarra* 15 [December 1979]) and foreign women were among those arrested in actions such as the occupation of Bilbao city hall (*Egin* [21 October 1979]). The French feminist review *des femmes en mouvement hebdo* covered the trial in detail. See the supplement to the first issue (26 October 1979).
35 Juan José Andrés and José Antonio Maisutxe, *El movimiento cuidadano en Euskadi* (San Sebastián: Txertoa, 1980), p. 97. The Basque mainstream, left-wing and radical nationalist press covered the trial and protests, as did the newsletters and journals of radical nationalist and far-left parties. For an example of celebrating the female defendants as a working-class challenge to the bourgeois State, see *Sugarra*, 14 (1979).
36 *Zuzen*, 3 (December 1980), and *Punto y Hora de Euskal Herria*, 201 (13–20 November 1980).
37 *Egin* (26 March 1982).
38 On 9 January 1980, Ana Tere Barrueta was raped and murdered in San Sebastián while on the way home from a Basque language class. On 13 January two young women were raped at gunpoint by a pair of men who allegedly asked their victims if they (the attackers) looked like members of a

far-right gang. On 13 April a young woman was raped at gunpoint in the coastal town of Bermeo, reportedly by a member of the Civil Guard, and finally on 8 May 16-year-old María José Bravo was kidnapped, raped and murdered in San Sebastián; Gestoras pro-amnistía, 'Relato diario de acontecimientos: detenciones, torturas, manifestaciones (1975–1980)'.
39 The rapes and murders were covered by the Basque mainstream, left-wing and radical nationalist press, and received some international coverage; *Anaitasuna*, 397 (February 1980); *des femmes en mouvement hebdo* , 9–17 (January–May 1980); *Punto y Hora de Euskal Herria*, 175 (14–21 May 1980); and *Zer Egin?*, 110 (31 May 1980).
40 *Ere*, 21 (6–13 February 1980), and *Egin* (17 January 1980). See also Gestoras pro-amnistía, 'Dosier sobre la represión' (1980).
41 Mujeres KAS, 'Bortxaketarik ez' (1980).
42 On the rapes of Serb women in Kosovo and the reactions of Serb nationalists, see Wendy Bracewell, 'Rape in Kosovo: masculinity and Serbian nationalism', *Nations and Nationalism*, 6:4 (October 2000), 572. For the different treatment of 'political' and 'social' rapes in Palestine, see Nahla Abdo, 'Nationalism and feminism: Palestinian women and the *Intifada* – no going back?', in Moghadam (ed.), *Gender and National Identity*, p. 162.
43 *Egin* (17 January 1980). See also Gestoras pro-amnistía, 'Dosier sobre la represión' (1980).
44 Andrew Parker *et al.*, 'Introduction' in Parker *et al.* (eds.), *Nationalisms and Sexualities* (New York: Routledge, 1992), p. 6. For the importance of the female body in discourses of modern nationalist movements, see Sumanthi Ramaswamy, 'Body language: the somatics of nationalism in Tamil India', *Gender and History*, 10:1 (April 1998), 78–109.
45 Lynda Edgerton, 'Public protest, domestic acquiescence: women in Northern Ireland', in Rosemary Ridd and Helen Callaway (eds), *Caught up in the Conflict: Women's Responses to Political Strife* (London: Macmillan, 1986), pp. 61–83; Monica McWilliams, 'Struggling for peace and justice: reflections on women's activism in Northern Ireland', *Journal of Women's History*, 6:4/7:1 (winter/spring 1995), 13–39; Ailbhe Smyth, 'Paying our disrespects to the bloody states we're in: women, violence, culture, and the state,' *Journal of Women's History*, 6:4/7:1 (winter/spring 1995), 190–215; and Simona Sharoni, 'El frente doméstico como campo de batalla,' *Viento Sur*, 28 (October 1996), 83–96.
46 Begoña Aretxaga, *Shattering Silence: Women, Nationalism and Political Subjectivity in Northern Ireland* (Princeton, NJ: Princeton University Press, 1997), pp. 50–1.
47 *Egin* (7 June 1979) and 'Una reivindicación de primer order: amnistía también para las mujeres', in booklet produced for Euskadiko Emakumeen Lehengo topaketak/Primeras jornadas de la mujer en Euskadi (Lejona, n.d.).
48 See, for example, Gillian Youngs, 'Private pain/public peace: women's rights as human rights and Amnesty International's Report on Violence against Women', *Signs*, 28:4 (2003), 1209–29.

49 Carrie Hamilton, 'Memories of violence in interviews with Basque nationalist women', in Katharine Hodgkin and Susannah Radstone (eds), *Contested Pasts: The Politics of Memory* (New York and London: Routledge, 2003), pp. 120–35.
50 Kristin Ross, *May '68 and its Afterlives* (Chicago: University of Chicago Press, 2002).
51 Margaret Randall, *Sandino's Daughters Revisited: Feminism in Nicaragua* (New Brunswick, NJ: Rutgers University Press, 1994), p. 64.
52 Ten years after this interview, women were in fact elected to 50% of the seats in the Basque parliament. See chapter 8.
53 MLNV = Movimiento de Liberación Nacional Vasco (Basque National Liberation Movement), an acronym sometimes used to denote the radical nationalist movement.
54 Jarrai was the radical nationalist youth movement at the time of the interview.
55 Cvetkovich, *An Archive of Feelings*, p. 210.

Chapter 8

1 *ABC, Deia, Egin* and *El Correo Español* (18 January 1986).
2 Begoña Aretxaga, *Los funerales en el nacionalismo radical vasco* (San Sebastián: Baroja, 1988).
3 Interview with Itziar Aizpurua, *Herria Eginez*, 31 (January 1996).
4 *Egin* (18 January 1986).
5 *Deia* (22, 24 and 25 January 1986) and *Egin* (19 and 21 January 1986).
6 As Begoña Aretxaga has written, '[I]n the funeral context, the death of a militant parallels the death of Jesus Christ; Aretxaga, 'The death of Yoyes: cultural discourses of gender and politics in the Basque Country', *Critical Matrix: The Princeton Journal of Women, Gender and Culture*, 1 (1988), 6.
7 *Egin* (26 January 1986).
8 For a brief biography of Yoyes in English, see Cameron Watson, 'The tragedy of Yoyes', in Cameron Watson and Linda White (eds), *Amatxu, Amuma, Amona: Writings in Honor of Basque Women* (Reno, NV: Centre for Basque Studies, 2003), pp. 134–56.
9 For example, the Spanish news weekly *Cambio 16*, which broke the story of Yoyes's return, predicted in an editorial that 'peace could be a matter of a few months'; *Cambio 16*, 727 (4 November 1985).
10 See ETA's communiqué claiming responsibility for the killing and an article defending the action in *Punto y Hora de Euskal Herria*, 444 (18–25 September 1986).
11 Two or three narrators expressed views along these lines. Yoyes herself denied revealing information to Spanish officials, and I have found no recorded evidence that she did so.
12 *ABC* (12 September 1986), *Cambio 16*, 773 (22 September 1986), and *Deia* (11 September 1986).

13 *Cambio 16*, 727 (4 November 1985), and *El Correo, Español* (11 September 1986); Aretxaga puts the total number of *reinsertados* at over 300; 'The death of Yoyes', p. 1.
14 *ABC* (21 November 1984); *Cambio 16*, 576 (13 December 1982); and *Punto y Hora de Euskal Herria*, 444 (18–25 September 1986).
15 Aretxaga, 'The death of Yoyes', p. 1.
16 *Yoyes: desde su ventana* (Pamplona, 1987).
17 Ibid., p. 166.
18 Conversation with narrator #14, June 1996. See also comments of a former male ETA member in Miren Alcedo, *Militar en ETA: historias de vida y muerte* (San Sebastián: Haranburu, 1996), p. 362.
19 For a description of the Goierri region as the prototype of the newly industrialised rural Basque country, and its historical importance as a base of ETA recruitment and support, see Robert P. Clark, *The Basque Insurgents: ETA, 1952–1980* (Madison: University of Wisconsin Press, 1984), pp. 198–203. Against Clark's claim that the Goierri provided an actual operational base for ETA, Francisco Letamendia Belzunce argues (correctly, I believe) that the importance of the Goierri in the radical nationalist community was a more a symbolic one, and that in the 1970s the region produced ETA members that became the 'ideal' activist type, revered by the radical nationalist community as a whole. Letamendia Belzunce, *Historia del nacionalismo vasco y de ETA*, 3 vols (San Sebastián: R&B Ediciones, 1994), vol. 1, p. 374.
20 Lorraine Dowler, 'The mother of all warriors: women in Belfast, Northern Ireland', in Ronit Lentin (ed.), *Gender and Catastrophe* (London: Zed Books 1997), p. 82.
21 Aretxaga, 'The death of Yoyes', p. 8. I wrote this section on the killing of Yoyes before I knew about Aretxaga's article. Although we reach similar conclusions about the incompatibility of motherhood and activism, Aretxaga's argument is additionally shaped by her anthropological research on Basque and Northern Irish republican women, as well as her direct experience of activism in the Basque country. Aretxaga's seminal work on women in the contemporary Basque and Irish nationalist movements, as well as her later study of youth cultures and violence in the Basque country, have been inspirational to me and many others working in these areas. Her early death in 2002 deprived Basque studies of one of its most original scholars, and one of its few feminist voices.
22 See Aretxaga, 'The death of Yoyes', p. 2, for a discussion of these reasons.
23 *El País* (22 May 2005). See also Arantxa Elizondo Lopetegi, *La presencia de las mujeres en los partidos políticos de la Comunidad Autónoma del País Vasco* (Vitoria-Gateiz: Eusko Jaurlaritza/Gobierno Vasco, 1999).
24 Percentages of female prisoners accused of ETA or ETA-related crimes rose from about 8 per cent in 1983 to 12 per cent in 2002. Throughout the 1990s the percentage fluctuated between 10 per cent and 13 per cent. See Appendix 2.

25 *ABC* (17 September 2001), *El Correo Español* (17 May 1992), *Guardian* (27 August 2002) and *El Mundo* (10 March 1999).
26 *Egin* (26 October 1999) and Carmen Gurruchaga, *Los jefes de ETA* (Madrid: La Esfera, 2001), p. 23. For a history of the ceasefire and the failed peace process, see William A. Douglass and Pedro Ibarra Güell, 'A Basque referendum: resolution of political conflict or the promised land of error', in Begoña Aretxaga *et al.* (eds), *Empire and Terror: Nationalism/ Postnationalism in the New Millennium* (Reno, NV: Centre for Basque Studies, 2004), pp. 137–62, and Ludger Mees, *Nationalism, Violence and Democracy: The Basque Clash of Identities* (Basingstoke: Palgrave Macmillan, 2003).
27 My analysis of the profiles of these fourteen women is based on press reports of police accusations, arrests and deaths between 1982 and 2003. For the sociological profile of ETA members from 1977 to 1998, see Fernando Reinares, 'Who are the terrorists? Analyzing changes in sociological profile among members of ETA', *Studies in Conflict and Terrorism*, 27:6 (2004), 465–88. See also Florencio Domínguez Iribarren, *ETA: Estrategia organizativa y actuaciones 1978–1992* (Bilbao: Universidad del País Vasco, 1998).
28 Reinares, 'Who are the terrorists?', p. 481.
29 Domínguez Iribarren, *ETA*, pp. 22–3, 76; Letamendia Belzunce, *Historia del nacionalismo vasco*, vol. 2, p. 249; Fernando Reinares, *Patriotas de la muerte: quienes han militado en ETA y por qué* (Madrid: Taurus, 2001).
30 See, for example, the biographies of dead ETA members in Editorial Txalaparta, *Euskadi eta Askatasuna/Euskal Herria y la libertad*, 8 vols (Tafalla: Editorial Txalaparta, 1993).
31 According to the Basque Government's Women's Institute (Instituto Vasco de la Mujer), in 1999 only 10 per cent of the Basque police force was female; Emakunde, *Cifras sobre la situación de las mujeres y los hombres en Euskadi* (Vitoria, 1999), p. 116.
32 Alizia Stürtze, 'Movimientos de liberación nacional y liberación de la mujer: aproximación al caso vasco', in Miguel Angel Barencilla *et al.*, *La mujer en Euskal Herria: hacía un feminismo propio* (San Sebastián: Basandere Argitaletxea, 2001), pp. 227–45.
33 Sharryn Kasmir, 'From the margins: punk rock and the repositioning of ethnicity and gender in Basque identity', in William A. Douglass *et al.* (eds.), *Basque Cultural Studies* (Reno: University of Nevada Basque Studies Program, 1999), p. 182.
34 *Ibid.*, p. 192.
35 Begoña Echeverria, 'Privileging masculinity in the social construction of Basque identity', *Nations and Nationalism*, 7:3 (2001), 339–63.
36 *Ibid.*, p. 361, n. 5.
37 *Ibid.*, p. 358.
38 This section focuses on press representations of women in ETA. Since the 1990s there have been several fictional portrayals of female ETA activists in novels and films. See, for example, Bernardo Atxaga, *Esos cielos* (Barcelona:

Ediciones B, 1996), *Días contados* (dir. Imanol Uribe,1994), *El viaje de Arián* (dir. Eduard Bosch, 2000) and *Yoyes* (dir. Elena Taberna, 2000). For an analysis of representations of imprisoned women activists in two Basque novels, see Linda White, 'Atxaga's *Lone Woman* and Mintegi's *Nerea eta biok*: two different views of the female Basque political prisoner', *Journal for the Society of Basque Studies in America*, 19 (1999), 17–35. While there is substantial overlap between fictional and newspaper representations of women in ETA, an analysis of the former lies beyond the parameter of this book.

39 *ABC* (26 August 1994); *El Mundo* (27 August 1994); Matías Antolín, *Mujeres de ETA: piel de serpiente* (Madrid: Temas de Hoy, 2002), p. 20; and Gurruchaga, *Los jefes de ETA*, p. 213. The information that López Riaño was known as 'the Tigress' inside ETA came from personal conversations.

40 *ABC* (26 August 1994). Similar descriptions were found in the British and Spanish press of another female ETA member after the arrest of ETA leaders in France in September 2000. This led to police speculation that Soledad Iparagirre, 'Amboto', would become the head of the organisation. An article in *The Daily Telegraph* focused on Iparagirre's appearance and personal relationships with male ETA members: 'Her dossier describes her as an elegant woman with good dress sense who, during her stay in the Spanish capital, frequented its trendier night spots wearing the latest fashions.' The article quoted Spanish police as saying, ' "This woman has been driven by hate following the death of her lover [a male ETA member killed by police in the 1980s]. But she is a vixen whose wiles have kept her from being captured" '. *The Daily Telegraph* (18 September 2000). An earlier article in *El Mundo* described Iparagirre as 'the bride of death' (9 May 2000).

41 Antolín, *Mujeres de ETA*, p. 21. Bat-Ami Bar On has shown that the 'symbolic refeminization' of the female combatant can also serve the opposite purpose, i.e. not to demonise the female 'terrorist' but to reclaim a female soldier whose actions would be labelled heroic in a man, but contradict popular images of femininity. She gives the example of an Israeli soldier presented in the media 'in a sexually suggestive manner wearing a sundress' and described as 'blonde and having a well-sculpted figure'; Bar On, *The Subject of Violence: Arendtian Exercises in Understanding* (Lanham, MD: Rowan and Littlefield, 2000), p. 160.

42 José María Calleja, *¡Arriba Euskadi! La vida diaria en el País Vasco* (Madrid: Espasa, 2001), p. 269. Like many popular books about ETA, this one does not provide evidence for many of its assertions. However, it is valuable as an example of the representations of female ETA activists that circulate, largely without criticism, amongst both general and more elite Spanish readerships. The book was awarded the prestigious Espasa essay prize in 2001 by a jury of Spanish intellectuals, including prominent critics of Basque nationalism Jon Juaristi and Fernando Savater. For a discussion of the work of Juaristi and Savater, see the Conclusion.

43 *El Mundo* (3 January 1996 and 12 May 2001). See Rosa Montero's critique of portrayals of López Riaño in the Spanish press in *El País* (9 April 2002).

Shortly after her arrest López Riaño herself responded to the press image of her as a 'man eater'; *Egin* (8 December 1994).

44 See, for example, the case of Nagore Mujika, arrested with her young daughter, in *Egin* (31 May 1996), and Marta Pikaza, detained while pregnant, in *Egin* (6 June 1998).
45 See the column by Mertxe Aizpurua in response to the death of Zeberio, in *Egin* (6 June 1998).
46 *Egin* (7 October 1987, 24 November 1990, 28 July 1996 and 30 August 2001).
47 Amnesty International, *Preocupaciones en Europa* (6 April 2000).
48 Antolín, *Mujeres de ETA*, p. 21. See also the report of Zeberio's death in *ABC* (6 June 1998).
49 See Appendix 2.
50 Shani D'Cruze and Anupama Rao, 'Violence and the vulnerabilities of gender', in Cruze and Rao (eds), *Violence, Vulnerability and Embodiment* (Oxford: Blackwell, 2005), p. 3.

Conclusion

1 Ilene Rose Feinman, *Citizenship Rites: Feminist Soldiers and Feminist Antimilitarists* (New York and London: New York University Press, 2000); Shani D'Cruze and Anupama Rao (eds), *Violence, Vulnerability and Embodiment* (Oxford: Blackwell, 2005); Frances S. Hasso, 'Discursive and political deployments by/of the 2002 Palestinian women suicide bombers/martyrs', *Feminist Review*, 81 (2005), 23–51; and Caroline O. N. Moser and Fiona C. Clark (eds), *Victims, Perpetrators or Actors? Gender, Armed Conflict and Political Violence* (London: Zed Books, 2001).
2 See various works by Begoña Aretxaga and Sharryn Kasmir listed in the Select Bibliography, as well as the work of Jacqueline Urla: especially 'Outlaw language: creating alternative public spheres in Basque free radio', in Lisa Lowe and David Lloyd (eds), *The Politics of Culture in the Shadow of Capital* (Durham and London: Duke University Press, 1997), pp. 280–300, and 'We too are Malcolm X: Negu Gorriak, hip-hop and the Basque political imaginary', in Tony Mitchell (ed.), *Global Noise: Rap and Hip-Hop outside the USA* (Middletown, CN: Wesleyan University Press, 2001), pp. 171–93.
3 Kasmir claims that, although women as well as men participate in youth demonstrations, more men than women participate directly in the violence; ' "More Basque than you": class, youth and identity in an industrial Basque town', *Identities*, 9:1 (January–March 2002), 50. This observation coincides with my own impression of the *kale borroka* from following media reporting and witnessing street violence in Bilbao in the mid-1990s, but further research would be required to substantiate this.
4 For a brief description of the activities of these groups since the 1990s, see Ludger Mees, *Nationalism, Violence and Democracy: The Basque Clash of Identities* (Basingstoke: Palgrave Macmillan, 2003), pp. 91–100.

5 Cynthia Cockburn, *The Space Between Us: Negotiating Gender and National Identities in Conflict* (London: Zed Books, 1998).
6 See, for example, Begoña Aretxaga *et al.* (eds), *Empire and Terror: Nationalism/Postnationalism in the New Millennium* (Reno, NV: Centre for Basque Studies, 2004); William A. Douglass *et al.* (eds), *Basque Politics and Nationalism on the Eve of the Millennium* (Reno: University of Nevada Basque Studies Program, 1999); and Mees, *Nationalism, Violence and Democracy*.
7 See, in particular, Juan Aranzadi *et al.*, *Auto de terminación* (Madrid: El País/Aguilar, 1994); Jon Juaristi, *El bucle melancólico: historias de nacionalistas vascos* (Madrid: Espasa, 1997) and *Sacra némesis: nuevas historias de nacionalistas vascos* (Madrid: Espasa, 1999); and Fernando Savater, *Perdonen las molestias* (Madrid: Aguilar 2001).
8 Juaristi, *El bucle melancólico*.
9 Carrie Hamilton, 'Melancholy men and mythic women: Jon Juaristi's *El bucle melancólico: historias de nacionalistas vascos*', *Hispanic Research Journal*, 3:1 (February 2002), 43–59.
10 See Juaristi's description of radical Basque nationalist politician Jone Goirizelaia in *El bucle melancólico*, 382–4, and also my critique in 'Melancholy men'.
11 See, for example, Juan Aranzadi, *El escudo de Arquíloco: sobre mesías, mártires y terroristas*, vol. 1, 'Sangre vasca' (Madrid: A. Machado Libros, 2001), p. 126.
12 Aranzadi himself criticises the conflation of anti-ETA and anti-nationalist positions among Spanish intellectuals, including Juaristi. *Ibid*, pp. 651–97.
13 Paul Julian Smith, *The Moderns: Time, Space and Subjectivity in Contemporary Spanish Culture* (Oxford: Oxford University Press, 2000), p. 83.
14 *Ibid.*, pp. 149–52. See especially Juaristi, 'Postnacionalismo' in Aranzadi *et al.*, *Auto de terminación*, pp. 97–113.
15 Smith, *The Moderns*, p. 152.
16 See Helen Graham and Jo Labanyi (eds), *Spanish Cultural Studies: An Introduction* (Oxford: Oxford University Press, 1995), p. 404.
17 Cameron Watson, 'Imagining ETA', in Douglass *et al.* (eds), *Basque Politics and Nationalism*, p. 110.
18 *Guardian* (23 October 2003).
19 Rob Stone, *Spanish Cinema* (Harlow: Pearson Education Limited, 2002), p. 139.
20 Nuria Triana Toribio has written of Medem's cinema that 'his films often directly engage with questions of Spanishness, of the nature of modern national identities, and the place of those identities in a wider European framework. Medem's oeuvre ... reveals a preoccupation with national/transnational subjectivity'; *Spanish National Cinema* (London: Routledge, 2003), p. 149.
21 Julio Medem, *La pelota vasca: La piel contra la piedra/Euskal pelota: lurrua*

harriaren kontra (Madrid: Aguilar, 2003).
22 Paul Julian Smith, 'The Basque ball: skin against stone', *Sight and Sound*, 14:5 (May 2004), 45.
23 Dominick LaCapra, *Writing History, Writing Trauma* (Baltimore and London: Johns Hopkins University Press, 2001), p. 196.
24 *Ibid.*, p. 104.
25 For a further discussion of this, see my 'Memories of violence in interviews with Basque nationalist women', in Katharine Hodgson and Susannah Radstone (eds), *Contested Pasts* (New York and London: Routledge, 2003), pp. 120–35.

Appendix 2

1 Editorial Txalaparta, *Euskadi eta Askatasuna/Euskal Herria y la Libertad*, 8 vols (Tafalla: Editorial Txalaparta, 1993), vol. 3, pp. 42–3, 86–7, 126–8.
2 *Ibid.*, vol. 4, pp. 268–74.
3 *Hitz*, 5 (January 1976).
4 Editorial Txalaparta, *Euskadi eta Askatasuna*, vol. 5, pp. 315–17.
5 Gestoras pro-amnistía, *Torturaren Aurka, Amnistiaren Alde* (1981).
6 Editorial Txalaparta, *Euskadi eta Askatasuna*, vol. 4, pp. 300–2.
7 Area Crítica 2 (July–August 1983). List provided by Gestoras pro-amnistía de Vizcaya.
8 For example, exiled members of ETA(pm) who voluntarily returned to Spain after their organization disbanded in 1982. See Deia (25 January 1984). In the majority of cases (i.e. those who returned anonymously) there is no written record of a woman's participation in the organisation. See also the list of 72 former ETA members from the Goierri region who condemned ETA's killing of Yoyes in *Deia* (13 September 1986). I have also consulted Patxo Unzueta's list of ETA members present at ETA's assemblies between 1966 and 1970. Unzueta, *Los nietos de la ira* (Madrid: El País/Aguilar, 1988), pp. 177–80.
9 See Cambio 16, 576 (13 December 1982), and *Interviu*, 156 (10–16 May 1979).
10 Editorial Txalaparta, *Euskadi eta Askatasuna*.
11 Robert P. Clark, *The Basque Insurgents: ETA, 1952–1980* (Madison: University of Wisconsin Press, 1984), pp. 283–5.
12 Editorial Txalaparta, *Euskadi eta Askatasuna*, vol. 4, pp. 300–2.
13 *Area Crítica*, 2 (July–August 1983).
14 *Dossier Represión. Monográfico Punto y Hora* (January 1987).
15 Editorial Txalaparta, *Euskadi eta Askatasuna*, vol. 8, pp. 257–62.
16 Gestoras pro-amnistía poster.
17 *Ibid*.
18 *Ibid*.
19 *El Mundo* (30 August 1994).
20 Gestoras pro-amnistía poster.

21 *Ibid.*
22 *Ibid.*
23 *Ibid.*
24 *Ibid.*

Select bibliography

Archival sources

i) Biblioteca y hemeroteca del convento de los Benedictinos de Lazkao (Guipúzcoa)
– Political pamphlets and other documents from radical nationalist organisations, including ETA, Gestoras pro-amnistía, Herri Batasuna and LAB; radical nationalist and other Basque and Spanish political newsletters and other publications
ii) Biblioteca y hemeroteca de la Diputación de Vizcaya (Bilbao)
– Basque and Spanish newspapers
iii) Centro de documentación de la mujer (Bilbao)
– documents and books on Basque women and feminism
iv) IPES – Biblioteca de la mujer (Pamplona)
– documents and books on Basque women and feminism
v) Koldo Mitxelena Kulturunea (San Sebastián)
– documents and books on Basque women and feminism

Private document collections

Documents of KAS Emakumeak, Aizan and Egizan – courtesy of various narrators

Newsletters and political publications (substantially consulted)

Arnasa (EIA) 1976–79
Berriak (ETA-VI) 1970–73
Bultzaka (EIA) 1977–78
Erne (LAIA) 1978–80
Gazte (Herri Gaztedi) 1966–72
Hautsi (ETA/ETA[pm]) 1972–79
Hertzale (HASI) 1977–79
Hitz 1975–82
Kemen (ETA[pm]) 1974–80

Saioak (ETA – Células Rojas) 1970–71
Sugarra (LAIA) 1974–82
Zer Egin? (MCE/EMK) 1970–82
Zutabe (ETA[m]) 1980–87
Zutik (ETA-VI-LCR/LKI) 1974–82
Zuzen (ETA[m]) 1980–83

Newspapers (substantially consulted)

ABC (Madrid) 1968–2003
El Correo Español (Bilbao) 1968–2003
Deia (Bilbao) 1977–86
Egin (San Sebastián/Hernani) 1977–98
Gara (San Sebastián/Hernani) 1999–2003
La Gaceta del Norte (Bilbao) 1968–77
El Mundo (Madrid) 1994–2003
El País (Madrid) 1976–2005

Journals (substantially consulted)

Anaitasuna 1953–83
Ateka 1983–84
Batasuna 1974–75
Berriak: Seminario vasco de información 1976–77
Cambio 16 1971–86
Cuadernos para el diálogo 1963–78
Enbata 1960–82
Ere 1979–81
des femmes en mouvement hebdo 1979–81
Garaia 1975–76
Interviu 1976–82
Muga 1979–80
Punto y Hora de Euskal Herria 1976–88
Zeruko Argia/Argia 1976–81

Films

El juicio de Burgos (dir. Imanol Uribe, 1979)
La pelota vasca: la piel contra la piedra (dir. Julio Medem, 2003)

Published primary sources

Amnesty International. *Preocupaciones en Europa.* 6 April 2000.
—— *Prisonniers politiques et torture sous le régime franquiste.* Brussels, 1975.

Asambleas de Mujeres de Euskadi y Aizan. *Ponencias de las II Jornadas Feministas de Euskadi (1984)*. Bilbao, 1986.
Documentos Y. 18 vols. San Sebastián: Hordago, 1979–81.
Editorial Txalaparta. *Euskadi eta Askatasuna/Euskal Herria y la libertad*. 8 vols. Tafalla: Editorial Txalaparta, 1993.
Emakunde (Instituto Vasco de la Mujer). *Cifras sobre la situación de las mujeres y los hombres en Euskadi*. Vitoria, 1999.
Euskadi: el último estado de excepción de Franco. Chatillon-sous-Bagneux: Ruedo Ibérico, 1975.
Forest, Eva (ed.). *Testimonios de lucha y resistencia: en la prisión de Yeserías*. Hendaye: Mugalde, 1977.
Gobierno Vasco. *Situación de la mujer en Euskadi*. 1982.
Herri Batasuna. *Euskadi 1982*. Bilbao: 1982.
—— *El pueblo vasco por su libertad*. Bilbao: 1985.
Krutwig, Federico. *Vasconia*. Buenos Aires: Ediciones Norbait, 2nd edition, 1973(1963).
Maspero, François. *Batasuna: la répression au Pays Basque*. Paris: Cahiers Libres, 1970.
Moreno, Neus and Montserrat Cervera. 'Algunas reflexiones sobre los 10 años de lucha feminista en el Estado Español (1975–1985)' in *Jornadas – 10 años de lucha del movimiento feminista*. Barcelona, 1–3 November 1985, pp. 65–71.
'Oharbide'. *Documentos de las cárceles 1975*. Brussels, 1975.
La tortura en Euskadi. Madrid: Editorial Revolución, 1986.
Yoyes: desde su ventana. Pamplona, 1987.

Secondary sources

Aguilar Fernández, Paloma. *Memoria y olvido de la guerra civil española*, Madrid: Alianza Editorial, 1996.
Alcedo, Miren. *Militar en ETA: historias de vida y muerte*. San Sebastián: Haranburu, 1996.
—— 'Mujeres de ETA: la cuestión del género en la clandestinidad', *La Factoria*, 4 (October 1997). Available online at www.lafactoriaweb.com/articulos/miren4.htm.
Alexander, Sally. 'Memory, generation and history' in *Becoming a Woman and Other Essays in Nineteenth- and Twentieth-Century Feminist History*. London: Virago, 1994, pp. 231–42.
Amigo, Angel. *Pertur: ETA 71–76*. San Sebastián: Hordago, 1978.
Anderson, Benedict. 'Exodus', *Critical Inquiry*, 20 (winter 1994), 314–27.
—— *Imagined Communities: Reflections on the Origins and Spread of Nationalism*. London: Verso, 1991 (1983).
Andrés, Juan José and José Antonio Maisutxe. *El movimiento cuidadano en Euskadi*. San Sebastián: Txertoa, 1980.
Antolín, Matías. *Mujeres de ETA: piel de serpiente*. Madrid: Temas de Hoy, 2002.

Aranzadi, Juan. 'Etnicidad y violencia en el país vasco' in Aranzadi *et al.*, *Auto de terminación*, pp. 201–33.
—— *Milenarismo vasco: edad de oro, etnia y nativismo*. Madrid: Taurus, 2nd edition, 2000.
Aranzadi, Juan, Jon Juaristi and Patxo Unzueta. *Auto de terminación*. Madrid: El País/Aguilar, 1994.
Aretxaga, Begoña. 'The death of Yoyes: cultural discourses of gender and politics in the Basque Country', *Critical Matrix: The Princeton Journal of Women, Gender and Culture*, 1 (1988), 1–10.
—— 'Hall of mirrors: on the spectral character of Basque violence' in William A. Douglass *et al.* (eds), *Basque Politics and Nationalism*, pp. 115–26.
—— *Los funerales en el nacionalismo radical vasco*. San Sebastián: Baroja, 1988.
—— 'Playing terrorist: ghastly plots and the ghostly state', *Journal of Spanish Cultural Studies* 1:1 (March 2000), 43–58.
—— *Shattering Silence: Women, Nationalism and Political Subjectivity in Northern Ireland*. Princeton, NJ: Princeton University Press, 1997.
Aretxaga, Begoña, Dennis Dworkin, Joseba Gabilondo and Joseba Zulaika (eds). *Empire and Terror: Nationalism/Postnationalism in the New Millennium*. Reno, NV: Centre for Basque Studies, 2004.
Arpal, Jesus. 'Solidaridades elementales y organizaciones colectivas en el País Vasco (cuadrillas, txokos, asociaciones)', *Euskal Herriko Soziologiazko Ikastaroa*, Cuaderno de Formación 3. Bilbao: IPES, n.d., 51–60.
Arriaga Landeta, Mikel. *Y nosotros que éramos de HB . . . sociología de una heterodoxia abertzale*. Alegia: Haranburu, 1997.
Bar On, Bat-Ami. *The Subject of Violence: Arendtian Exercises in Understanding*. Lanham, MD: Rowan and Littlefield, 2000.
Barencilla, Miguel Angel, Roslyn M. Frank, Ann Marie Lagarde *et al*. *La mujer en Euskal Herria: hacía un feminismo propio*. San Sebastián: Basandere Argitaletxea, 2001.
Ben-Ami, Shlomo. 'Basque nationalism between archaism and modernity', *Journal of Contemporary History*, 26 (1991), 493–521.
Benison, Saul, Studs Terkel, Jan Vansina *et al*. 'It's not the song, it's the singing. Panel discussion on oral history' in Grele *et al.*, *Envelopes of Sound*, pp. 50–105.
Benson, Mike, Mariah Evans and Rita Simon. 'Women as political terrorists', *Law, Deviance and Social Control*, 4 (1982), 121–30.
Benton, Sarah. 'Women disarmed: the militarization of politics in Ireland 1913–23', *Feminist Review*, 50 (summer 1995), 148–72.
Bracewell, Wendy. 'Rape in Kosovo: masculinity and Serbian nationalism', *Nations and Nationalism*, 6:4 (October 2000), 563–90.
Buckley, Suzann and Pamela Lonergan. 'Women and the Troubles, 1969–1980' in Yonah Alexander and Alan O'Day (eds), *Terrorism in Ireland*. Aldershot: Croom Helm, 1984, pp. 75–87.
Bullen, Margaret. 'Gender and identity in the *Alardes* of two Basque towns' in Douglass *et al.* (eds), *Basque Cultural Studies*, pp. 149–77.

Calleja, José María. *¡Arriba Euskadi! La vida diaria en el País Vasco*. Madrid: Espasa, 2001.
Carr, Raymond and Juan Pablo Fusi. *Spain: Dictatorship to Democracy*. London: George Allen and Unwin, 1979.
Casquete, Jesus. *El poder en la calle: ensayos sobre acción colectiva*. Madrid: Centro de Estudios Políticos y Constitucionales, 2006.
Cassinello Pérez, Andrés. 'E.T.A. y el problema vasco' in Salustiano del Campo (ed.), *Terrorismo internacional*. Madrid: Instituto de Cuestiones Internacionales, 1984, pp. 265–308.
Cerdán, Manuel and Antonio Rubio. *Lobo: un topo en las entrañas de ETA*. Barcelona: Plaza & Janés, 2003.
Christian, William A., Jr. *Visionaries: The Spanish Republic and the Reign of Christ*. Berkeley and Los Angeles: University of California Press, 1996.
Clark, Robert P. *The Basque Insurgents: ETA, 1952–1980*. Madison: University of Wisconsin Press, 1984.
—— *The Basques: The Franco Years and Beyond*. Reno: University of Nevada Press, 1979.
Condren, Mary. 'Sacrifice and political legitimation: the production of a gendered social order', *Journal of Women's History*, 6:4/7:1 (winter/spring 1995), 160–89.
Conversi, Daniele. *The Basques, the Catalans and Spain: Alternative Routes to Nationalist Mobilization*. London: Hurst & Company, 1997.
Cooper, H. H. A. 'Woman as terrorist' in Freda Adler and Rita James Simon (eds), *The Criminology of Deviant Women*. Boston: Houghton Mifflin Company, 1979, pp. 150–7.
Craske, Nikki. *Women and Politics in Latin America*. Cambridge: Polity Press, 1999.
Cvetkovich, Ann. *An Archive of Feelings: Trauma, Sexuality and Lesbian Public Cultures*. Durham, NC: Duke University Press, 2003.
Cueva, Justo de la, José Luis Morales, Grupo de Médicos contra la tortura, *et al*. *Tortura y sociedad*. Madrid: Editorial Revolución, 1982.
D'Cruze, Shani and Anupama Rao. 'Violence and the vulnerabilities of gender' in Cruze and Rao (eds), *Violence, Vulnerability and Embodiment*, pp. 1–18.
D'Cruze, Shani and Anupama Rao (eds). *Violence, Vulnerability and Embodiment*. Oxford: Blackwell, 2005.
Deleuze, Gilles and Félix Guattari. *Anti-Oedipus: Capitalism and Schizophrenia*. London: The Athlone Press, 1984 (1972).
Díez Medrano, Juan. *Divided Nations: Class, Politics, and Nationalism in the Basque Country and Catalonia*. Ithaca, NY and London: Cornell University Press, 1995.
Domínguez Iribarren, Florencio. *ETA: estrategia organizativa y actuaciones 1978–1992*. Bilbao: Universidad del País Vasco, 1998.
Douglass, William A. *Death in Murélaga: Funeral Ritual in a Spanish Basque Village*. Seattle: University of Washington Press, 1969.

Douglass, William A. and Joseba Zulaika. *Terror and Taboo: The Follies, Fables and Faces of Terrorism*. New York and London: Routledge, 1996.
Douglass, William A., Carmelo Urza, Linda White and Joseba Zulaika (eds). *Basque Cultural Studies*. Reno: University of Nevada Basque Studies Program, 1999.
—— *Basque Politics and Nationalism on the Eve of the Millenium*. Reno: University of Nevada Basque Studies Program, 1999.
Dowler, Lorraine. 'The mother of all warriors: women in Belfast, Northern Ireland' in Ronit Lentin (ed.), *Gender and Catastrophe*. London: Zed Books, 1997, pp. 77–90.
Dyer, Richard. *Stars*. London: British Film Institute, revised edition, 1998.
Echeverria, Begoña. 'Privileging masculinity in the social construction of Basque identity', *Nations and Nationalism*, 7:3 (2001), 339–63.
Edgerton, Lynda. 'Public protest, domestic acquiescence: women in Northern Ireland' in Rosemary Ridd and Helen Callaway (eds), *Caught up in the Conflict: Women's Responses to Political Strife*. London: Macmillan, 1986, pp. 61–83.
Eisenstadt, S. N. 'Introduction' in Max Weber, *On Charisma and Institution Building*. Chicago and London: University of Chicago Press, 1968.
Elorza, Antonio. *Ideologías del nacionalismo vasco 1876–1937 (de los 'euskeros' a Jagi Jagi)*. San Sebastián: Haranburu, 1978.
—— 'Some perspectives on the nation-state and Autonomies in Spain' in Graham and Labanyi (eds), *Spanish Cultural Studies*, pp. 332–6.
Elorza, Antonio *et al*. *Historia de ETA*. Madrid: Temas de Hoy, 2000.
Enders, Victoria Lorée and Pamela Beth Radcliff (eds). *Constructing Spanish Womanhood: Female Identity in Modern Spain*. Albany: State University of New York Press, 1999.
Etxezarreta, Miren. *El caserío vasco*. Bilbao: Elexpuru Hnos., 1977.
'Feminismo e izquierda abertzale en Hego Euskal Herria', *Ezpala* 0 (1996), 30.
Fentress, James and Chris Wickham. *Social Memory*. Oxford: Blackwell, 1992.
Folguera, Pilar (ed.). *El feminismo en España: dos siglos de su historia*. Madrid: Pablo Iglesias, 1988.
Franco, Jean. 'Gender, death, and resistance: facing the ethical vacuum' in Juan E. Corradi, Patricia Weiss Fagen and Manuel Antonio Garretón (eds), *Fear at the Edge: State Terror and Resistance in Latin America*. Berkeley: University of California Press, 1992, pp. 104–18.
—— 'Going Public' in George Yudice, Jean Franco and Juan Flores (eds), *On Edge: The Crisis of Contemporary Latin American Culture*. Minneapolis and London: University of Minnesota Press, 1992, pp. 65–83.
Fusi, Juan Pablo. 'The Basque question 1931–37' in Paul Preston (ed.), *Revolution and War in Spain 1931–1939*. London: Methuen, 1984, pp. 182–201.
—— *Franco: A Biography*. London: Unwin Hyman, 1987.
Garmendia, José María. *Historia de ETA*, 2 vols. San Sebastián: Haranburu, 1980.

Graham, Helen. 'Gender and the state: women in the 1940s' in Graham and Labayni (eds), *Spanish Cultural Studies*, pp. 182–95.
Graham, Helen and Jo Labanyi (eds). *Spanish Cultural Studies: An Introduction*. Oxford: Oxford University Press, 1995.
Granja Sainz, José Luis de la. *El nacionalismo vasco: un siglo de historia*. Madrid: Tecnos, 1995.
Grele, Ronald J. 'Private memories and public presentation: the art of oral history' in Grele *et al.*, *Envelopes of Sound*, pp. 242–83.
Grele, Ronald J., with Studs Terkel, Jan Vansina *et al. Envelopes of Sound: The Art of Oral History*. New York: Praeger, 2nd edition, 1991.
Grugel, Jean and Tim Rees. *Franco's Spain*. London: Arnold, 1997.
Gurruchaga, Ander. *El código nacionalista vasco durante el franquismo*. Barcelona: Anthropos, 1985.
Gurruchaga, Carmen. *Los jefes de ETA*. Madrid: La Esfera, 2001.
Haen Marshall, Ineke, Vincent Webb and Dennis Hoffman. 'A review of explicit and implicit propositions about women as terrorists', *Resources for Feminist Research*, 14:4 (1986), 20–2.
Hamilton, Carrie. 'Changing subjects: gendered identities in ETA and radical Basque nationalism' in Jordan and Morgan-Tamosunas (eds), *Contemporary Spanish Cultural Studies*, pp. 223–32.
—— 'Género y nacionalismo: una nueva área de estudio', *Inguruak*, 22 (1998): 163–74.
—— 'Melancholy men and mythic women: Jon Juaristi's *El bucle melancólico: historias de nacionalistas vascos*', *Hispanic Research Journal*, 3:1 (February 2002), 43–59.
—— 'Memories of violence in interviews with Basque nationalist women' in Hodgkin and Radstone (eds), *Contested Pasts*, pp. 120–35.
—— 'Re-membering the Basque nationalist family: daughters, fathers and the reproduction of the radical nationalist community', *Journal of Spanish Cultural Studies*, 1:2 (autumn 2000), 153–71.
Hasso, Frances S. 'Discursive and political deployments by/of the 2002 Palestinian women suicide bombers/martyrs', *Feminist Review*, 81 (2005), 23–51.
Hobsbawm, Eric. 'Introduction: inventing traditions' in Eric Hobsbawm and Terence Ranger (eds), *The Invention of Tradition*. Cambridge: Cambridge University Press, 1997 (1983), pp. 1–14.
Hodgkin, Katharine and Susannah Radstone (eds). *Contested Pasts: The Politics of Memory*. New York and London: Routledge, 2003.
Hollander, Nancy Caro. 'The gendering of human rights: women and the Latin American terrorist state', *Feminist Studies*, 22:1 (spring 1996), 41–80.
Horne, John. 'Masculinity in politics and war in the age of nation-states and world wars, 1850–1950' in Stefan Dudink, Karen Hagemanna and John Tosh (eds), *Masculinities in Politics and War: Gendering Modern History*. Manchester: Manchester University Press, 2004, pp. 22–40.

Huston, Nancy. 'The matrix of war: mothers and heroes' in Susan Ruben Suleiman (ed.), *The Female Body in Western Culture: Contemporary Perspectives*. Cambridge, MA and London: Harvard University Press, 1985, pp. 119–36.

Ibarra Güell, Pedro. *La evolución estratégica de ETA*. San Sebastián: Kriselu, 1989.

Iztueta, Paulo. *Sociología del fenómeno contestario del clero vasco, 1940–1975*. San Sebastián: Elkar, 1981.

James, Daniel. *Doña María's Story: Life History, Memory and Political Identity*. Durham, NC and London: Duke University Press, 2000.

Jáuregui Bereciartu, Gurutz. *Ideología y estratégia política de ETA 1959–1968*. Madrid: Siglo XXI, 1981.

Jelin, Elizabeth. *State Repression and the Struggles for Memory*. London: Latin American Bureau, 2003.

Jones, Anny Brooksbank. *Women in Contemporary Spain*. Manchester: Manchester University Press, 1997.

Jordan, Barry and Rikki Morgan-Tamosunas (eds). *Contemporary Spanish Cultural Studies*. London: Arnold, 2000.

Juaristi, Jon. *El bucle melancólico: historias de nacionalistas vascos*. Madrid: Espasa, 1997.

—— 'Postnacionalismo' in Aranzadi *et al.*, *Auto de terminación*, pp. 97–113.

Jurado, Nekane. 'Mujer vasca: aportación oculta a la economía' in Miguel Angel Barencilla *et al.*, *La mujer en Euskal Herria*, pp. 163–206.

Kaplan, Gisela. *Contemporary Western European Feminism*. London: UCL Press Limited, 1992.

—— 'Feminism and nationalism: the European case' in West (ed.), *Feminist Nationalism*, pp. 2–40.

Kaplan, Temma. 'Reversing the shame and gendering the memory', *Signs*, 28:1 (2002), 179–99.

Kasmir, Sharryn. 'From the margins: punk rock and the repositioning of ethnicity and gender in Basque identity' in Douglass *et al.* (eds), *Basque Cultural Studies*, pp. 178–204.

—— '"More Basque than you": class, youth and identity in an industrial Basque town', *Identities*, 9:1 (January–March 2002), 39–68.

—— *The Myth of Mondragón: Cooperatives, Politics and Working-Class Life in a Basque Town*. Albany: State University of New York Press, 1996.

Kerber, Linda K. 'Separate spheres, female worlds, woman's place: the rhetoric of women's history', *Journal of American History*, 75:1 (June 1988), 9–39.

Klein, Kerwin Lee. 'On the emergence of *memory* in historical discourse', *Representations*, 69 (winter 2000), 127–50.

Kristeva, Julia. *Strangers to Ourselves*. New York and London: Harvester Wheatsheaf, 1991.

Krylova, Anna. 'Stalinist identity from the viewpoint of gender: rearing a generation of professionally violent women-fighters in 1930s Stalinist Russia' in D'Cruze and Rao (eds), *Violence, Vulnerability and Embodiment*, pp. 132–60.

LaCapra, Dominick. *Writing History, Writing Trauma*. Baltimore and London: Johns Hopkins University Press, 2001.

Lannon, Frances. 'Catholicism and social change' in Graham and Labanyi (eds), *Spanish Cultural Studies*, pp. 276–82.

—— *Privilege, Persecution and Prophecy: The Catholic Church in Spain 1875–1975*. Oxford: Oxford University Press, 1987.

Letamendia Belzunce, Francisco. *Historia del nacionalismo vasco y de ETA*, 3 vols. San Sebastián: R&B Ediciones, 1994.

Leydesdorff, Selma, Luisa Passerini and Paul Thompson. 'Introduction', *International Yearbook of Oral History and Life Stories*, vol. 4 'Gender and Memory'. Oxford: Oxford University Press, 1996.

Linz, Juan. *Conflicto en Euskadi*. Madrid: Espasa Calpe, 1986.

Lloyd, Genevieve. 'Selfhood, war and masculinity' in Carole Pateman and Elizabeth Grosz (eds), *Feminist Challenges: Social and Political Theory*. Boston: Northeastern University Press, 1987, pp. 63–76.

MacClancy, Jeremy. 'At play with identity in the Basque arena' in Sharon Macdonald (ed.), *Inside European Identities: Ethnography in Western Europe*. Oxford: Berg, 1993, pp. 84–97.

McClintock, Anne. *Imperial Leather: Race, Gender and Sexuality in the Colonial Contest*. New York: Routledge, 1995.

MacDonald, Eileen. *Shoot the Women First*. London: Arrow, 1991.

McWilliams, Monica. 'Struggling for peace and justice: reflections on women's activism in Northern Ireland', *Journal of Women's History*, 6:4/7:1 (winter/spring 1995), 13–39.

Mata López, José Manuel. *El nacionalismo vasco radical*. Bilbao: Universidad del País Vasco, 1993.

Matsell, Catherine. 'Spain' in Joni Lovenduski and Jill Hills (eds), *The Politics of the Second Electorate: Women and Public Participation*. London: Routledge & Kegan Paul, 1981, pp. 134–52.

Medem, Julio. *La pelota vasca: La piel contra la piedra/Euskal pelota: lurrua harriaren kontra*. Madrid: Aguilar, 2003.

Mees, Ludger. *Nationalism, Violence and Democracy: The Basque Clash of Identities*. Basingstoke: Palgrave Macmillan, 2003.

Miguel, Amando de. 'Estructura social y juventud española', *Revista del Instituto de la Juventud*, 0 (1965).

—— 'Religiosidad y clericalismo en los jovenes españoles', *Revista del Instituto de la Juventud*, 8 (1966), 67–70.

Moghadam, Valentine M. 'Introduction and overview: gender dynamics of nationalism, revolution and Islamization' in Valentine Moghadam (ed.), *Gender and National Identity: Women and Politics in Muslim Societies*. London: Zed Books, 1994, pp. 1–17.

Morán, Gregorio. *Los españoles que dejaron de serlo: Euskadi 1937–1982*. Barcelona: Planeta, 1982.

Morcillo, Aurora G. *True Catholic Womanhood: Gender Ideology in Franco's Spain*. DeKalb: Northern Illinois University Press, 2000.
Moreno, Amparo. *Mujeres en la lucha: el movimiento feminista en España*. Barcelona: Anagrama, 1977.
Morgan, Robin. *The Demon Lover: The Roots of Terrorism*. London: Piatkus, 2001 (1989).
Munck, Ronaldo. 'Deconstructing terror: insurgency, repression and peace' in Ronaldo Munck and Purnaka da Silva (eds), *Postmodern Insurgencies: Political Violence, Identity Formation and Peacemaking in Comparative Perspective*. Basingstoke: Macmillan, 2000, pp. 1–13.
Parker, Andrew *et al.* 'Introduction' in Andrew Parker *et al.* (eds), *Nationalisms and Sexualities*. New York: Routledge, 1992, pp. 1–18.
Passerini, Luisa. *Autobiography of a Generation: Italy 1968*. Hanover and London: Wesleyan University Press, 1996.
—— *Fascism in Popular Memory*. Cambridge: Cambridge University Press, 1987.
—— 'Introduction' in Luisa Passerini (ed.), *International Yearbook of Oral History and Life Stories*, vol. 1 'Totalitarianism'. Oxford: Oxford University Press, 1992, pp. 1–19.
—— 'Lacerations in the memory: women in the Italian underground organizations', *International Social Movement Research*, 4 (1992), 161–212.
Payne, Stanley. *Basque Nationalism*. Reno: University of Nevada Press, 1975.
Peiss, Kathy. 'Gender relations and working-class leisure: New York City, 1880–1920' in Carol Gronemon and Mary Beth Norton (eds), *'To Toil the Livelong Day': America's Women at Work, 1780–1980*. Ithaca: Cornell University Press, 1987, pp. 93–111.
Pérez-Agote, Alfonso. *La reproducción del nacionalismo: el caso vasco*. Madrid: Centro de Investigaciones Sociológicas, 1984.
Pérez Pérez, Carmen. 'Historia y actualidad del movimiento feminista en Euskadi', *Inguruak* (December 1987), 53–9.
Portell, José María. *Los hombres de ETA*. Barcelona: Dopesa, 1974.
Portelli, Alessandro. 'The peculiarities of oral history', *History Workshop*, 12 (autumn 1981), 96–107.
Preston, Paul. *The Politics of Revenge: Fascism and the Military in 20th Century Spain*. London: Routledge, 2nd edition, 1995.
—— *The Triumph of Democracy in Spain*. London: Routledge, 1993 (1986).
Radstone, Susannah. 'Social bonds and psychical order: testimonies', *Cultural Values*, 5:1 (January 2001), 59–78.
Ramírez Goicoechea, Eugenia. 'Cuadrillas en el País Vasco: identidad local y revitalización étnica', *Revista Española de Investigaciones Sociológicas*, 25 (January–March 1984), 213–20.
Randall, Margaret. *Sandino's Daughters Revisited: Feminism in Nicaragua*. New Brunswick, NJ: Rutgers University Press, 1994.
Reinares, Fernando. *Patriotas de la muerte: quienes han militado en ETA y por qué*. Madrid: Taurus, 2001.

—— 'Who are the terrorists? Analyzing changes in sociological profile among members of ETA', *Studies in Conflict and Terrorism*, 27:6 (2004), 465–88.

Richmond, Kathleen. *Women and Spanish Fascism: The Women's Section of the Falange 1934–1959*. London: Routledge, 2003.

Rooney, Eilish. 'Political division, practical alliance: problems for women in conflict', *Journal of Women's History*, 6:4/7:1 (winter/spring 1995), 40–8.

Ross, Kristin. *May '68 and its Afterlives*. Chicago: University of Chicago Press, 2002.

Sangster, Joan. 'Telling our stories: feminist debates and the use of oral history' in Robert Perks and Alistair Thomson (eds), *The Oral History Reader*. London: Routledge, 1997, pp. 85–100.

Scanlon, Geraldine M. *La polémica feminista en la España contemporánea 1868–1974*. Madrid: Akal, 1976.

Scarry, Elaine. *The Body in Pain: The Making and Unmaking of the World*. New York and Oxford: Oxford University Press, 1985.

Sharoni, Simona. 'El frente doméstico como campo de batalla', *Viento Sur*, 28 (October 1996), 83–96.

Smith, Paul Julian. 'The Basque ball: skin against stone', *Sight and Sound*, 14:5 (May 2004), 44–5.

—— *The Moderns: Time, Space and Subjectivity in Contemporary Spanish Culture*. Oxford: Oxford University Press, 2000.

Smyth, Ailbhe. 'Paying our disrespects to the bloody states we're in: women, violence, culture, and the state', *Journal of Women's History*, 6:4/7:1 (winter/spring 1995), 190–215.

Stacey, Judith. 'Are feminists afraid to leave home?' in Juliet Mitchell and Ann Oakley (eds), *Who's Afraid of Feminism? Seeing Through the Backlash*. New York: Pantheon Books, 1986, pp. 208–37.

Stone, Rob. *Spanish Cinema*. Harlow: Pearson Education Limited, 2002.

Stürtze, Alizia. 'Movimientos de liberación nacional y liberación de la mujer: aproximación al caso vasco' in Barencilla et al., *La mujer en Euskal Herria*, pp. 227–45.

Sullivan, John. *ETA and Basque Nationalism: The Fight for Euskadi 1890–1986*. London: Routledge, 1988.

Summerfield, Penny. *Reconstructing Women's Wartime Lives*. Manchester: Manchester University Press, 1998.

Talbot, Rhiannon. 'Myths in the representation of women terrorists', *Eire-Ireland*, 35 (autumn/winter 2000/01), 165–86.

Taylor, Diana. *Disappearing Acts: Spectacles of Gender and Nationalism in Argentina's Dirty War*. Durham, NC: Duke University Press, 1997.

Theweleit, Klaus. *Male Fantasies*, 2 vols. Cambridge: Polity Press, 1987, 1989.

Thompson, Paul. *The Voice of the Past: Oral History*. Oxford: Oxford University Press, 2nd edition, 1988.

Triana Toribio, Nuria. *Spanish National Cinema*. London: Routledge, 2003.

Ugalde, Mercedes. *Mujeres y nacionalismo vasco: Emakume Abertzale Batza 1906–1936*. Bilbao: Universidad del País Vasco, 1993.

Ugalde Solano, Mercedes. 'The discourse of gender and the Basque nationalist movement in the first third of the 20th Century', *History of European Ideas*, 15:4–6 (1992), 695–700.

—— 'La historia de las mujeres y la historia del nacionalismo: una convergencia necesaria', *Revista de Extremadura*, 13, Segunda Época (January-April 1994), 33–42.

—— 'Notas para una historiografía sobre nación y diferencia sexual', *Arenal*, 3:2 (July-December 1996), 217–56.

Unzueta, Patxo. *Los nietos de la ira*. Madrid: El País/Aguilar, 1988.

Valle, Teresa del. *Korrika: rituales de la lengua en el espacio*. Barcelona: Anthropos, 1988.

Valle, Teresa del, *et al*. *Mujer vasca: imagen y realidad*. Barcelona: Anthropos, 1985.

Watson, Cameron. 'Imagining ETA' in Douglass *et al.* (eds), *Basque Politics and Nationalism*, pp. 94–114.

—— 'The tragedy of Yoyes' in Cameron Watson and Linda White (eds), *Amatxu, Amuma, Amona: Writings in Honor of Basque Women*. Reno, NV: Centre for Basque Studies, 2003, pp. 134–56.

West, Lois A. 'Introduction: feminism constructs nationalism' in West (ed.), *Feminist Nationalism*, pp. xi–xxxvi.

—— (ed.). *Feminist Nationalism*. New York and London: Routledge, 1997.

Yuval-Davis, Nira. *Gender and Nation*. London: Sage, 1997.

Yuval-Davis, Nira and Floya Anthias (eds). *Woman–Nation–State*. London: Methuen, 1989.

Zirakzadeh, Cyrus Ernesto. *A Rebellious People: Basques, Protests and Politics*. Reno: University of Nevada Press, 1991.

Zulaika, Joseba. *Basque Violence: Metaphor and Sacrament*. Reno: University of Nevada Press, 1988.

Zwerman, Gilda. 'Conservative and feminist images of women associated with armed, clandestine organizations in the United States', *International Social Movement Research*, 4 (1992), 133–59.

—— 'Mothering on the lam: politics, gender fantasies and maternal thinking in women associated with armed, clandestine organizations in the United States', *Feminist Review*, 47 (summer 1994), 33–56.

Index

Note: 'n.' after a page reference indicates the number of a note on that page

Aberri Eguna 59, 65, 208n.64
abortion 224n.31
   Basauri trial 154–5, 224n.35
   law 155, 224n.30
   see also Catholic Church; class;
      feminism; prisoners
agency, political 182
   women's activism and 111–16, 145,
      166
Aizan see feminism
Aizpurua, Itziar 59, 82, 134, 166,
   214n.2, 214n.15, 220n.52
amnesty, political 140, 149,
   212n.29
   feminism and 149, 150, 157
Arana, Sabino 20, 36, 54, 55, 67, 85,
   180, 199n.3, 199n.4
armed activists, female 106, 108, 114,
   119–23, 143–4, 177,
   215n.24
   motherhood and 118–19
   representations of 106–7, 110–11,
      118, 120, 121, 215n.26,
      215n.29, 216n.32
   see also ETA activists
arrest 126
   of female ETA members 110, 113,
      127, 136, 138–40, 144, 174
Arruti, Arantza 82, 214n.2, 215n.25,
   216n.40
Arzelus, Bakartxu 165–7

baserri (Basque farmstead) 23–4, 53
Basque conflict 179
   during transition to democracy 156
   gender and 171, 177–8
   interviews and 9, 10
   possible resolution 178
   victims and perpetrators 15
   see also media; violence
Basque country, definition 194n.1
Basque language see *euskera*
Burgos trial (1970) 62, 71, 77–83,
   86, 96, 100, 102, 127, 180,
   189
   defendants 76, 82, 105, 207n.44
   female 105, 109, 140, 210n.37,
      214n.2, 214n.15, 216n.40
   see also *Juicio de Burgos, El*; media

Carlism 31, 32, 200n.17, 202n.48
Catholic Church
   abortion and 153–4
   anti-Franco opposition and 40
   association with Basque identity
      44
   Basque 2, 18, 30–1, 40
   Basque culture and language and
      41–3, 58
   divorce and 153
   early Basque nationalism and
      199n.4
   education and 41, 42–3, 45

family and 41, 45
feminism and 45
Franco regime and 40, 63
influence on ETA and radical nationalism 39–45, 60, 71, 88
interviews and 41, 46
PNV and 21, 39
reforms of 1960s 43
sexual repression and 41–5
women and 20, 134, 199n.13
youth groups 58 40, 45
see also media; nuns; priests; religion
CC.AA. (Comandos Autónomos) 196n.29
CC.OO. (Comisiones Obreras) 55
childless women
ETA and 35
political activism and 35, 166
children
in interviews 158
of ETA activists 90–2, 94, 98
Church *see* Catholic Church
Civil Guard (Spanish) 72
deaths of ETA activists and 72, 165–6
as ETA targets 213n.47
GAL and 9
repression and 59, 68, 208n.64, 210n.40
torture of female detainees 132, 136
see also Franco dictatorship; police and security forces; violence
class
abortion and 115, 224n.35
Catholic youth groups and 40–1
development of ETA and 54–5, 72, 74–5, 85
early Basque nationalism and 21, 23–4
ETA membership and 72, 142
feminism and 151
interviews and 12, 37
prison and 142

radical nationalism and 12
see also labour movement, Basque; socialism
clothing
Church attitudes to 44, 114
female activist identities and 44, 109, 114
prison and 143
contraception 143, 154, 159
see also abortion; sexuality
cuadrilla 68, 205n.18
definition and activities of 46–7
ETA and 39, 46–8, 60, 88, 171
exile and 95–6, 97
gender and 46–7, 96, 205n.30, 206n.41
see also masculinity
cultural activities 208n.65
nationalist politics and 58–9, 204n.8
women and 53, 57–60
culture, Basque, association with women 39, 53, 55–7, 94, 176

daughters
fathers and 28–34, 92
mothers and 28, 30, 33, 34, 36, 91, 158–9, 174
Dorronsoro, Jone 82, 136, 214n.2

EAB (Emakume Abertzale Batza) 21–2, 27, 58, 60, 202n.36
economy
Basque 11–12, 20, 23, 29, 46, 52, 74, 85, 198n.44
Spanish 2, 29, 11, 48–9, 74
education
Franco dictatorship and 63–4
gender segregation and 42, 50, 206n.38
of girls and women under Franco 42, 44, 49
see also Catholic Church; nuns; priests; universities
EGI (Eusko Gaztedi del Interior) 67

Egizan *see* feminism
Ekin, 29, 54, 55, 200n.43
Elkarri 178, 230n.4
emotion
  activism and 17, 31, 72, 134, 144, 149, 159–60, 164
  emotional evidence and interviews 130
  as factor in ETA activism and support 106–7, 162–3
  feminism and 149, 159–64
  gender and 107
  nationalism and 17, 159
  oral history and 164
  prison and 130–1, 143
  torture and 134
ETA (Euskadi ta Askatasuna)
  founding 1, 19, 29
  political and strategic development 54
  split between ETA-V and ETA-VI (1971) 139–40
  split between ETA(m) and ETA(pm) (1974) 139
  see also Basque conflict; ETA activists; ETA-V; ETA-VI; ETA(m); ETA(pm); violence
ETA activists 2, 15, 78, 80–1, 113, 165, 183, 208n.65, 211n.29
  female 1, 3, 4, 32, 36, 41, 52, 53, 56, 57, 59, 60, 70, 72–3, 82, 86, 89, 94, 95, 96, 98, 102, 104, 141, 160, 196n.29
  in academic studies of ETA 106
  ages of 189–90
  attitudes to ETA violence 121, 167, 169
  as collaborators 190, 192
  deaths of 165–70, 173–4
  'double life' of 114–15
  feminism and 151, 166, 168
  in fiction and film 228n.38
  gender fantasies of 119, 123
  generations and 174
  leaders 167–9, 170, 192
  male fantasies about 173
  motivations for entering ETA 123, 177
  numbers of 105, 170, 188
  occupations 190–1
  participation in armed actions 140, 170
  proving themselves 116–18
  recruitment patterns different from men's 51–3, 170–1, 177
  reportedly more dangerous than men 109–11, 173–5, 176–7
  representations of 107–11
  roles 70–1, 105–6, 107, 113, 120, 140, 143–4, 192
  weapons and 110, 111, 113, 117–18
  see also arrest; mothers; prison; torture
  male 4, 9, 13, 50, 62, 70, 71, 72–7, 80–2, 86, 87–8, 90–3, 94, 96–101, 103, 107, 108, 167, 210n.39, 211n.25
  participation in armed actions 175
  representations of 109, 127
  sociological profiles of 171, 228n.27
ETA-V 73, 85, 139–40
ETA-VI 73, 85, 139–40
ETA-Berri 55, 72
ETA-militar (ETA[m]) 85, 140, 196n.29, 223n.18, 223n.20
  feminism and 152, 155
  killing of Yoyes 167–9, 226n.10
ETA-político-militar (ETA[pm]) 85, 140, 196n.29, 232n.8
  dissolution of (1982) 167
  feminism and 223n.19
  support for campaign against sexual violence 155
  women in 118
'ethnic Basque', definition 199n.8
Etxebarrieta, Txabi 73, 74, 84
  death of 72, 77, 78, 166

euskera 3, 31, 41, 59, 172, 197n.33, 208n.65
  ETA and 54–5
  feminism and 150
  masculinity and 172–3, 177
  prohibitions against under Franco 22–3, 58, 64, 81
  teaching of 58, 60, 208n.66
  women and 21, 57, 60
exile
  of ETA members in French Basque country 13, 86, 91, 94–9, 211n.25, 211n.29, 211n.30
  gender divisions and 94–9, 169
  national identity and 94–5
  see also families; GAL; González Catarain, Dolores; memory; nostalgia

Falange (Spanish) 81, 200n.16
families
  Basque nationalist under Franco 25–38, 50–1
  development of ETA and 60
  early Basque nationalism and 2, 19–22
  exile and 94–9, 211n.29
  feminist theory and 26
  importance in ETA recruitment 171, 191, 228n.30
  in ETA rhetoric 56
  radical nationalism and 39, 91, 102–4, 165, 176
  women and 20
fatherhood
  ETA and 29, 89–94, 165
  postnationalist critique and 178
  radical nationalism and 6, 177
  see also fathers; masculinity
fathers
  male ETA activists as 88, 90, 103, 177, 211n.25
  see also children; daughters; fatherhood; masculinity

feminism 82
  abortion rights campaign 149, 150, 153–5, 157, 162, 224n.33
  anti-militarism and 123
  Basque women's movement 56, 150, 176, 222n.12
    Women's Assemblies 150
  consciousness-raising groups 143
  'dual activism' 149, 150
  early Basque nationalist rhetoric against 153
  ETA and 108
  Franco dictatorship and 221n.6
  interviews and 9
  memories of 149, 158–64
  nationalist movements and 3, 148, 221n.1
  prison and 140–2, 146
  radical nationalism and 2, 9, 18, 108, 162–4
    resistance to 149, 152, 161–3, 171–2
  radical nationalist 128–9, 133, 144, 149–53, 222n.16, 223n.17
    Aizan 133, 151–3, 154, 161
    campaign against sexual violence 155–7
    Egizan 133
    KAS Emakumeak 128–9, 151–3, 155, 156, 223n.24, 224n.33
    'triple oppression' 151–2
  Spanish women's movement 56, 143, 149–50, 221n.7
  under Franco 149
  see also abortion; Catholic Church; class; emotion; ETA-militar; ETA-político-militar; ETA members; *euskera*; generations; González; Catarain, Dolores; motherhood; sexuality; transition to democracy; violence against women
foral laws *see fueros*
Forest, Eva 133–4

Franco, General Francisco 1, 22, 31, 63, 81, 85, 100, 149, 182
Franco dictatorship (1939–75) 2, 3, 9, 10, 11, 20, 28–9, 43, 62, 65, 66, 71, 74, 75, 83, 84, 96, 108, 137, 139, 142, 149, 154, 176
  gender and 25, 48, 50, 79, 219n.39
  violence and repression under 16, 18, 22–3, 24, 25, 40, 46, 54, 57, 58–60, 63, 65, 69, 70, 72, 78, 79, 81, 98, 132, 133, 197n.33
  women under 25, 34, 44, 48, 61, 79, 89, 107, 141, 221n.6
  see also media; motherhood
French Basque country (*Iparralde*) 30, 44, 60, 100, 113
  definition 194n.1
  ETA exile community in 86, 94–9, 102, 168, 197n.37
  feminist movement in 151
fueros 200n.22
  gender and 23, 24, 200n.26
funerals, of ETA activists 165

GAL (Grupo Anti-terrorista de Liberación) 9–10, 11, 14, 90, 91, 97, 167, 197n.37
gender
  arrest and torture and 131
  death of Yoyes and 168–9
  divisions in ETA 53, 60–1, 123, 127
  early nationalist language and 20–1
  gendered binary of pain 135
  identities 45
  in ETA rhetoric 55–7
  nation-building and 76
  nationalist movements and 67–9, 94
  political violence and 118–24
  radical nationalism and 1
  roles 3, 5, 21, 33, 71, 76, 93–6, 108, 102–4, 108, 113, 129, 140
    'complementary' 98–9, 120

  support for radical nationalism and 214n.48
  war and 103
  see also Basque conflict; *cuadrilla*; ETA activists; education; emotion; exile; Franco dictatorship; *fueros*; generations; gun; *ikurriña*; leisure; masculinity; media; memory; militarisation/militarism; oral history; *Pelota vasca, La*; prison; postnationalism; rebel identity; sexuality; torture; violence; work
generations
  Basque nationalism and 19
  childless women and 34
  ETA founding and 29, 202n.44
  exile and 96–7
  feminism and 149, 158–9
  Francoist families and 202n.41
  historical interpretation and 29–30
  memory and 33–4
  prison and 127–30, 142, 145–6
  women's activism and 33–4
  see also ETA activists; feminism; gender
Gesto por la paz 178, 230n.4
Gestoras pro-amnistía 126, 127, 163
  prisoners' lists of 188, 189
  women and 178
Goenaga, María Asunción 214n.2
GRAPO (Grupo Revolucionario Anti-fascista Primero de Octubre) 220n.55
  female prisoners 143–4, 145, 220n.56
gun, as gendered symbol 92–3, 117–19, 120, 122
González, Belén 109, 170, 174, 215n.20
González Catarain, Dolores ('Yoyes') 41, 106, 174, 226n.8, 226n.11

death of 166–70, 214n.3, 227n.18, 227n.21, 232n.8
exile of 167
feminism and 168
silence about in interviews 169
see also ETA activists; ETA-militar; mothers

HASI (Herriko Alderdi Sozialista Iraultzalea) 151, 223n.18, 223n.19
HB (Herri Batasuna) 134, 151, 163, 165, 223n.18
women and 166, 223n.19
Herri Gaztedi 40–1, 204n.6
HOAC (Hermandad Obrera de Acción Católica) 40–1
home
defined in opposition to ETA 87–9, 93, 98–9, 118, 168
home/prison dichotomy 125–6, 129, 145–6

ikastola 64
origins 60, 208n.66
privileging of masculinity in 172–3
women and 60
see also euskera
ikurriña
as nationalist symbol 46, 66–8, 70 208n.65
as gendered symbol 67–9, 93
industrialisation
in Basque country 11, 19, 52–3, 53
see also economy
interviews
age and 120
with Basque nationalist women 7–15
see also Basque conflict; Catholic Church; children; class; emotion; feminism; González Catarain, Dolores; media; memory; nostalgia; oral history; prisoners; rebel identity; religion; violence
Iparagirre, Soledad 170, 229n.40
Iparralde *see* French Basque Country

JOC (Juventud Obrera Católica) 40–1
Jarrai 163, 226n.54
Juicio de Burgos, El (dir. Imanol Uribe) 180, 210n.37

KAS (Koordinadora Abertzale Sozialista) 152, 223n.19, 223n.20
KAS Emakumeak *see* feminism
kale borroka see violence

LAIA (Langile Abertzale Iraultzalean Alderdia) 151, 223n.18
labour movement, Basque 72
ETA and 54–5, 85
leisure
gender divisions and 26, 31, 47, 201n.31, 205n.28
see also cuadrilla
López Riaño, Idoia 173, 174

Madrid commando (ETA-m) 108–9, 170, 173
Manzanas, Melitón 78–80, 115
masculinity
Basque nationalism and 6, 21, 172–3, 196n.22
masculinity (*cont.*)
charisma and 73–7, 80
cuadrillas and 47–8
ETA and 35, 48, 196n.22
nationalist movements and 35
political leadership and 72–7
representations of Spanish police and 215n.20
sport and 48, 82, 205n.32
war and conflict and 6, 101, 196n.196
women's memories and 177

masculinity (cont.)
  youth culture and 172
  see also euskera; fatherhood; fathers; ikastola; militarisation/militarism; youth culture, radical nationalist
maternity see motherhood
matriarchy see motherhood
Medem, Julio 179–82
media
  activist identities and 114
  Basque conflict and 10, 62, 70
  Burgos trial and 77–83, 114
  Catholic Church and 24
  construction of nationalism and 31–2, 70, 81
  Franco dictatorship and 63
  gender and 70, 79–80, 102
  interviews and 70
  memory and 73–7, 80–1, 114–15
  popular culture in 1960s and 44
  radical nationalism and 8
  reports of 'terrorism' vs sexual violence 156, 225n.42
  sensationalising of 'terrorism' 156
  silence about sexual torture 175
  see also press reports; radio; television
memory 6, 15, 16, 131, 218n.19
  academic debates around 5, 131
  Basque nationalism and 2, 4
  collective 5, 196n.17
  exile and 129, 146
  feminist history and 33–4
  gender and 4–6, 45, 76–7, 82, 90, 92, 177
  interviews and 7–8
  motherhood and 92, 141
  nationalism and 5
  of male political leaders 72–7
  oral history and 4–5
  peace processes and 183
  prison and 126, 129–31, 162
  recent memories of torture 138, 144
  memories of sexuality 143
  Spain and 18, 182–3, 198n.57
  transnational 72
  truth and 131, 218n.20
  violence and 15–17
  see also generations; interviews; media; nostalgia; oral history; Spanish Civil War; trauma; victims
militarisation/militarism
  of ETA and radical nationalism 3, 54, 61, 83–5, 86–9
  gender and 18, 69–70, 83, 86–9, 93–4
  masculinity and 6, 69–70, 87–94, 96, 106, 110, 118, 123, 205n.32
  violence against women and 156
motherhood
  authoritarianism and 201n.33
  Basque matriarchy theory 24, 25, 102–3, 201n.27, 210n.28
  as constructed 177
  early Basque nationalism and 20–2, 23–5, 36, 200n.26
  ETA and 54–5, 86, 89, 103–4, 106, 152
  feminism and 157
  Franco dictatorship and 25
  incompatibility with ETA activism 119, 168–9, 174
  metaphor for nation 99–100
  'militant motherhood' 128
  narrators' ambivalence towards 145–6, 177
  nationalist movements and 2, 35–6, 101–2, 194n.7
  pacificism/peace and 119, 121–2
  'patriotic motherhood' 101–2, 177
  radical nationalism and 1, 2, 3–4, 8, 36, 92–3
  suffering and 134–5, 157

war and 87, 101–2
see also gender; memory; mothers
mothers
  as archetypal nationalist figures 92, 122, 174, 177
  as ETA activists and supporters 102–3, 119, 168–9, 174, 217n.49, 230n.44
  of female ETA activists 165
  of male ETA activists 29–30, 36, 86, 90, 99–102, 104, 165, 213n.40
  of male prisoners 126, 127, 135, 145
  narrators' memories of 25–8, 76–7, 102–3, 158–9
  in prison 145
  see also daughters; ETA members; gender; motherhood
Mujika, Nagore 230n.44

National Catholicism (Spanish) 23, 48, 62, 63, 64
national liberation movements
  influence on ETA 57, 72, 84–5
nationalist movements
  women and 8, 176–7
Nieva, Pilar 108
nostalgia
  activism and 160
  exile and 97–8
  interviews and 13, 164
nuns 65, 70, 114, 204n.10
  Basque nationalism and 203n.53
  different roles from priests 40
  education of Basque girls 42–3, 49, 50
  see also Church; religion; priests

oral history 4–17, 113
  activism and 149
  ethics of 13–14, 16
  feminist 6–7, 195n.13
  gender and 77, 90
  language and 75
  methodology 37

silence and 15–17, 169
  see also emotion; interviews; memory

PCE (Partido Comunista de España) 12, 139, 140–1
  feminist activists in 141, 150
peace movements
  women and 178
  see also motherhood
Pelota vasca, La (dir. Julio Medem, 2003) 179–82
  gender representations in 180–1
  portrayal of victims in 182
perpetrators
  ethics of listening to 182–3
  see also ETA activists; victims
PNV (Partido Nacionalista Vasco) 1, 2, 19, 22, 23, 29, 31, 32, 39, 54, 58, 67, 68, 85, 89, 98, 113, 165, 172, 180, 200n.17, 203n.49, 222n.11
  founding 20
  women and 202n.36, 222n.13
  see also rural society, Basque
police and security forces
  actions in demonstrations 128
  Basque police 210n.40
  as ETA targets 213n.46, 213n.47
  operations against ETA 108–9, 115, 116, 146
  police station as male space 138
  predominantly male 138, 171, 176, 228n.31
  radical nationalist representations of 103, 109, 215n.20
  Spanish National Police 210n.40
  see also Civil Guard; Franco dictatorship; torture; violence
politics, women's participation
  Basque country 170–1
  elections
    Basque country 170, 226n.52
    Spanish 222n.9
  in radical nationalism 170

postnationalism
  gender and 18, 178–9
  see also fatherhood
PP (Partido Popular) 9
press reports
  of death of Yoyes 167–8
  of deaths of female ETA activists 166–8
  of domestic violence 157, 175
  of ETA as masculine 109, 127
  of female ETA activists 171, 173–5, 229n.40, 229n.42, 229n.43
  of mothers and widows of victims of Basque conflict 102
  of violence against women 224n.38
  see also media; radio; television
priests
  education of young Basque men and 41–2
  role in development of ETA 41, 90
  support for Basque nationalism and 40, 203n.53
  see also Church; masculinity; nuns; religion
prison 139–41
  activism in 139, 146
  as gendered space 126–9
  as political and social education 140–2, 146
  in radical nationalist iconography 125
  women's solidarity work in 26–7, 35, 100, 103, 127–9
  Yeserías women's prison 126, 140
  see also class; emotion; feminism; generations; home; memory; mothers; prisoners; torture
prisoners
  Basque nationalist under Franco 26
  ETA prisoners 11, 126
    and support for radical nationalism 129, 163
    in interviews 130, 146

female prisoners 18, 96, 138–47
  and abortion offences 224n.31
  communist 140–1, 220n.52
  ETA activists and collaborators 113–14, 126–7, 134, 139–40
    statistics 127, 188, 227n.24
  GRAPO 143–4, 145, 220n.56
  lesbians 141–2
  prostitutes 141–2
  under Franco 131, 218n.18
  interviews and 26–7, 129–30
  male 139
  'social reinsertion' of 167–9, 227n.13
  see also amnesty; Gestoras pro-amnistía; mothers
PSOE (Partido Socialista Obrero España) 9, 11, 12, 54, 153, 222n.9
  feminist activists in 150
  GAL and 197n.37

radical Basque nationalism
  definition 194n.2
radio 31–2, 80–1
  see also media; press reports; television
rape see sexual violence
rebel identity
  agency and 116
  Church and 43–4, 113
  female ETA activists and 112–16, 117
  gender and 113, 115–16, 120
  in interviews 37, 43–4, 112
  torture testimonies and 136–8
religion
  interviews and 8
  see also Catholic Church; nuns; priests; rural society, Basque
representation see armed activists; ETA activists; masculinity; media; *Pelota vasca, La*; police and security forces; press reports; radio; television;

transition to democracy;
victims; victims of ETA violence
rural society, Basque
  association with Basque identity 44,
    55, 168, 172, 180
  early nationalism and 23, 180
  ETA recruitment and 52–3
  PNV and 23
  religion and 40
  women and 24, 53
  see also baserri
Sección Femenina de Falange 57,
  207n.60
Second Republic, Spanish (1931–36)
  48, 208n.66
  Basque Church and 43
  Basque nationalists and 22, 39, 54,
    200n.15, 202n.36, 202n.48
  women and 22
sexual violence 69, 131
  war rape 155–6, 225n.42
  see also feminism; torture; violence;
    violence against women
sexuality
  censorship and 160
  as feminist issue 153, 159–60
  heterosexual couples and ETA
    91–3, 94, 96–8, 106–9, 115,
    140, 145, 171, 211n.29;
    212n.30, 215n.18
  'couple terrorism' 106–7, 171
  nationalist movements and 36
  nationalist attitudes to 20
  in prison 141–3
  'sexual revolution' 142, 154
  women's sexuality as explanation
    for ETA activism 106, 111,
    123, 173–5, 215n.26
  see also abortion; contraception;
    feminism; memory; sexual
    violence; transition to
    democracy
single women 34–7
  political activism of 35
  as role models 34

socialism
  early Basque nationalism and 20–1,
    54, 199n.4
  ETA and 54–7, 73, 75, 85
  radical nationalism and 28
  see also class; labour movement,
    Basque
Spanish Civil War (1936–39) 2, 21,
  22, 24, 27, 29, 33, 34, 63, 89,
  98, 127, 129, 202n.48
  memory and 182–3
  women and 22, 141, 195n.10,
    199n.14, 202n.37

television 32, 80–1, 204n.13
  see also media; press reports; radio
torture
  of Basque activists 112, 125
  construction of sexual difference
    and 135–8
  of female activists 131–38, 175
  as gendered and sexualised
    performance 137–8
  as human rights issue 157
  sexual 3, 132–3, 135–8, 175, 177
  of male detainees 133, 137,
    219n.39
  women and 3, 18, 126
  women's testimonies of 131–4,
    136–7, 181
  see also Civil Guard; emotion;
    gender; media; memory; rebel
    identity; sexual violence;
    transition to democracy;
    victims; violence
transition to democracy (Spain,
  1976–82) 1, 12, 85, 153, 176
  Basque politics and 150
  feminism and 150, 154
  representation of sexuality and
    women 153
  security forces and state violence
    155, 156, 219n.36
  torture of political prisoners 132,
    156

transition to democracy (cont.)
  women in Parliament 222n.9
  see also Basque conflict; violence
trauma 131, 164
  memory studies and 15, 16–17
  see also memory

universities
  ETA recruitment and 49
  women and men in 49–50, 206n.38

victims
  ethics of representation 181–2
  identification with 15, 182
  memory studies and 15
  political positions of 183
  problem of claiming ETA activists as 123, 166, 169–70, 175
  representations of women as 181
  torture and victim label 138
  victim/perpetrator dichotomy 170
  see also Basque conflict; *Pelota vasca, La*; perpetrators; press reports; victims of ETA violence
victims of ETA violence
  female 213n.47
  pain of 124, 170, 182
  victims of state violence and 181–2
  wives and widows of 102, 181
  statistics (1968–98) 213n.47
violence
  anti-terrorist 140, 162
  ETA 1, 2, 3, 10–11, 15, 17, 32, 36, 62, 69, 70, 72, 75, 84, 86, 93, 100–1, 118, 120, 140, 167, 170, 182
    associated with the feminine 179, 231n.10
    ceasefires 170, 183 (2006), 228n.26
    critiques of 11, 130, 178
    during transition to democracy 156
    effects of 170
    as political not personal 121–2

gender and 16
interviews and 9–10
state 85, 129, 170, 175
  see also Franco dictatorship; GAL; memory; police and security forces; torture
street violence (*kale borroka*) 10, 11–12, 178, 197n.41
  gender and 230n.3
  ultra-right-wing 155, 156, 224n.38
  see also sexual violence; torture; violence; violence against women
violence against women
  feminist campaign against 149, 150, 153, 155–7
  see also sexual violence; torture

women's movement see feminism
work
  domestic
    men and 32–3, 92, 112, 158
    ETA recruitment and 52–3
    gender divisions in 24–6, 39, 52
    migrant workers 119n.8
    ETA and 54, 57, 171
    political activism and 51–2
    women and 2, 6, 26, 34, 48–53, 58, 206n.41
    in industry 26, 53
    as schoolteachers 34
    in war 86–7

youth culture, radical nationalist 178
  masculinity and 172
  street violence and 178
  women and 172
'Yoyes' see González Catarain, Dolores

Zeberio, Iñaxi 173–4, 230n.45, 230n.48

EU authorised representative for GPSR:
Easy Access System Europe, Mustamäe tee 50,
10621 Tallinn, Estonia
gpsr.requests@easproject.com

www.ingramcontent.com/pod-product-compliance
Ingram Content Group UK Ltd.
Pitfield, Milton Keynes, MK11 3LW, UK
UKHW021836140426
5217IPUK00021B/1480